W9-AHA-922

BERSERK STYLE IN
AMERICAN CULTURE

Also by Kirby Farrell:

Cony-Catching (1971)
Shakespeare's Creation: The Language of Magic and Play (1976)
Play-Death and Heroism in Shakespeare (1989)
The American Satan (1990)
Women in the Renaissance: Selections from English Literary Renaissance, ed. Kirby Farrell,
Elizabeth Hageman, and Arthur F. Kinney (1990)
Snuff (1991)
Post-Traumatic Culture: Injury and Interpretation in the 90s (1998)
Critical Essays on Shakespeare's Richard II, ed. Kirby Farrell (1999)
The Mysteries of Elizabeth I, ed. Kirby Farrell and K. Swaim (2003)

BERSERK STYLE IN AMERICAN CULTURE

Kirby Farrell

First published in 2011 by
PALGRAVE MACMILLAN® in the United States – a division of
St. Martin's Press LLC, 175 Fifth Avenue, New York, NY 10010.

Where this book is distributed in the UK, Europe and the rest of the
world, this is by Palgrave Macmillan, a division of Macmillan Publishers
Limited, registered in England, company number 785998, of
Houndmills, Basingstoke, Hampshire RG21 6XS.

Palgrave Macmillan is the global academic imprint of the above
companies and has companies and representatives throughout the
world.

Palgrave® and Macmillan® are registered trademarks in the
United States, the United Kingdom, Europe and other countries.

ISBN: 978–0–230–11663–4

Library of Congress Cataloging-in-Publication Data

Farrell, Kirby, 1942–
   Berserk style in American culture / Kirby Farrell.
      p. cm.
      ISBN 978–0–230–11663–4 (hardback)
   1. American literature—20th century—History and criticism.
2. Psychoanalysis and literature—English-speaking countries.
3. Psychic trauma. 4. Suffering in literature. 5. Wounds and injuries
in literature. I. Title.
   PS228.P74F36 2011
   810.9'0054—dc22   2011002902

A catalogue record of the book is available from the British Library.

Design by MPS Limited, A Macmillan Company

First edition: August 2011

10 9 8 7 6 5 4 3 2 1

Printed in the United States of America.

CONTENTS

List of Figures	vi
Preface	vii
Acknowledgments	x
Introduction	1
1 Berserk Style	13
2 At War with Style	55
3 Making a Killing	93
4 Booty and the Beast	125
5 Rage for Order	147
6 The Living End	181
Conclusion	211
Notes	215
Index	241

List of Figures

0.1   A Pontiac 2000 Grand AM advertisement   ix
1.1   A Lexus SUV advertisement   17

PREFACE

This book grew out of *Post-Traumatic Culture* (1998), which explores the concept of trauma in the 1890s, when its modern form first crystallized, and in 1990s America, when the concerns of Vietnam veterans, feminists, and many clinicians brought post-traumatic stress to public awareness. Symptoms of traumatic stress cluster around depressive and aggressive behaviors. One person may be immobilized, another panicked, while a third may become furiously charged—berserk. As the psychiatrists say, much depends on how you are wrapped.

Much depends, too, on how you conceive of your experience. Traumatic stress is profoundly psychosomatic: the injury entails an interpretation of the injury. How you understand what is happening to you affects your susceptibility to particular symptoms. Your past history, expectations, and convictions influence the effects of stress. But the process can be turned inside out too. Under stress we may turn to available narratives of trauma to account for disturbances. Whatever the physiological contribution, even extreme behavior takes shape through cultural influences.

For this reason *Post-Traumatic Culture* explored the way ideas about traumatic injury and symptoms seeped out of the doctor's office and into everyday life. In the final decades of the twentieth century, trauma became a supercharged buzzword even as symptoms proliferated. While much suffering was undoubtedly real, the terminology and medicalization of distress showed that trauma could function as an explanatory tool that could be used to make a host of unrelated problems more manageable. People and prosecutors thronged into court seeking justice or compensation for traumatic injuries that in many cases proved to be unverifiable. Appeals to medical authority promised to relieve suffering and injured self-esteem. Some psychiatrists pursued preposterous specters such as satanic ritual abuse. And societies as well as individuals have used past traumas to explain today's passions and distress.

Aggressive responses to traumatic stress make headlines as rampage killing in a war zone, a workplace, or a school. The extreme violence signifies a do-or-die effort to remake reality: to obliterate all conflict and restore—or impose—a sense of order. For all its sensational horror, the imaginative model has familiar variants all around us in everyday life, from apocalyptic religion to the shootouts that climax uncountable movies. Journalism uses the idea of running amok to describe excesses or loss of control in all sorts of endeavors, from the playing field to Wall Street and the gaming table.

When we become aware of these models, berserk behavior becomes berserk style. This book has two premises that will need periodic reemphasis. As an idea, the berserk state is radically equivocal and ambivalent: horrific in its potential for destruction but also alluring as a promise that the overthrow of inhibitions can open up access to extraordinary resources. In Hollywood thrillers, villains and heroes as well accomplish amazing feats by throwing restraint to the wind, and emerge unscathed.

The second premise is that as a style, berserk abandon can be used for all sorts of ends. The idea of uncontrollable frenzy can be a tool, a role, a means to manage morale or to influence others. It can be personal, conscious or not, and it can be cultural, shared by a group, even contagious.

These premises are tools that the present book uses to examine particular expressions of American culture from the Vietnam War era to the economic crisis that closed the first decade of the new century. As the world rebalanced following World War II, America's dominance came under increasing stress. In areas as far-flung as corporate finance, the post-September 11 wars, the changing status of gambling, and the assumptions of apocalyptic religion, this book traces ways in which abandon shaped behavior.

The idea of berserk abandon is so capacious that any analysis has to be frustratingly selective. The same ambiguities that make berserk style seductively potent in the world outside your window also challenge a tidy argumentative frame. What's more, in the new century the pace of change accelerated as I wrote, with events a moving target.

The book's subject is emotionally charged, and its focus on extremes means that it risks misinterpretation. An account of soldiers and policy makers who have run amok in Iraq, for example, cannot do justice to individuals or to the tragic complexities that may overtake them. Likewise, the premise that mafia tropes are widespread in economic life is not an indictment of all businessmen or a Spenglerian disquisition on the decline and doom of American culture. The allure of abandon for Americans has been ecstatic as well as sinister.

Berserk style takes a variety of historically particular forms in cultures around the world. And given the urgent character of the core ideas,

Figure 0.1   A Pontiac 2000 Grand AM advertisement

those forms are volatile. In the go-go 1990s, for example, Detroit
sold thrilling themes. In a magazine advertisement a new Pontiac
tears across a no-man's land spiked by giant saw blades, its windshield
and wheels jagged with saw toothed reflections, its caption defying
danger "When the Road Bites, Bite Back" (fig. 0.1). As in action
comics, the daredevil motorist could be dashing through enemy lines
in a war movie, triumphantly invulnerable.

With terrorism and the Bush administration's actual wars in the
news, marketers toned down the thrills. But by 2008, ads were pumping
adrenaline again, showing a slow-motion fist punching a board, shattering the wood, and turning into a new Acura sedan. But the long
post-Vietnam recovery and boom was about to crash. A year later,
not only was the death-defying Rambo-like Pontiac muscle car gone,
the whole Pontiac division had been liquidated by a bankrupt General
Motors reorganizing on the lip of a financial precipice.

Still, berserk style does not vanish; it mutates.

It adapts.

It bites back.

ACKNOWLEDGMENTS

When writing a book about styles of abandon, it helps to have wise friends and colleagues holding onto your shirttails to keep you grounded. In this expedition I've been fortunate to have the support of Neil Elgee and the Ernest Becker Foundation, and the canny insights of Kay Smith, Steve Helmling, Rob Carrion, Bob and Claire Hopley, Naomi Ossar, Barbara Ravelhofer, Frank Brownlow, Michael Telles, and Bruce Wilcox.

In different forms some of the book's arguments have appeared in *Bang Bang, Shoot Shoot!: Essays on Guns and Popular Culture*, ed. Murray Pomerance and John Sakeris (Boston, 2000); *Bad: Infamy, Darkness, Evil, and Slime on Screen*, ed. Murray Pomerance and John Sakeris (Albany, 2004); and, from the same editors, *Popping Culture* (Boston, 2007, 2010). Excerpts from my essay "Berserk Style in American Culture" have been reprinted with the permission of *Cultural Critique* and the University of Minnesota Press.

INTRODUCTION

You went berserk . . . you'll probably be liable to fits of it all your life.

Rudyard Kipling

To be berserk is to be on the edge of control. The term came into American headlines with the massacre of civilians in the Vietnam War and the rash of workplace and school rampages in the 1980s, but the idea is venerable. Dictionaries define the berserk state as frenzied, violent, or deranged. The original berserker was "A wild Norse warrior of great strength and ferocious courage, who fought on the battlefield with a frenzied fury known as 'the berserker rage'; often a lawless bravo or freebooter." The term may refer to a Norse hero who "never fought in armor but in his *ber sark,* which means 'bearskin' in the Nordic languages. Thus the term berserk became synonymous with reckless courage. During the Saga time in Iceland and in the Scandinavian countries (AD 870–1030) . . . the Berserks, apparently bearing the same name as the legendary warrior, arose as a predatory group of brawlers and killers who disrupted the peace of the Viking community repeatedly."[1] Some sources suggest that the Viking fury was a temporary psychosis induced by eating the mushroom *Amanita muscaria* (Fabing, 239).

The term is not just an antique curiosity. Based on his clinical work with Vietnam War veterans, the psychiatrist Jonathan Shay concludes that in combat today soldiers may experience the same icy rage that Homer describes in *The Iliad.* The Vikings were hardly the only warriors who plunged into battle without armor, as if the bear sark or shirt gave them the bear's ferocity.[2] Lacking claws and a carapace, humans have long relied on prosthetic weapons and a shell of animal hides or armor, or on symbolic protection such as talismans. Even today military units and sports teams commonly take the name of a fearsome animal.

By sharing the uncanny potency of wild predators, warriors want to frighten enemies, suppress their own terror, and pump up "fighting spirit"—their willingness to kill without compunction. Soldiers may believe they are restoring order or honor through revenge or sacrifice; mystically replenishing life by slaughtering enemies; or commanding death itself through their superhuman wrath. In such fantasies emergency physiology combines with creaturely compulsion—biting aggression and hunger for life—to energize warrior culture. In peril, soldiers may feel a supernatural agency guiding their behavior as the Greek warrior felt Athena directing his spear. Homer's word for Achilles' rage—*menis*—implies cosmic wrath. Berserkers may feel transported, in touch with uncanny powers and luck: open to the beyond. In that supercharged state, godlike but also beastlike, they are apt to feel invulnerable, throw off their armor, and attack the threat head on.

These terms might appear to be merely colorful abstractions. But consider Milton Blahyi, former rebel commander in Liberia's ghastly civil war, who "has admitted to taking part in human sacrifices as part of traditional ceremonies intended to ensure victory in battle. He said the sacrifices "included the killing of an innocent child and plucking out the heart, which was divided into pieces for us to eat"—as a bear might. Blahyi literally stripped off his armor: he "is better known in Liberia as 'General Butt Naked' because he went into combat with no clothes on, to scare the enemy." Blahyi's ordination at age 11 as "the traditional priest of my tribe" may have prepared the ground for the godlike conviction berserkers report, while his current calling as an Evangelical preacher may be functioning to pacify or magically undo that conviction.[3] Fundamental to the behavior either way is an exceptional need for a conviction of rightness or what is right.

Conventional wisdom nowadays associates berserk behavior with rampage killing. When the post-Vietnam era created an economic "rust-belt" and a more stressful workplace, a string of post office shootings gave us the idiom to "go postal." The final year of the twentieth century began with gunfire blazing in a Salt Lake City television station and ended in November with seven Honolulu office workers dead. On April 20, at Columbine High School in Colorado, 2 students slaughtered 15 people and wounded 23 before taking their own lives. A month later a discharged Marine killed four Las Vegas supermarket employees. Before the year was out, the carnage reached an Atlanta day trading firm, a Los Angeles day care center, and a church in Fort Worth, Texas, where seven worshipers died during a service.

A study by the *New York Times* (April 8, 2000) tallied 102 rampage attacks in the United States since 1949, when a World War II veteran named Howard B. Unruh murdered 13 people on a residential street in Camden, New Jersey.[4] The database spotlights some important characteristics that distinguish rampage killing from what the *Times* calls "regular homicides." Although most kinds of murder decreased in the 1990s, "the incidence of . . . rampage killings appears to have increased, according to a separate computer analysis by The *Times* of nearly 25 years of homicide data from the Federal Bureau of Investigation." Between 1976 and 1989 the number of incidents averaged "about 23 a year," whereas between 1990 and 1997, "the number averaged over 34, dipping below 30 only once, in 1994."

Still, the report concludes, "[T]hese killings remain extremely rare, much less than 1 percent of all homicides." They are also not peculiar to the United States. In a larger perspective, "the best scientific thinking, in a field that is admittedly understudied, now holds that multiple public murder occurs at a fairly constant level across time and cultures. What some people call 'running amok,' a term first used in Malaysia to describe frenzied, indiscriminate killing, has been observed in many cultures."[5] That conclusion needs to be qualified, since the American civilian's unusual access to multiple combat-style weapons raises the prospect of mass killing. In Britain, where gun ownership is tightly restricted, firearms deaths are rare, with fewer than 100 gun murders annually.

Rampage killers are overwhelmingly male. In the military of course, berserkers are mostly young men, though in a developmental perspective they also fit Charles Silberman's observation that males are most susceptible to violence and prison from late adolescence to their mid-twenties, at which time demography shows a mate and family likely to help them—in the wisdom of slang—to "settle down."[6]

When women do commit multiple murders, their victims are likely to be family members, as in Andrea Yates's murder of her five children in Houston (June 20, 2001).[7] In the worst women's rampage on record (January 30, 2006), a former postal employee, Jennifer San Marco, murdered a neighbor and six coworkers in Goleta, California, then took her own life. In American culture media accounts are disposed to construe men's violence as explosive rampage behavior, and to report signs of mental illness in cases involving women. Journalists recognized that Andrea Yates had a history of grave depression and religious delusions, and noted evidence suggesting that Jennifer San Marco had suffered paranoid and possibly psychotic symptoms. In media accounts women killers are apt to be mad; men, mad dogs.

The *Times* database calls attention to some surprising characteristics. Rampage killers show "few of the demographic patterns of poverty and race associated with regular crime." They are more likely than other murderers to be apprehended by police (100 percent to

76 percent) and to be suicidal (33 percent to 3 percent). They are more likely to be military veterans (52 percent to 20 percent), better educated (35 percent to 2 percent college graduates), and out of work (57 percent to 26 percent). They usually act less on impulse than out of long-seething frustration and rage. More than half "had histories of serious mental health problems—either a hospitalization, a prescription for psychiatric drugs, a suicide attempt or evidence of psychosis." The students who massacred classmates at Columbine High School (1999) and Virginia Tech (2007) also acted on "long-seething frustration and rage," marching into a killing zone with godlike indifference to the law and police bullets.

While the database does not pretend to absolute truth, it does bring order to a terrifying phenomenon. Yet its categories are broad, discrete, and static. Its clarity is at best a matter of percentages, and from the vantage point of this book, its focus on pathological violence screens out a wide complex of related behaviors that require a much-expanded investigation. Bullets and body bags command attention, but they are not the whole story.

On January 8, 2011, an attack on an admired Congresswoman in Tucson killed six bystanders and wounded fourteen. The young killer imagined himself heroically striking at a hated figure and evil government. In turn the public celebrated the heroes who disarmed him on the scene. In the media storm that followed, public voices debated whether a culture of political vitriol and plentiful guns had influenced the mentally disturbed killer. Reactions were starkly ambivalent. Even as the president led a mourning service, gun sales spiked in Arizona. Politicians and talk show hosts famous for whipping up outrage suddenly denied that outrage had any effect on behavior, and attacked anyone who claimed otherwise. Efforts to tame the shock labeled the killer insane and the rampage senseless. Everyone needed to feel innocent, yet the violence was familiar—and acceptable—enough that Americans took for granted that nothing would be done to control access to guns or to improve mental health services. In coping with terror, disavowal of violence could not compete with convictions that personal weapons and a vigilant mindset can master extreme violence.

ABANDON AS BEHAVIOR AND TROPE

Rampage is an action but also an idea about action. This book considers thought and actions at the edge of conventional reality as boundary behaviors. "The edge" is of course just a crude metaphor for experience in which autonomic forces overtake conscious self-control.

Fight-or-flight physiology may produce the mix of panic or rage spotlighted in the news, but "the edge" can also be—for example—an experience of manic play, discovery, and visionary ecstasy. This book's argument contends that the concept of berserk abandon is far more pervasive than conventional wisdom recognizes. Soldiers and fired employees may go berserk, but so do politicians, cancer cells, and financial markets.[8] The term implies a clinical category but also a trope that shapes a wide range of personal and cultural fantasies.

As a trope, the term berserk is strikingly volatile and ambiguous. It can apply to almost any loss or overthrow of control. In everyday speech to be berserk is to be carried away or "unhinged." While psychiatry refers to the berserk "state," the term "berserking" responds better to the headlong motion implied, as in to "run" amok, to go "over the edge," "over the top," "off the deep end," or "out" of your mind." You can "go for broke," "go rogue," go "hog wild," "haywire," or "ballistic"; "freak" or "flip" out, "lose it," or "fly off the handle" or off your predictable rocker. In love and war "anything goes" with "no holds barred." Slang reveals the violent fantasies implied. In a "winner take all" competition the athlete with the "killer instinct" triumphs. You can be "wildly" successful or "shop till you drop," spend "like there's no tomorrow," and "blow your mind." At a bar you can drink "car bombs." Getting "high" can be a chemical shortcut to the berserker's sense of godlike exaltation. So can binge gambling or orgasmic recklessness in an era of AIDS. Beauty can be a "knockout." A good time can be a "blast."

As slang shows, we are seriously ambivalent about berserk abandon. When the scale, pace, or complexity of things overwhelms cognitive resources, the response can be panic or fury, but also ecstatic release. Mystics and warriors both report a conviction of transcendence or access to the beyond. Traumatic stress can be berserk, but so can a soccer riot. Going "over the edge" can be frightening but also alluring as an access to uncanny power and heroic expansiveness. Facing death, soldiers may charge into enemy fire with suicidal daring—and possibly survive. Since a failure of nerve can be fatally paralyzing, such recklessness may be seen as lifesaving courage and stamina. For survivors it may have the color of miracle or magic, and make them heroes.

How can we not be of two minds about a behavior as dangerously equivocal as abandon? Viking berserkers could be bestial marauders or legendary heroes. If it doesn't get you killed on the battlefield, reckless fury may stun and scatter your enemies. Abandon may culminate in mad folly, or it may bring triumph and more life—and the symbolic equivalents of more life: loot, sex, land, marble statues, and apotheosis. The ambivalence is vivid in the reaction to crowd disasters such as a stadium or a post-Thanksgiving shopping crush. Scientific studies show that such disasters are caused by miscommunication and laws of physics, not by abandon. Yet when a Wal-Mart employee died trying to manage a throng of shoppers in 2008, media voices reacted with vehement horror. One letter writer to the New York *Post* condemned "the animals (you know who you are) who stampeded that poor man at Wal-Mart on Black Friday. You are a perfect example of the depraved decadence of society today."[9] The popular misconception is that the shoppers were recklessly greedy for loot—like berserk Vikings—and that "depraved" consumerist America is terrifyingly drawn to abandon.

LOSING TO GAIN

Abandon takes many forms. It can be sublime, as in trance or the New Testament injunction to lose yourself in order to find yourself, but it can also be terrifying or even ridiculous, as in sales pitches urging you to "find the new you!" with the swipe of a credit card. The assumption is that extraordinary resources lie within us and just beyond us, accessible if we could only shed the inane inhibitions that hold us back. Go "over the edge" or "outside the box" and you may experience an abyss—failure, guilt, and social death—that triggers suicide or rage. It can also be the ecstatic abandon of lovers: Tristan and Iseult, Thelma and Louise, and lovers' leap.

But there is another outcome to consider: the conviction that self-loss opens access to superhuman resources. Fans scream for an athlete to "break" a record and become a cosmic "star." In darkened movie theaters spellbound audiences watch as a mild-mannered citizen turns into Superman. Wall Street wizards report stupefying profits from "lightning" trading software and derivatives whose algorithms defy plodding analysis and mock the salaried employee caged in a cubicle. The shared fantasy is that various styles of abandon open up extraordinary resources that are more authentic than the everyday self. This conviction plays out in religious rapture and in Plato's vision of creativity as divine frenzy.

Those desirable powers—fearlessness, strength, and uncanny instinct—have the potency and allure of magic. Athletes try to psych it out or attain it with steroids. Superheroes and Harry Potter gratuitously command it. Fulfilled, that magical connection is the stuff of comedy. When it fails or proves vicious, tragedy prevails. Little wonder that efforts to master berserk abandon are at the heart of culture, whether tribal elders are initiating the young through extreme tests or performers are ritually pumping up backstage. And no wonder popular culture obsesses over the theme. Stevenson's Dr. Jekyll destroys himself attempting to master the berserk Mr. Hyde within him. Ang Lee's film of the Marvel comic *Incredible Hulk* (2003) updates the same struggle. Made susceptible to berserk transformation by radiation poisoning, Bruce Banner (Eric Bana) periodically becomes the Hulk: his eyes glow with alien fury, and his body swells to superhuman proportions. He becomes indomitable but also abominably dangerous. The story is a parable about the risk of self-destruction in the struggle to master heroic autonomy.

Hollywood's *Hulk* openly retails heroic aggrandizement to audiences, as in a blurb promising viewers "A super powered adrenaline blast" (Peter Hammond). The "adrenaline blast" is of course an advertising fiction: an idea about berserk frenzy. Nobody expects fans to storm out of the theater uprooting telephone poles and throwing cars about. But insofar as it pumps up morale and sells tickets, the "blast" is using the idea to evoke at a tame distance the uncanny powers associated with abandon.

This is berserk style.

BERSERK STYLE

A story about the experience of berserk abandon is not the same thing as the experience itself. The story represents and interprets the experience. In the blurb for *Incredible Hulk* just mentioned, an advertisement is representing and interpreting a story (movie) that is representing and interpreting in theaters a berserk experience (the Hulk's) that is frankly fictional, from a screenwriter's conception of berserk experience. We need not be mesmerized by the infinite regression. Rather, the crucial point is to see that people *use the idea* of abandon in all sorts of ways, often unwittingly, and the experience and the story about it can be bewilderingly entangled.

In James Toback's documentary film *Tyson* (2009), for example, the champion boxer Mike Tyson uses a version of the Hulk's story to stabilize an explosive personality torn by "extremes" (his word) of violent exaltation and demonic chaos. From childhood terror, humiliation, predatory fury, and prison, Tyson rose to dominate the ring. As he tells it, his powers came from harnessing the fury of berserk abandon, thanks to the boxing skills and warrior ethos—the heroic story—instilled in him by his fatherly trainer Gus D'Amato. In prefight publicity and in the ring, Tyson was able to dramatize a threat of wild force that intimidated opponents and excited fans, yet his focus on the warrior story kept him in control. At his peak he enjoyed the berserker's conviction of godlike invulnerability, with spectacular fame, loot, and sexual conquests as a reward. As time went on, however, the champ increasingly cycled between monstrous appetite—drugs, rape, profligacy, egomania—and collapse. Style proved unable to manage his furies.

After more time in prison Tyson attempted a comeback, trying to relive the story of warrior poise "on the edge." But in a classic plot line, his heart was no longer in it, and in 1997 the story fell apart in his desperate title match with Evander Holyfield. When both fighters began to lose control, Tyson wildly bit off a piece of his antagonist's ear as berserk soldiers may bite or even eat parts of slain enemies. As if fighting for his life in a teenage gang brawl, he ran amok. The abandon thrilled and outraged the boxing world. In the film Tyson takes a penitent, confessional role to come back from failure. He advances a new story created out of family bonds and psychotherapy to substitute for the mirage of uncanny powers.

Tyson himself lived through some berserk moments. But in *Tyson* we are mostly looking at examples of berserk style: "berserk" because some of the recounted actions entail self-abandon, and a "style" insofar as the *idea* of abandon is being used in stories that shape everyday experience. Tyson and his trainer relied on the idea of mastered abandon as a goal in training and as a tool for supporting morale under stress. For fans and advertisers the material functioned as an elixir enhancing excitement, million-dollar purses, and golden glories.

A core premise of this book is that this is a cultural process. Fascination with berserk powers is variously personal and collective, but also crucially conditioned by fantasies that are pervasive if often unacknowledged in American culture. Mike Tyson attributes his toxic rage to the humiliation and terror of urban poverty—a "toxic" environment. The Hulk's superhuman force is the product of toxic radiation. Like Tyson's rage, radiation made the nuclear weapons that promised the United States godlike dominance after the horrors of World War II, and implied a prosperous future of unlimited cheap power. Once "harnessed," as propaganda used to put it, radiation would be akin to Tyson's fantasy of warrior mastery. The "world champion" was entitled to boast that nobody could beat him. In effect, the relation was reciprocal: the boxer and the country drew on a cluster of fantasy materials signifying supremacy.

Yet like Tyson's career, that magical prospect proved to be painfully equivocal for the nation as challenges to nuclear supremacy proliferated. By the time investment guru Warren Buffett spoke of Wall Street's fabulously profitable, stupefyingly destructive derivatives as "financial weapons of mass destruction, carrying dangers that, while now latent, are potentially lethal" (2002), his allusion to nuclear superiority was meant to evoke menace.

Buffett recognized the berserk quality in Wall Street's behavior. And true to the symbolic logic, the 2008 financial crisis did in fact pose the "mega-catastrophic risk" for the economy that Buffett foretold (March 4, 2003), a tale taken up in later chapters. For now it is enough to note that berserk style operates in intimate personal thought but also in the more abstract reaches of cultural fantasy. And it implies belief. The belief may be woozy, fanatical, or outright magical thinking. Or in countless movies—and in life—it may be a visionary commitment to a seemingly impossible project "worth fighting for." Carried beyond conventional safeguards, the risk is always the sway of delusion. "During the housing bubble," said James Surowiecki tartly in 2009, "the financial sector essentially tried to create reality."[10]

This expanded conception of berserk behavior and style requires an expanded investigation. Psychiatry conceives the berserk state as a pathological response to traumatic stress. The core experience of trauma, says the textbook, is "intense fear, helplessness, loss of control, and threat of annihilation."[11] In combat, berserking is an emergency response to stress physiology. Overtaken by terror and exhaustion, soldiers may charge into enemy fire, indiscriminately violent. They appear carried away or deranged. Fight overcomes flight. "It is plain," says the psychiatrist, "that the berserker's brain and body function are as distant from everyday function as his mental state is from everyday thought and feeling."[12]

In the words of one Vietnam veteran, "I was a fucking animal. When I look back on that stuff, I say, 'That was somebody else did that'" (83). He speaks as if he was out of control, really not there, yet he recognizes his behavior—"that stuff"—clearly enough to reject it as "not me." The behavior is alien but not meaningless. The behavior may be recklessly impulsive or chaotic, yet combat soldiers who have run amok may report a feeling of godlike invulnerability and purposefulness. Some rampage killers make cunning plans and even advertise their exploits. Dr. Shay calls their cold rage "flaming ice," evoking the contradictory sense of actions coldly willed yet wild. "The true physiological relationship between the burning rage of the berserker and his icy deadness remains uncharted territory" (93).

Where in this "uncharted territory" is individual responsibility? This is the familiar challenge posed by trauma. Since traumatic injury entails an interpretation of the injury, to what extent is it beyond control?

Stress physiology and individual make-up determine behavior, but not in a vacuum. Why does berserk behavior take one particular form and not another? The complication, as witnessed by the law's long struggle to clarify accountability, is that everyday thought shades into self-abandon, richly conditioned by autonomic or unconscious qualities, not least of all denial. Berserk behavior may be erratic or even suicidally reckless, but that need not rule out some degree of premeditation and strategic awareness. Rampage killings such as the Columbine High School massacre (April 20, 1999) often have a copycat character, with the killers consciously trying to capture record-breaking head-line attention. Almost a decade later, half a world away in Finland, a 22-year-old culinary arts student gunned down ten vocational school students after posting on YouTube video clips of himself dressed in black like a professional assassin in a movie thriller, and revealing his fascination with video clips from the Columbine attack.

Copycat behavior shows that the *idea* of abandon can be objectified, imitated, and manipulated. What's more, the idea may condition actions. Copycats are aware of precedents as models to be repeated and outdone. Fantasizing about spectacular revenge, copycats are not (yet) physically amok. They may be seething or brooding, on the edge of self-control. They may be aware of their rage and gratified by the prospect of sensational violence, even if they have not (yet) decided to act. But they may also be only half-aware, in denial or self-deceived, trying out the possibilities of abandon.

This book treats that mode of being on the edge as a style. The term is appropriate because it connotes casual as well as formal behav-ior—which is critical, because casualness and routine readily mask denial and manipulation. As a boxer, Mike Tyson could be conscious of living close to the edge while trying to be relaxed about it in his social life. At this distance it is impossible to gauge the quality of his awareness of his potential for rage. If berserk behavior falls along a continuum, then when style predominates, abandon takes on the quality of role-playing. When style is minimal, impulse and emergency physiology are prominent.

In style meanings proliferate. Comedy has traditionally exploited berserk excess in exploding stale pieties for laughs. Even the terminology such as a "punchline" or "gallows humor" reveals the violence lurking in comic imagination. Chaplin, Buster Keaton, Keystone cops, and other comedians systematically made mayhem and reckless physical daring triggers for hilarity. Verbal jokes likewise breach boundaries and turn humdrum reality upside down. When clowns run amok in a slapstick melee, they burlesque berserk aggression. Tamed for the spectators, and especially for children, who are still wrestling with self-control, the freewheeling assaults and harmless pratfalls are an act, conventionalized as style. The clowns break all the rules, triumph over pain and fear, and fascinate everyone.

But impulsive violence may also be ambiguously conditioned by style, since even an action that is "out of control" raises the question: why did the action take this particular form? Who or what "chose" or predisposed it? At a hockey practice a suburban father argues with his son's coach, leaves the arena for a few minutes, and on his return, before bystanders and his own children, beats the smaller man to death.[13] Granted, the father was enraged. But why act it out as a fight to the death? Many of the likely forces shaping the behavior are grounded in routine cultural fantasies. Bizarre as the attack is, it played out the underlying structure of sport as combat. "Body contact" sports are less sublimated than some others, but all draw on a cluster of metaphors for deadly struggle and self-esteem. Even in the dignified Olympics commentators enthuse about athletes "killing," "dominating," "attacking," "defending," and the like. Games may end in "sudden death" overtime. Verbal assault on an umpire is a personal contest and may be surreptitiously regarded as a game or rite. But then, the experience of play is associated with enchantment because it can be all-absorbing.

Assimilated to the headline news topic "sports violence," the hockey murder becomes part of a genre with its own explanatory system: a warning to impassioned fans but also proof that sports is serious, even heroic in its ability to evoke tragic passions as the irate fan defends his son or his team. "Show me your budget, and I'll tell you what you hold most dear. And as long as the NFL's propaganda wing, NFL Films, shows you every brutal takedown in super slo-mo, from nine different angles, and glorifies brutes . . . we'll know what this league is all about. . . . The actuary tables for NFL players are horrifying. The men who play this game die much younger, on average, than most other groups of men. But out of sight, out of mind. Goodell knows that while the players are in full view, they have to be considered modern gladiators, impervious to normal levels of pain and fatigue." The sports writer is well aware of the role of style as a disguise: "I say this in shuddering admiration of the league's PR skills, so powerful that they have made millions of people believe they cannot live without the three hours of carnage brought to their living rooms."[14]

By extension, sports combat is grounded in a structure of self-esteem. Winners are culture heroes and larger than life. Losers stand for failure, inadequacy, and social death. Identifying with his son, the hockey dad wanted to win. Overridden by the coach—the smaller man invested with authority—the hockey dad very likely felt humiliated or vengeful on behalf of his own imagined rightness. By temporarily leaving the rink, he may have tried to save face or perhaps cool his indignation. Returning to pick up his son, he acted out the drive to revenge prominent in many workplace and combat rampages. However deliberately, by grappling with the coach, he was engaging in—staging—a primitive athletic agon, showing his son and the crowd that he could win.

To complicate matters, our capacity for ambivalence means that in the father's eyes the combat could be both a heroic contest and appalling murder. For another, insofar as he "lost" his temper and was "carried away," the hockey dad could claim he was momentarily "beyond" self-control, outside the magic circle of everyday life. In that state, where inhibitions and safeguards fall away, our ancient survival physiology goes into emergency overdrive. We behave like predators—housecats as well as tigers—in the throes of seizing and killing prey.

Did the man intend to murder the coach? The question leads into a maze, with criticism following on a string.

CHAPTER 1

BERSERK STYLE

Nothing succeeds like excess.

Oscar Wilde

Ideally readers will look up from the last page of this book and see many unexpected examples of berserk style at work around them. Yet the phenomenon is not a particular butterfly that can be pinned to a specimen board once and for all. The difficulty lies in the comprehensive and interactive nature of the problem. As style, abandon is thoroughly psychosomatic and psychocultural. Its feedback mechanisms mean that it is richly volatile, readily self-intoxicating, and contagious. Conditioned by style, berserk behavior becomes self-conscious. But since it is also usually richly conflicted, it also invites doublethink or another mode of denial. And since it affects the creaturely ground of personality—fear of death and appetite for life—it can be as inexhaustible as it is intractable.

Though the consequences of abandon can be appalling, its allure can be irresistible, and the difficulties it presents to analysis can be as disorienting as a carnival funhouse. The challenge for the critic is to range far enough afield to evoke the scale and scope of the phenomenon while at the same time working to integrate the findings. This book combs through cultural materials for tropes that foster and manage abandon. It asks how and why the stories we live by come to be infused with explosive potential.

THE INTERPRETED BODY

In berserk abandon body and mind interact in an escalating feedback loop. A woman imprisoned for violence against a partner reports that in rage "I cry because there is no other outlet. I get hot and sweaty, clench my fists . . . I take my glasses off and tell people, 'I'm having a bi-polar moment.' It's my trigger to warn people before I explode . . . In rage, I'm intense . . . I'm afraid of myself—I'm going to kill you because you did something to me . . . I just get relief after rage." Another woman said, "I get red, shake and cry. My legs shake, I'm pacing, I get red. I look for something to hit, and it's a warning to people. I look for an object to destroy."[1]

The way the women interpret the ostensibly irresistible rage is shaping it. One decides that her rage "has no other outlet," but knows it will give her relief. They both warn bystanders and look for things to destroy. In effect, like the fantasy figure the Hulk, they take on the heroic role of publicly trying to master their superhuman wrath. They are both proud of it and afraid of it—and assume others will be as well. Is the nervous system storm real? Yes. Is imagination complicit in it? Also, yes.

The women say they feel as if an alien force intrudes on them. Conventional wisdom unfailingly treats rage as an aberration associated with beasts and gods. The body appears to have a perverse will of its own. But abandon is functional. Diminished conscious control enables emergency physiology to direct behavior—eminently desirable if you encounter a grizzly bear. The crucial question is whether abandon is appropriate. The conventional answer is that in a complex modern society, rage is best switched off. In reality, berserk experience persists all around us. But as history shows, it has also been progressively sublimated, seeping into remote symbolic areas of culture. If anything, the problem of appropriateness requires more acute interpretation than ever.

In his well-known studies psychologist Dolf Zillmann finds escalating anger to be "a sequence of provocations, each triggering an excitatory reaction that dissipates slowly."[2] As Daniel Goleman elaborates, "every successive anger-provoking thought or perception becomes a mini trigger for amygdala-driven surges of catecholamines, each building on the hormonal momentum of those that went before" (61). The eventual eruption of unreasoning rage entails a high level of excitation that "fosters an illusion of power and invulnerability" (62)—core symptoms of the berserk state. This physiology, with the help of illusion, makes rage a process.

Berserk dynamic is seductive in part because it is self-intoxicating and contagious. As in mania, the conviction of purpose may grow stronger even as the behavior becomes more erratic and unrealistic. In a treacherous paradox, greater momentum appears to stabilize resolve, whether as obsession or as fatalism. The effect is like pedaling faster on a bicycle. Greater speed increases the bike's gyroscopic stability and momentum, but also the danger. The bike becomes more committed to its trajectory, but emergency steering and stopping become harder to control.

Short of a blackout, imagination mediates physiology. And no matter how idiopathic the disturbance, culture affects the interpretation. Rampage killers and warriors often explain their fury as a defense of what they believe is right, or as retaliation against injustice. For the women inmates above, rage is "a bi-polar moment" or a "trigger" because "you did something to me." The example shows the need to feel right to be physiological as well as cognitive. Understandably, since it is more than "just" an idea, it is associated with the beyond inhabited by gods, demons, and heroes. Several women in the prison study compared rage to a supernatural force. One said, "It's more than anger. It felt like an evil spirit was in me." Another drew on the familiar ideation of religious hysteria: "My hands shake, my jaw clenches together. It's like the devil is crawling up my back. It's a horrible experience. I hate when I feel like that."

But these reports of intrusive forces expose another troublesome ambiguity, since the demons are also an outcome of faltering impulse control. In turn a failure of self-control can result from weak inhibitions against harming others, but it can also result from anticipating the release from inner conflict that an explosion of fury affords. The inmate "just get[s] relief after rage." This sort of self-abandonment or letting go can play out a tacit death and rebirth. The trope takes all sorts of guises. Bungee jumpers dive into a chasm in a mock suicide, letting go of self (and fear) when they plunge into a symbolic beyond and rebound from this play-death feeling more keenly alive. Like high-wire daredevils in the circus, they dramatize the possibility of mastering the edge of doom. Such a raid on the beyond can be a purgation, a release, a transformation, or a rebirth. The suicidal disposition of many rampage killers is very likely related to that deep fantasy that fatal release is somehow a new life.

With the body in emergency mode, behavior can feel as if it is beyond control and nevertheless be a role. In *Drunken Comportment,* Craig MacAndrew and Robert B. Edgerton describe an encounter with a tribesman in Kenya who interrupted a rampage to greet the visitor, then resumed his "drunken rage" and the berserk interpretive frame.[3] In colonial Indonesia, the syndrome of running amok "essentially disappeared" when the Dutch administration insisted that berserkers no longer be killed but instead taken into custody and sentenced to lifetime penal servitude.[4] With no suicidal blaze of glory to discharge rage and preempt second thoughts, potential assailants chose to be more strategic about their heroic desperation.

Conventional wisdom forces experience into one category or another, for simplicity's sake or in denial. But inhibitions are not a simple on-off switch, all or nothing. Under extreme conditions people do black out or dissociate, but more likely some form of role-playing or doublethink will complicate awareness. Even researchers may be dubiously definitive. Alcohol, for example, "makes the thing in the foreground even more salient and the thing in the background disappear." This myopia puts a drinker "at the mercy of whatever is in front of him."[5] This description could apply to the fixation and self-intoxication in berserk behavior. But it may be more accurate to say that intoxication makes the thing in the background dim or change shape rather than disappear. Which is one reason that intoxication is so fascinating.

THE USES OF ABANDON

Once style conditions emergency physiology, imagination radically complicates the possible outcomes. You can pretend, disguise, or deny berserk abandon. You can project it onto others, or use it to smear them. In fact, people use abandon or the idea of abandon for countless ends. As a style berserk intensity can become a powerful tool, and enticing. In the popular mind it is a weapon, the rage that obliterates threats and enemies. That intensity can also be treated as a catalyst, dissolving inhibitions, overriding worries, and enabling change, as civilians often discover in wartime. Like a forbidden steroid, it can tap reserves of energy and confidence. The rush of arousal can shake off uncertainty and inner conflict, and the result can be heroic selflessness as well as sadistic fury or the folly of "go for broke" gambling or a drug binge.

Culture is continually assimilating and taming abandon to make use of its energy or to defuse it. Where "going postal" initially signified horrific workplace murders, now it is also a mailing business franchise, "Goin' Postal: Your Friendly Neighborhood Shipping Center." Consider the way fight and flight combine in an advertisement for luxury SUVs that ran at the time of the Columbine slaughter (fig. 1.1). A street of identical suburban houses sports an army tank in each driveway, its cannon pointed at an invisible neighborhood off the page. In one driveway sits a Lexus SUV, and the caption promises that a smart consumer can combine security; lethal threat display;

Figure 1.1   A Lexus SUV advertisement

and elite, stylish comfort. The neighbors are allies or enemies, and driving is war.

An article in *The Atlantic* reported in 1998 that road rage is largely a media myth created by journalistic hype feeding on itself.[6] Allusions to apocalypse and berserk frenzy stand out in Michael Fumento's quotations from the Associated Press ("ROAD WARRIORS ... TURN FREEWAYS INTO FREE-FOR-ALLS"), *Newsweek* ("ROAD RAGE: WE'RE DRIVEN TO DESTRUCTION"), the *San Francisco Examiner* ("TWO-THIRDS OF ALL AUTO DEATHS BLAMED ON STRESSED-OUT, AGGRESSIVE DRIVERS"), the Albany *Times Union* ("SEETHING MOTORIST MAKES CARS WEAPONS"), and a study released by the American Automobile Association Foundation for Traffic Safety ("What used to be just two people screaming at each other is now one person losing it and pulling the trigger").

In these examples berserk style is used to manage morale. It gives humdrum highway frustration thrilling significance even as it reinforces cautionary self-control. In road rage headlines the driver is an incipient psychopath related to tabloid monsters such as the office rampage killer. In the films of Quentin Tarantino the vocabulary of heroism and evil is cooked as in a drug lab to giddy, magical purity by dramatizing low-life psychopaths "on the edge," capable of anything.

In "shock jock" attack broadcasting, "rant" makes berserk style a naively explicit genre. The manipulation of outrage serves transparent partisan politics, but it also functions as a technology for morale management. As the host pumps up indignation at the scapegoat du jour, audiences can use the dose of outrage as a stimulant to counter boredom, anxiety, or depression. It can be self-medicating behavior, mildly addictive, using anger as some people use coffee, alcohol, or drugs, to stimulate, soothe, or impose order on inner life. In practice the broadcast content is secondary, as it is in supermarket tabloids whose headlines screech exciting improbabilities.

When the use of abandon becomes obvious and dull, style has to escalate. In the movies the conventions of berserk abandon are continually evolving, pushing hyperbole, violating taboos, searching out new avenues to arousal. This year's over-the-top sensation is next year's routine brawl. Today the fistfights and decorous bullet wounds of classic crime and cowboy sagas have given way to exploded bodies, crime lab evisceration, and in a film such as Roland Emmerich's wildly popular *Independence Day* (1996), urban cataclysm.

When use becomes especially sophisticated, style can make it possible to scoff at our fascination with violence while indulging it. In a Toyota advertisement from the spring of 2005, we are in the control booth at an indoor laboratory test track. Two young boys urge the lab technician to crash one car after another into a wall while a voiceover sums up the safety features of each model. The crashes delight the kids, and the ad climaxes when they beg, "Come on, Bob. Do another one." Bob replies, "There are no more." The kids then deliver the enthusiastic punch line, "What about your car?" Violence can be self-intoxicating, pumping up toward the berserk state. The more the kids see, the more they want. This is the subtext of the sales pitch in the voiceover, that the Toyota "has everything kids want." How much is enough? The escalation becomes berserk style in the kids' punch line, which would take the destruction outside the lab and destroy "Bob's" car. The advertisement uses berserk style to sell safety by reminding us of our childlike appetite for violence and inviting us to enjoy it vicariously.

AMBIVALENCE AND ALIENATION

As awareness and abandon become more complexly entangled, use opens toward incalculable consequences. Body and soul in turn conspire to exploit that opening to the beyond. In the potential for chaos and madness also lies ecstasy. Lovers have probably always used berserk style as an aphrodisiac. As in bungee jumping, we "fall" in love. And as in Renaissance wordplay on "dying" as sexual climax, erotic desire from time immemorial has joined orgasm to self-abandonment. From Romeo and Juliet and Wagnerian love-death to the orgiastic, alcoholic self-destruction in Mike Figgis's *Leaving Las Vegas* (1995), erotic passion has been associated with reckless orgasmic apotheosis and doom. As the perils of the AIDS epidemic emerged in the 1980s, survival ecstasy intensified the allure of risky promiscuity in some areas of gay culture.[7] As in warfare, death can give risky sex an incomparable larger-than-life urgency. In all its varieties sexual abandon can be calculated—a sort of erotic bungee jumping into the arms of death—but it is also akin to religious rituals that seek to relinquish or dissolve the self in order to induce a conviction of renewal.

At this point the uses of the berserk enter a zone of paradox and perversity where criticism struggles to keep a clear head amid dissolving preconceptions. A simple example can be seen in rock concerts whose promise of liberation and creativity climaxes with stoned audiences, ear-splitting amplifiers, and musicians smashing their instruments as The Who did in the 1960s until that became tamely predictable. At the famous Altamount Speedway concert (December 6, 1969) the Rolling Stones played through a set unaware that in the surrounding mayhem a fan high on methamphetamine had drawn a pistol in a skirmish with a Hell's Angel and been stabbed to death.

In *Hated*, Todd Philips' 1993 documentary about the marginal punk rocker GG Allin and the Murder Junkies, the camera catches Allin acting out suicidal rage onstage in his performances. His performances were symbolic rampage killing. Naked, defecating and hurling excrement, chairs, and the microphone stand, Allin assaulted audiences, tacitly inviting violent retaliation. In one melee with fans he suffered a broken arm. Toward the end of his short career he repeatedly vowed to kill himself onstage, and in 1993 did die of a drug overdose. Allin seems trapped in compulsive, fixated behavior characteristic of mental illness. Yet the performer, fans, and rival musicians all monotonously interpreted his behavior in crude ideological terms, as a struggle for freedom. Even on a network television talk show no one challenged Allin's boasts that he represented total freedom.

Allin and his fans grew up in the psychic aftermath of the Vietnam War. His rant about total freedom can be seen as a grotesque mutation of Cold War anticommunist hysteria and the utopian promises of a dying counterculture. As if in combat, Allin combined paramilitary fantasies with the berserker's feeling of magical invulnerability. "My mind is a machine gun," he tells the film maker, "my body the bullets and the audience is the target." Apparently high on drugs, he claims he wants "to conquer the world—not to entertain but to annihilate." This self-intoxicating rant acts out the suicidal anger blazoned in Allin's tattoo "Life Sucks." It also resonates with the malevolent depression that Dylan Klebold expressed in his journal in the months before carrying out the Columbine High School massacre.

The drive toward ecstasy and blackout in the arts is a form of play-death. Once the curtain falls, the tragic heroine will get to her feet and be applauded back to life. The allure of vampires is symptomatic. Traditionally vampires act out the berserker's cold survival rage. They and their victims struggle in a shadowy zone between life and death. Their violence fractures daylight reality but stops short of annihilation. In the popular revision represented by Stephanie Meyer's *Twilight* (2005) and Alan Ball's HBO series *True Blood* (2008), vampire eros is about sharing liberating transgression and the dream of immortalizing abandon. Vampires are "like the supernatural version of rock 'n roll bad boys," says Ball. "They have special powers, they're forever young and they don't play by the rules. No wonder so many people have sexual fantasies about them."[8] That is, these vampires are excuses to shed inhibitions, in the tradition of femme fatales such as Carmen. And yet from time to time people "on the edge" do act out such stories in real life. Even impulsive behaviors have some sort of models conditioning them.

These behaviors raise momentous questions. If berserkers "put on" their fury as they once did bear or jaguar skins, to what extent are they role-playing? Is berserk fury a technic for inducing acute physiological arousal akin to ceremonies such as a war dance that sharpen fighting spirits and turn warriors into weapons? We think of rage as autonomic: a bizarre interruption of everyday serenity, something that happens to someone under stress. But the Norse warriors deliberately shed inhibitions, pumping up morale and muscle. Warrior frenzy was also a tactic and a tool—berserk style.

Warrior abandon has always aroused acute ambivalence. After the capture of Antioch in 1098 during the First Crusade, the daughter of the Byzantine emperor reported that the Franks "have no military discipline nor strategic skills." In battle "a raging fury seizes their hearts and they become implacable, common soldiers and leaders alike. They hurl themselves with invincible impetus into the midst of the enemy ranks as soon as the latter give a little ground." The Emir Ousama-ibn-Munquidh summed up the ambivalence: "Anyone who knows anything about the Franks looks on them as beasts, outdoing all others in courage and warlike spirit, just as animals are superior when it comes to strength and aggression."[9] The warriors' abandon was a cultural practice, a style that felt natural to them. It functioned as a tool akin to "shock and awe" today. Intimidating propaganda can also be a motivational technique and one solution to problems of competition and hierarchy within a group of high-strung and well-armed males. Such abandon is a window on questions underlying all creativity and atrocity: How do we sort out heroic and vicious motivation, symbolic and neurophysiological components? Is there an identifiable threshold or "edge" marking off the berserk state?

The psychiatrist Jonathan Shay acknowledges the equivocal god-like or beastlike ambiguity that makes the berserk state fascinating: "A soldier who routs the enemy single-handedly is often in the grip of a special state of mind, body and social disconnection at the time of his memorable deeds. Such men, often regarded by commanders as 'the best,' have been honored as heroes . . . the word *berserk* is the most precise term available to describe the behavior." He acknowledges "the ambiguous borderline between heroism and a blood-crazed, berserk state in which abuse after abuse is committed" (77).

That "borderline" is treacherous. Recall the hockey dad who murdered his son's coach. A psychiatrist might classify him as a "sadistic borderline personality" or an "explosive psychopath": someone calm enough to cope with daily life most of the time, though subject to sudden episodes of hostility.[10] But of course this terminology is just a label, and a self-evident label at that. It is safe to say that the "borderline" father saw himself as a hero defending his son, his own self-esteem, and justice, or attacking the coach as a rival, bad father. He may have identified so closely with his son—the "victimized" child in himself—that he felt as if he was suffering the son's unjust defeat, perhaps in the way that some abortion opponents so closely identify with the unborn that they call themselves "survivors" and have bombed clinics and murdered doctors. Claiming self-defense and that the death was accidental, the hockey dad was convicted of involuntary manslaughter: a judgment allowing for diminished responsibility.

Fury readily preempts responsibility—hence the design of Dante's Hell. Once beyond cultural controls, abandon can be self-intoxicating and more autonomic. As one Vietnam veteran described a crisis in combat, "I just went crazy. . . . I lost all my mercy. I felt a drastic change after that. I just couldn't get enough. I built up such hate. I couldn't do enough damage. . . . Got worse as time went by. I really loved fucking killing, couldn't get enough. For every one that I killed

I felt better. Made some of the hurt went away" (Shay, 78). Based on his clinical work with veterans, Shay calls the berserk state "ruinous," concluding that it usually leads to the soldier's maiming or death in battle, and to lifelong psychological and physiological injury if he survives (98).

This view is based on painful evidence and not to be gainsaid. Its limitation is the core problem of berserk style. The borderline between heroism and berserk frenzy is not only ambiguous, as Shay says, but insolubly ambivalent. We fear the berserk as a kind of madness; but we also associate it with exceptional powers. Deeds may be disgusting yet charged with heroic meaning on the battlefield under the pressure of death. The Vietnam veteran quoted at the outset bitterly recollects: "I became a fucking animal. I started putting fucking heads on poles. Leaving fucking notes for the motherfuckers. Digging up fucking graves. I didn't give a fuck anymore. Y'know, I wanted—They wanted a fucking hero, so I gave it to them. They wanted fucking body count, so I gave them body count. I hope they're fucking happy. But they don't have to live with it. I do" (83). The man feels he was out of control, icily indifferent—"I didn't give a fuck anymore"—yet he "couldn't get enough" and was also guided by what "they" wanted: by the values and feelings of his culture, by the demands of home no less than of his superiors. "They" are tacitly a voice in his head shaping his behavior. Being starkly ambivalent about what "they" demand of him, he is agonizingly alienated now, whether he recognizes it or not, about the culture—the home—he had been prepared to die for.

The tormented and alienated hero goes back through Shakespeare's Coriolanus and Macbeth to Homer's Achilles. In vernacular American culture a representative figure would be the Vietnam vet John Rambo in Ted Kotcheff's First Blood (1982). Rambo (Sylvester Stallone) runs amok after police in a small town abuse him. His one-man war against police injustice escalates to a fiery climax yet is scripted to harm no one. Rambo is a traumatized renegade yet also the archetypal frontiersman. His actions bespeak rage, but also an adolescent fantasy of omnipotence: Don't mess with me or I'll destroy your entire town. In many ways he resembles the Gulf War veteran Timothy McVeigh, who reacted to the government's brutal annihilation of the Branch Davidian religious sect in Texas by bombing a Federal office building, killing hundreds of innocent people and going to his death coldly convinced of his righteous purpose. First Blood camouflages Rambo's wrath as the last-ditch self-defense of a naturally composed man, so that moviegoers identify with behavior that would otherwise be richly contaminated by terrorist fury.

The berserk warrior may be a revered hero or a crazed killer, and those categories may tragically blur, especially if frenzy becomes a usable tool or role. Rambo's cold violence is a public part of his warrior identity. Timothy McVeigh self-consciously proclaimed his radical alienation. "Putting on" the bear's skin, so to speak, can be—to some extent, always is—a style. To be clear about it: berserk style can be an innocuous facsimile or a way of mediating or sublimating action. But it also contains the potential for towering fury.

The veterans' psychiatrist understandably protects the idea of a healthy norm and emphasizes the "ruinous" effects of the berserk state. "If a soldier survives the berserk state, it imparts emotional deadness and vulnerability to explosive rage to his psychology and a permanent hyperarousal to his physiology—hallmarks of post-traumatic stress disorder (PTSD) in combat veterans" (98). But combat frenzy is the most extreme form of the syndrome, since the soldier is fighting for his life. Framed as style, the berserk is more likely to hold in suspension the pressure of the appetite for survival that is built into us.

Before pursuing the problem of style any further, we need to examine our survival instincts and other creaturely motives. We are unique among the animals in our awareness of death. As Ernest Becker puts it: "to live a whole lifetime with the fate of death haunting one's dreams and even the most sun-filled days" creates "an impossible situation for an animal to be in. I believe that those who speculate that a full apprehension of man's condition would drive him insane are right, quite literally right."[11]

CREATURELY MOTIVES

We have evolved as radically conflicted beings. We kiss to make love with the same mouth that bites to feed and destroy. The part of us that speaks is also a weapon. We are not *given* life: on the contrary, we live by corralling, slaughtering, chewing, digesting, and excreting other lives, plundering their nutrients and fortifying ourselves to search for more life to consume. Although cultures celebrate good table manners, eating is not a chosen pastime: like breathing and mating, it is a compulsion. If we resist or fail to satisfy the compulsion to kill and feed, we die.

In this perspective "frenzied fury," the Oxford English Dictionary's (OED's) definition of the berserk state, resembles a "feeding frenzy" in the animal world. And this is the motive that applies to the OED's secondary example of the berserker: "a lawless bravo or freebooter." After all, Norse "warriors" were also plunderers, exacting "tribute," taking slaves, and sometimes stealing land to settle on. Like other voracious raiders of history, they fed on the vitality of others. The Vikings were impressive predators. They fascinate us like dinosaurs, whose epoch, says Becker, "is an epic food orgy with king-size actors who convey unmistakably what organisms are dedicated to."[12]

Although we are usually less volatile than our primate cousins, we do share some of their violent traits. Adolescent male chimps are prone to spells of berserk frenzy in which they will indiscriminately dominate others. Males undertake organized lethal raids on their neighbors as humans do. The bipeds may see themselves as "jaguar warriors" in Mesoamerica or as gang members claiming "their" urban turf, but the deep affinity is unmistakable. What's more, in the berserk state chimpanzees can be systematically cruel. A group may spread-eagle a captured victim and inflict lethal bites on his face and exposed body, exulting in the torture.

Still, Becker reminds us, we are also symbolic animals. More than extinction, we fear extinction with insignificance. We want our lives to matter. The wish to be heroic is also the wish not to be nothing: to be bigger than death. Karen Horney sees the temptation to falsify the self through inflated claims on the world as a form of the ancient "devil's pact" that haunts all human development. Since we begin life as helpless infants, we grow up fearing and hating our vulnerability. We love godlike parents and symbols. We emulate "big shots." We want to share their powers and importance, but we also fear and hate the possibility of their rejection or failure.

This helps to account for the ambivalence of berserk motives. The behavior can be all-out striving for heroic significance—to make life matter. Yet it may also develop the physiology and themes of the child's tantrum. In moments of all-encompassing panic and rage, character dissolves into primal appetite for life: a demand for superhuman action and attention. In this context rampage killing is a desperately perverse form of heroic striving. Extraordinary murder forces the world to recognize the murderers and their grievances. Murder proves that the killer exists, even as its evil confirms the ultimate, often suicidal futility of the act.

Operating at the limits of control, striving to overcome death, berserk abandon acts out insolubly ambivalent creaturely motives. Massacre and feeding frenzy, rage and greed for life, are two faces of the same creaturely appetite, and the more ambivalent because greed for life can sometimes include sacrifice: self-abandon for the sake of others. In an age of agribusiness and microwaved instant meals we still celebrate the great predators, including wolves and tigers. In nature documentaries featuring thrilling fangs, we are fascinated by predatory compulsions. And not without reason. Since we too can be eaten, we turn bears into harmless teddy bears.

Anxiety spurs us to generate cultural forms that shelter and empower us. At the dinner table you can "attack your food with gusto," converting aggression into healthy desire just as "fighting a cold" makes combat salubrious. A supermarket is a storehouse of symbolic vitality that includes plants and animals shrink-wrapped and colorfully labeled to screen out awareness of the killing that brought them to the shelves. The market's brightly lit, aesthetic displays, trustworthy cash register, and cornucopia of immortality markers—vitamins, cleaning agents, beauty magazines, and the like—assure us that life is plentiful, under control, and enduringly meaningful. Canned singers fill the aisles with vows to "love you forever," appealing to your sexual appetite for more life.

We ennoble appetite through denial. The far-reaching preoccupation with dieting regulates desire and imagines an ideal kind of consumption. Nevertheless, we are meat eating meat, splitting off guilt and rage by killing other creatures offstage at the slaughterhouse. The clever animal that digests other creatures into foul-smelling excrement is able to repudiate its animal origins by using "the Purist Hatbox," the Kohler Corporation's toilet in the shape of a hatbox that "aims to bring the throne to your home into the 21st Century,"[13] offering you regal elevation above your animal mortality. The reflex of this denial is scatological rage: the use of "shit" as an all-purpose insult and marker for nemesis, and the hatred of "assholes." In extreme forms it underlies the combat berserker's attack on the bodies of enemies through mutilation and collecting body parts. Likewise cannibalism, in which eating another's body incorporates its vitality, in effect converting deadly flesh into magical life.

Research shows that we respond viscerally to immortality symbols such as the flag and the cross.[14] In a crisis we will kill for them. They stand for enduring life the way monuments and even bones concretize the inconceivable nothingness of death. As long as we believe, our lives feel purposeful: we feel *right*.[15] The problem is that cultural guarantees are as mortal as our bodies, always in need of renewal. When enchantment falters, creaturely survival motives surge into action. Think of the famous photo of the doomed Hitler in his bunker transfixed by architectural models of his immortal dream city as death chewed apart the real city overhead. Cornered, facing death, he struggled to stay enchanted by his monumental immortality fantasies even as he was ordering the annihilation of enemies and his own people.

Even when it is suicidal, sadistic aggression can generate immortality fantasies. Erich Fromm held that sadism "is the passion to have absolute and unrestricted control over a living being. . . . To force someone to endure pain or humiliation without being able to defend himself is one of the manifestations of absolute control." Fromm anticipates Becker in recognizing that "[t]he experience of absolute control over another being, of omnipotence . . . creates the illusion of transcending the limitations of human existence."[16]

Fromm's definition resonates with the "godlike" and "beastlike" characteristics of the berserk state. The extremes are intimately connected. The great conquerors of history have been monsters of appetite, swallowing land and people and as it were excreting corpses, compulsively expanding their life-space. Conquest explicitly counters the fear of being nobody, alone and helpless: the fear of social death.[17] And given the hero-worship that binds followers to leaders, the leader's motives magnify the concerns of the group. Reciprocally, those on the bottom facing social death aspire to immortalizing glory. The pattern turns up again and again in rampage killing. One day after a military officer killed 13 people at Fort Hood, Jason Rodriguez opened fire at the engineering firm that had let him go two years earlier. He was divorced, in debt, with past indications of mental disturbance. As if colleagues had killed him two years before the incident, he reentered the scene with guns blazing, "Because they left me to rot."[18]

While there is no practical way to inventory all the forms berserk style takes, there are revealing clusters of language and fantasies that stand out. Since eating entails killing, it can be no surprise that one cluster of signs originates in the hunt. Throughout history hunters have had to manage conflicted and violent creaturely motives. Evolving cultural controls helped hunters to master fear, greed, and hunger pangs, especially in the supercharged, dangerous moments when the prey fights for its life and triggers the conclusive burst of ferocity. Early hunters had to learn to summon—and then calm—the "killer instinct." In sharing out the kill afterward they had to develop heroic roles as providers that could tame greed.

Cultural controls were survival tools also because they helped to regulate competition for food that could trigger warfare—another cluster of berserk signs. Successful hunters and warriors who could provide more life for the group came to dominate the group and its fertility. In this way predation has been an important adaptive strategy in human evolution, "providing benefits for genetic fitness (passing on one's genes) in forager, pastoral, and urban societies, and its enjoyment is a 'culturally elaborated' manifestation of the initial predatory adaptation."[19] The potency of the legendary hunter or warrior such as Gilgamesh shimmers in the king's scepter, which originated as the hunter's club and the warrior's mace, and in the prodigious harems of history's great warlords. The hunt had mythic status for New England Puritans, drawing "strength from its relevance to traditional Indian-war writing.[20]

This is not simply a colorful historical detail. "As part of an instruction course named 'Combat Hunter,' the Marines have brought in 'big-game hunters' to school their snipers in the better use of 'optics.' According to a September 2007 article by Grace Jean in *National Defense Magazine*, '[T]he lab conducted a war game with Marines, African game hunters and inner city police officers to search for ways to improve training.' The program included a 15-minute CD titled 'Every Marine a Hunter.'"[21] A Marine team forms a hunting pack, ritualized at the end of briefings when "Marines put their hands together and shout, 'Kill!'"[22]

Like hunters, ancient warriors overcame fellow animals fighting for their lives, harvesting life in the frenzied climax to battle. Victors regularly exterminated rival males, enslaving women and children, hauling off food, livestock, and valuables—the adversary's "livelihood." In many traditional cultures throughout the Americas victors ceremonially cannibalized slain enemies to acquire their vital qualities. In subsuming their rivals' women, warriors acted out a godlike power to propagate more life: creating more children or slaves to extend a master's will. Even when the hunter-warrior role is only nominal, as in racist lynching, the mob acts to strengthen its feeling of dominance—its self-feeling—by running down, torturing, and destroying the scapegoat, mutilating his body and especially his genitals, supposedly to protect "its" women and children.[23]

A third cluster of markers for berserk style is associated with religion. Since religions are a primary tool for managing the insoluble problems of death and creaturely ambivalence, they are always susceptible to panic and rage. Although Christians worship a single all-loving God, for example, under stress they have invoked the rival Satan to account for evil and mobilize wrath against scapegoats. Christ's sacrifice is supposed to stop that murderous cycle, but sometimes the contemplation of His suffering and persecution has incited rampages. From the First Crusade through the schismatic massacres of the early modern period, Christian Europe was intermittently amok, vanquishing enemies of Christ. In the witchcraft panics that persisted into the seventeenth century Christians attacked neighbors and even family members in judicial killing frenzies that combined elements of the hunt, warfare, and religious quest.[24] In the nineteenth century American lynch mobs believed they were good Christians killing for a sacred cause, even as Christian white supremacist groups and Islamic terrorists consecrate violence today. As Otto Rank explained, "the death fear of the ego is lessened by the killing, the sacrifice, of the other; through the death of the other, one buys oneself free of the penalty of dying, of being killed."[25] A Chapter 6 shows how some forms of today's "end times" fantasies act out this principle as a berserk rampage that annihilates the unsaved and secures the immortality of the righteous.

The dilemma, then, is that the religious materials used to regulate creaturely appetites can also inflame survival greed. "Surrender" to the divine is an impossibly volatile concept since by definition it has no natural limits. Religious ideas are richly ambiguous and plastic. Messianic delusions show up regularly in rampage killers with a history of mental illness. The devout reasonably protest that these are distortions of "true" religion. But of course religions around the world continually suffer sectarian conflict and blend into other cultural forms. In Nazi esoterica Parsifal, the Christian knight, continued his quest for the pure blood of the holy grail through the gas chambers. "Killer groups engaging in groupthink have an illusion of invulnerability and moral righteousness that leads to excessive risk-taking. . . . Genocides, viewed this way, constitute a virulent form of social hysteria, one with a hapless target group for extreme aggression."[26]

Behind all of these creaturely motives is the most comprehensive force of all: the compulsion to organismic expansion. Groups fight to the death over food and mates and territory, including claims to the beyond. Unchecked, appetite for life can produce epidemic obesity and addiction syndromes. As a species we are built to reproduce, with no reliable means of managing runaway overpopulation. UN population conferences usually wind up with pledges of self-restraint, paranoid glances at fertile rivals, and continued expansion. Proponents of sustainable development warn that in the past two centuries growth of cheap hydrocarbon energy has become exponential, and the approaching era of energy and resource scarcity forecasts grave conflicts. The impact is especially forbidding because current economic systems are based on debt and boundless expansion, by warfare if necessary.

Greed seems natural when markets assume that more is always better. The prejudice is built into us. As Becker puts the question, "Whoever gets enough life?" The question leads to everyday "Faustian economics" which, says Wendell Berry, is "not only prodigal extravagance but also an assumed limitlessness," as if we are gods, open to the beyond, and not creatures who must live in a finite world.[27] Faustian greed for life grips history's maniacal conquerors. Harder to grasp is the exponential change that has been accelerating at a mind-boggling pace in the past few centuries. Abandon and the beyond are not simply spatial concepts, terra incognita on the map, but shadows in motion.

FIGHTING TO BELIEVE

Rampage killers are said to "seethe" at injustice; soldiers fight and die for "God and country," religious crusaders and martyrs fight and die for "faith." Belief in "what's right" is psychosomatic. It makes you and your world *feel* coherent and therefore is the ground of self-esteem. When belief frays or mental processes are impaired, world and self suffer a "nervous breakdown." Hence Otto Rank 's pithy remark that "[e]very conflict over truth is in the last analysis just the same old struggle over . . . immortality." As Becker elaborates in *Escape from Evil*, "If anyone doubts this, let him try to explain in any other way the life-and-death viciousness of all ideological disputes. . . . No wonder men go into a rage about fine points of belief: if your adversary wins the argument about truth, you die. Your immortality system has been shown to be fallible, your life becomes fallible" (64).

Perversely, that is, failure of "what's right" produces not problem-solving behavior but emergency reactions. Psychic defenses that should support the self can put it at risk. Feeling victimized, righteousness lashes out. History abounds in vicious battles over purity. Righteousness cults that fixate on a particular belief system predictably become punitive or self-destructive when it fails. Decades after the war some Germans looked back in bewilderment at their roared assent to Goebbels' famous "Total War" speech ("Do you want total war?") at a moment when havoc was raining down on Germany and it was obvious that the war was lost. The berserk final ten months of World War II claimed as many lives as all the preceding years of carnage. This is the dynamic figured in the Cold War fantasy of the Doomsday Machine in Stanley Kubrick's *Dr Strangelove* (1964): a weapon that cannot be disarmed once an attack is launched, as in "we've gone too far to stop now."

To "go into a rage about fine points of belief" is to be in the grip of "life-or-death" greed for meaning—and for survival. The problem is not that berserk fury eliminates meaning, but that it condenses and fixates on it. The moral world shrinks. Amok, the rampage killer hates globally, absolutely, and without mercy. For the seething rampage killer injustice comes to tyrannize identity. Amy Bishop, the biology professor who gunned down three colleagues at the University of Alabama when she was denied tenure, once punched a woman in a dispute over a child's seat in a restaurant, shouting "I'm Dr. Amy Bishop!" "Over the years, Dr. Bishop had shown evidence that the smallest of slights could set off a disproportionate and occasionally violent reaction, according to numerous interviews with colleagues and others who know her." Echoing the anthrax terrorism of 2001 and periodic headline fears of rogue epidemics, she fantasized about using a virus to carry out mass killing.[28]

This is a familiar pattern: inner life is a survival struggle between godlike self-righteousness—Greek tragedy calls it hubris—and madness or social death. For one side or the other, in war or peace, winner-take-all contests end in real or symbolic death. Durkheim held that when cultural meanings fail, the victims are reduced to the animal level of chronic fighting or fornication. Conversely some people try to reduce experience to animal instinct in order to block the anguish of failed meaning. "Alcoholism, drug addiction, sexual obsessions, and adventurousness—in which meaning remains, but only while engaged in extreme and risky activities, including violence—have all been attributed to misguided and finally self-destructive attempts to suppress the question of meaning by drowning in instinctual behavior."[29] In berserk hands guns similarly compress unruly meanings into an instinct.

The deep problem is that the self, too, is a story, and the failure of a story can mean a breakdown of self and human connectedness. When the Vietnam War lost its conviction, desperate soldiers not only ran amok against enemies and civilians, but sometimes against their own leaders. The public has never been made fully aware that in the final years of the Vietnam War soldiers assassinated their officers on a scale that helped bring about Washington's decision to withdraw. In Sen. John Kerry's challenge during Congressional testimony as a Vietnam Veteran against the War, "Who wants to be the last man to die for a mistake?"

A striking example of the cross-relation between war and civilian culture, and between self and story, is E. J. Leed's recognition of an intimate "interaction between German cultural categories and German soldiers' experiences of the Great War." He concludes that "the effect of combat was a disintegrative personal experience which rendered the self instinctively meaningless." A "disintegrative personal experience" is a definition of madness, whether expressed as catatonic depression or fury. How did such damage come about? "Going into the war, German culture comprehended battle as a test of self that could resolve the pressing contradictions of modernity. Instead, the harsh reality of battle marginalized its participants, its trenches ironically objectifying the very labyrinth that the experience of modernity had come to seem."[30] It goes without saying that these dynamics had a lasting effect on the veterans—Hitler, for one, acted out berserk themes for the rest of his life. Across the globe cultures are still struggling to "resolve the pressing contradictions of modernity," in the United States no less than in tribal societies and in the hotbeds of terrorist jihad.

The crucial point is that a loss of belief can lead to despair or fury—or to despairing fury. The failure of a crucial life story can disembed the self and poison basic trust in the world. The reaction may be physical violence among terrorists, criminals, and desperate employees, but it may also unleash the mayhem of rogue bankers and executives operating within a shrunken moral and social narrative. Even when genius disregards conventional reality to make new discoveries, the process can be berserk: hence the trope of the mad scientist memorably dramatized in *Frankenstein*.

The point is not only that disenchantment guts one particular belief or value, but that it deranges creaturely equilibrium. Under too much stress, basic trust breaks down and all values seem artificial and empty, leaving death and loss to terrorize the mind. This is the critical risk in military culture, since armies have to break down the new recruit's basic trust to create the belief that fellow humans are enemies who must be killed. Likewise, gang initiations deliberately subvert trust in outsiders by demanding that new members kill for the group. Religious fanaticism poses a similar danger.

FIGHTING FOR SANITY

Almost half of the rampage killers in the *New York Times* study—47— "had a history of mental health problems before they killed; 20 had been hospitalized for psychiatric problems; 42 had been seen by mental health professionals. Psychiatric drugs had been prescribed at some point before the rampages to 24 of the killers, and 14 of those people were not taking their prescribed drugs when they killed. Diagnoses of mental illness are often difficult to pin down, so *The Times* tabulated behavior: 23 killers showed signs of serious depression before the killings, and 49 expressed paranoid ideas."[31]

Some rampage killers present unambiguously paranoid psychotic symptoms. In December 1993, for example, the Jamaican immigrant

Colin Ferguson murdered five commuters in a Long Island Railroad coach believing that he was participating in an apocalyptic race war. At his trial Ferguson was obstreperously psychotic. Misfortunes and his distorted judgment had crippled him. According to the (black) landlord who had to evict him, "Ferguson bought a gun" and "talked in the third person about some apocryphal [apocalyptic]-doom scenario." In his room he chanted "mantras all night about 'all the black people killing all the white people.'"[32]

Meaning may be distorted in mental illness yet remain crucial. Beyond his personal grievances and the internal pressure of illness, Ferguson also drew on berserk style in the culture around him. He echoed salient themes of the day, from workplace shootings and ethnic cleansing around the world—as in Bosnia—to the fear of race war that Rev. Jim Jones used to lure victims to his Peoples Temple church and eventual murder in Guyana (1979). The billionaire Fred Koch, one of the original members of the John Birch Society, held that "[t]he colored man looms large in the Communist plan to take over America," and "Welfare was a secret plot to attract rural blacks to cities, where they would foment 'a vicious race war.'"[33] Adapted to serve white supremacists' survival anxieties, apocalyptic race war is a cardinal belief of Christian identity adherents and others on the radical right.

When government offices denied Ferguson's grievances, he took the role of messianic warrior with a chaotic discharge of emotions. His fantasy of race war replaced the lost meaning in his life. It condensed his actual experiences into a parable that orchestrated chaos and converted terror into tragic rage that he could act on. The parable substantiated his inner life, and the homicidal assault in turn substantiated the parable. Paradoxically, the man was fighting off social death, plunging into a delusional story in a desperate effort to keep—or make—himself real.

At this distance we can only glimpse the inner turmoil of a Colin Ferguson. The critical point is that what Becker says of schizophrenia can apply to anybody under sufficient stress: "He has to contrive extra-ingenious and extra-desperate ways of living in the world that will keep him from being torn apart by experience, since he is already almost apart."[34] Once in motion, emergency physiology and momentum can give the berserk state the trancelike quality of psychosis. In 1995, 56-year-old James Davis returned to the Union Butterfield tool company in Asheville, NC, where he had been fired two days earlier for fighting. Firing 50 rounds from a semiautomatic rifle and pistol, he killed three employees. Witnesses reported that he "walked with calm determination [and afterward] lit a cigarette and quietly surrendered to police."[35]

Davis apparently set out to get revenge for the fights and termination two days earlier, fixated on feelings of betrayal and injustice. But a closer look reveals an ungrounded personality that had long been using a combative attitude to make "fighting for his life" a story that could give him coherence. Coworkers had nicknamed him Psycho, because he "repeatedly picked fights at the tool warehouse . . . and had often told colleagues that if he were ever fired, he would return to kill his bosses. He had seen combat in Vietnam and been hospitalized with schizophrenia after the war. He lived alone, and co-workers knew he owned a .44 Magnum with a scope and had practiced firing it in his basement."[36]

Needless to say, Davis had strong incentives to believe that he was not responsible for his actions. But the dissociated, psychotic quality of his account is compatible with other descriptions of the berserk state. From death row he wrote: "I was calm. I was no longer me. Like someone else in my brain took over." He "went from tunnel vision to total blackout. When I got my vision and my mind back, I looked and seen what had happened. I did not know who I was. In the end, I self-destructed."[37]

To hold himself together Davis organized his life around fighting off threat. In themes (conflict, defiance, revenge) and practice (gun-use) he focused on mastering violent abandon. To interpret his experience, however, he seized on Jekyll-and-Hyde ideas about dissociative states that have been influential in many movies such as *The Manchurian Candidate* (1962, 2004). The blackout has long been a favorite plot device of screenwriters. "I was no longer me. Like someone else in my brain took over." However responsible for his actions he may have been, Davis felt—and needed to believe that he felt—"carried away." Concluding that he "self-destructed," he was describing the sort of "disintegrative personal experience which rendered the self instinctively meaningless" that overtook soldiers in World War I. What is striking is Davis's inability to find a story that could give his life coherence: not just in jail but long before, in the Vietnam War, during his treatment (or lack of treatment) for schizophrenia, and finally on the job.

Whatever its cause, mental illness challenges the integrity of the self. Indiscriminate aggression against others can be an effort to fight off or to master threats to the self: threats that reflect the internal symptoms of illness, whether recognized as such or not. Before his rampage in Tucson, Jared Loughner fixated on ideas about the disintegrating ground of reality. He began to find waking and dreaming blurring into one another. He feared that words were losing their meaning and that without a gold standard, government was destroying the currency. On the Internet he posted mystifying tutorials about his beliefs and burned with resentment that the Army and Pima Community College had rejected him. He had two nine-millimeter bullets tattooed on his back, and photographed himself posing in a G-string with a pistol strapped to his body. Stripping off his social identity, he was in effect making himself a powerful weapon instead of an alienated young man threatened by derealization and slipping toward madness.

About two-thirds of the rampage killers in the *Times* database "made general threats of violence to others in advance." Of the 100 killers, 55 "regularly expressed explosive anger or frustration," while 35 had a history of violent behavior and assaults. "They were so noticeably unstable that even in their very separate circles they had been awarded similar nicknames: 'Crazy Pat,' 'Crazy John,' 'Crazy Joe.'"[38] Expecting a violent reaction from the man coworkers called "Psycho," James Davis's bosses broke the news of his termination in a room with a table they could use as a shield if necessary. Campus police brought backup officers when they told Jared Loughner that he had been suspended from Pima Community College.

But not everyone under stress runs amok. And not everyone will run amok in the same way. Much depends on how particular individuals are wrapped. In an individualistic culture with limited health care resources people have limited options in dealing with an ambiguously threatening person. Although some experts are more optimistic about prediction,[39] psychology has no foolproof tools for predicting violent behavior. Most threats turn out to be only threat displays. In hindsight life histories may well reveal an alarming pattern, but even then intervention is no simple matter. Speculation about neurophysiology is as venerable as Galenic humors theory and remains as tantalizing as it is inconclusive. As witnessed by the bizarre Satanic ritual abuse fad in 1980s and 1990s psychiatry, theories of demonic possession still persist in a scientific age.

Generations of theorists since Lombroso have tried to establish a taxonomy of criminal types.[40] And animal breeding shows that genetic makeup strongly influences aggressiveness. In the 1970s, genetic studies promised to show that a particular chromosomal abnormality such as the XYY or "double Y" configuration could identify males prone to violent crime. The evidence was seductive but finally unpersuasive.[41]

Research into traumatic stress has produced insights into brain chemistry and structures such as the amygdala, which processes alarm, and the dorsal striatum, which releases neurotransmitters such as dopamine associated with pleasure and safety. Psychopharmacology has produced psychotropic agents judged to be effective in treating symptoms of anxiety and aggression in PTSD, although PTSD "is heterogeneous in its nature, and often presents with other psychiatric comorbidities. As a result, empirical research on effective pharmacotherapy for PTSD has produced complex findings."[42] When paranoid schizophrenics commit violent acts, it often turns out that they have stopped taking antipsychotic medication—which may be proof of the drugs' effectiveness but also of the harrowing ambiguities at work.

It would be a mistake to focus on mental illness as the primary driver in berserk behavior. In the right circumstances anyone is capable of atrocity, as Donald Dutton's survey shows. The "sadistic borderline personality" and the "explosive psychopath" are not alone "on the edge." We are always only a personal or vicarious step away from death-awareness. Even without organic illness, says Becker, humans drive themselves "into a blind obliviousness with social games, psychological tricks, personal preoccupations so far removed from the reality of [their] situation that they are forms of madness—agreed madness, shared, disguised and dignified madness, but madness all the same" (27).

The full-blown berserk state emerges when that agreement, disguise, and dignity break down. The "seething" that explodes is in effect a super story that tries to make sense of the disjunction and a self beset by stress or illness. So charged with conflict is the story that it resembles a dream in retrospect. Sitting on death row, trying to be cogent for his interviewer and for himself, James Davis experienced his murderous transformation as a spell now broken. "I did not know who I was," he reported as if waking from a dream state. "In the end, I self-destructed." Waiting in prison to be killed, having come face-to-face with his doom, he had no place left to go. No longer inside the shelter of everyday reality, he relates himself as a story—"In the end, I self-destructed"—in effect, seeing himself already dead.

The crucial point is that we are psychosomatic creatures, and whether it is primarily symbolic or neurophysiological, a threat to the self can trigger fury. When Davis fumed that "[i]f they ever decide to fire me, I'll take two or three of them with me," he was interpreting job loss as social death. His reply echoes war movies as well as the basic idea behind the Cold War nuclear doctrine of Mutual Assured Destruction (MAD): kill me and we all die. The underlying theme, that is, reveals a zone in human behavior in which lockstep logic and insanity fuse. Davis's fear of social death exacerbated what must have been tormenting fears of psychotic disintegration—literally self-destruction—that in turn reinforced the spiral of survival rage. In holing up with weapons, he acted like a soldier under fire in a fox-hole. The "blackout" of abandon momentarily resolved his turmoil. On death row he is amazed to find he is once again alive and in distress.

As a "break out," berserk abandon implies losing yourself. As a result it has much in common with behaviors such as mania, frantic grief, and religious ecstasy. In American culture, with the popular awareness of bipolar disorder, berserk abandon and mania commonly overlap. Mania can include indifference to risk and pain as well as heightened impulsivity signaling an acute focus on the instant but also on the beyond—a focus that seems to call for maximum exertion. Whatever the differences in physiology—conventional wisdom imagines berserk violence driven by hatred and fear, mania by elation—nervous system arousal enters a zone of shadowy paradoxical ambiguities. In Oliver Sacks's description of manic-depressive illness, his language resonates with characteristics of the berserk state: "One may call it mania, madness, or psychosis—a chemical imbalance in the brain—but it presents itself as energy of a primordial sort." He goes on to quote Michael Greenberg, who "likens it to 'being in the presence of a rare force of nature, such as a great blizzard or flood: destructive, but in its way astounding too.' Such unbridled energy can resemble that of creativity or inspiration or genius . . . not an illness, but the apotheosis of health, the release of a deep, previously suppressed self." [43]

Sacks calls attention to the alien quality of that manic energy, drawing on the title of Edward Podvoll's *The Seduction of Madness*. Recounting a therapist's treatment of mania, Greenberg observes that she speaks as if it were a lion or another being inside the patient. "Mania is a glutton for attention. It craves thrills, action, it wants to keep thriving, it will do anything to live on" (60). This sounds like the berserk state in its "beastlike" wrath (the lion), rage for risk-taking, alienation, and tyrannical sway over the personality. Most significantly, the therapist's "lion" illustrates Becker's recognition of survival appetite as a primary creaturely motive: in mania, unstoppable (godlike, beastlike) emergency survival greed. Greenberg's account of his daughter Sally puts it eloquently in Sacks's description: "Mania . . . is by no means all pleasure, as Greenberg continually observes. He speaks of Sally's 'pitiless ball of fire,' her terrified grandiosity,' of how anxious and fragile she is inside the 'hollow exuberance' of her mania. When one ascends to the exorbitant heights of mania, one becomes very isolated from ordinary human relationships, human scale—even though this isolation may be covered over by a defensive imperious-ness or grandiosity" (60). This too sounds like the berserk state: and also like the vulnerability that threatens to undo character after fury passes, in post-traumatic stress.

Just as traumatic injury entails an interpretation of the injury, even victims of psychosis have to interpret their experience using the cultural materials available to them. The "voices" they hear may be delusional, but they try to make sense of them in cultural narratives, from lions to race war. Tragically, even an evil rage can act to focus reality and what feels right.

SACRIFICE, TRANSFERENCE, AND THE ROMANCE OF ABANDON

Mental illness is not a neat fingerprint at the scene of a crime or a pathogen under a microscope. The label can put the phenomenon of berserk abandon into a conceptual straitjacket. The wish is to find someone totally mad or totally sane. But if killers such as James Davis are classified as indisputably ill and not responsible for their actions, then society's most radical defense of what's right—capital punishment—would itself be a form of vindictive rampage. Monstrous transgression—or the fear of it—brings out demands for monstrous revenge, a rage for order. At the same time the punishment of others can be a means of policing the self. Night after night television audiences watch cops subdue criminals, vicariously exercising and taming antisocial impulses in themselves. In this way media melodrama is a popular form of scapegoat ritual. More perversely, rampage killings too act out scapegoat fantasies in an effort to purge toxic fury. And the "sacrifice" is treacherously equivocal, since the suicidal recklessness of the killer plays out fantasies of martyrdom. Having turned over his belongings to a nephew, James Davis was suicidal in his role as avenger, as if emulating the grim heroism honored in countless war movies.

We want to be bigger, stronger, and more enduringly significant than we are. We want to be substantiated by the attention of others. Hence the lure of the beyond and the dream of controlled abandon. It may take the form of selfless rescue, but it can also be grandiose fury. In 2007 the Carnegie Hero Fund Commission selected recent heroes who had been able to "run into burning buildings and cars," "fight off men with knives and snapping dogs," and "go after people hanging off cliffs." The deeds "must be done by a 'civilian who knowingly risks his or her own life to an extraordinary degree while saving or attempting to save the life of another person.' To underscore the point, three winners died while saving someone else."[44]

What kind of work does heroic abandon do? Insofar as habit and the rules of reason impose limits, they are reminders of the unwelcome ultimate limit, death. By contrast, as in shamanism, ventures into the beyond can make life feel boundless and exhilarating. Losing and recovering the self creates a conviction of survival magic. To the extent that the behavior goes "beyond," it expands the self by pushing back anxieties and unfreezing personal resources. As in repeated drug trips, letting go becomes easier. And as in the treacherous paradox of sacrifice, the loss of self promises to substantiate the self yet can also lead to madness and suicide. The beyond can be paradise but also an abyss. The psychologist Karen Horney sees human development threatened by motives she relates to stories of the devil's pact in which an evil figure tempts a mortal with infinite glory and an easy way out.[45]

In a related way the idea of abandon can be a means of managing morale. For someone at the edge of endurance, abandon can be means of relieving despair, paralysis, or panic, which can be as life-threatening as a do-or-die break-out. Recall the Vietnam veteran who confessed: "I just couldn't get enough. I built up such hate. I couldn't do enough damage. . . . Got worse as time went by. I really loved fucking killing, couldn't get enough. For every one that I killed I felt better. Made some of the hurt went away" (Shay, 78). The man's language is self-intoxicating, an incantation. Even looking back from a safe distance he is psyching himself up, resisting the anguish and depression implied in "the hurt." In berserk style the fantasy of cutting loose can function as self-encouragement, even modeling action that could be taken. It can also shape transference relationships with powerful others.

As in the devil's pact, the mortal who appears to master the beyond whets the appetite of followers for boundless life. Alexander the Great and Napoleon left a trail of loyal corpses. Germans succumbed to the fatal allure of the absurd Hitler. What makes homicidal communities such as the Manson family so terrifying, says Becker, is that "they exaggerate the dispositions present in us all. Why should they feel guilt or remorse? The leader takes responsibility for the destructive act, and those who destroy on his command are no longer murderers, but 'holy heroes.' They crave to serve in the powerful aura that he projects and to carry out the illusion that he provides them, an illusion that allows them to heroically transform the world."[46]

While the Manson family and Hitler's Germany make lurid examples, what needs emphasis is the ordinariness—the naturalness—of berserk fantasy in transference. When Arnold Schwarzenegger entered politics, journalists regularly associated him with the Terminator cyborg he played in the movies, yet voters preferred to see his undying strength rather his icy rage. For them he was more St. George, who kills the voracious dragon of death, marries the rescued princess, and becomes the city's new ruler.

As gender roles have modulated in recent decades, berserking has replaced motherly empathy in some popular entertainment. Instead of being depicted as victims of demonic fury, many Hollywood heroines are now as violent as men. And so the scriptwriters send the glamorous Uma Thurman on a "vengeful rampage" to *Kill Bill* (2003), "the worldly father figure of a pack of crack assassins." In *Salt* (2010), Angelina Jolie is a spy and an unstoppable supercharged killer. Steig Larsson's Lisbeth Salander is grotesquely persecuted but more than equal to her tormenters.

The romantic killer can be attractive as a fresh face when news and movies have been crowded with soldiers and male psychopaths. And once established as berserk style, the role is endlessly adaptable. To roaring approval at the Republican 2008 convention the attractive vice presidential nominee Sarah Palin, the "hockey mom" governor of Alaska, sought to establish her leadership credentials by associating herself with brute ferocity. "You know what they say is the difference between hockey mums and a pit bull?" she joked. "Lipstick." Pit bulls are known for frenzied killing, and as a middle-class woman suddenly in line to be a global leader, Governor Palin, nicknamed "Sarah Barracuda," deliberately chose to play underdog and attack dog—and to permit her admirers to identify with the implied capacity for unstoppable rage. Thereafter, Peggy Noonan began an October 3, 2008 *Wall Street Journal* column about the Palin-Biden vice presidential debate by gushing that Mrs. Palin "killed" Biden. By the end of the campaign, Secret Service agents revealed, "Sarah Palin's attacks on Barack Obama's patriotism provoked a spike in death threats against the future president." The attacks "provoked a near lynch mob atmosphere at her rallies, with supporters yelling 'terrorist' and 'kill him' until the McCain campaign ordered her to tone down the rhetoric."[47] On her Website two years later she put hunters' gunsight icons over the names to "target" political enemies.[48]

For followers, abandon can be proof of a leader's alpha status and immortality magic. The supreme rulers' orgiastic grandiosity, licentiousness, and waste prove their potency. The violation of limits models the insatiable appetite for life that lurks in every heart at some point. Followers let such leaders live life for them while they experience it vicariously from a safe distance. When an Osama bin Laden publicizes his daunting austerity, the impact is the same, since the supposed self-denial points to saintliness and survival in the cosmic realm. The martyr's sacrifice testifies to a transcendent spiritual form of the berserk state's self-forgetfulness and fierce purpose.

Since transference relationships are always in play, the element of abandon contributes to their volatility. All parties to hero-worship have reason to love, fear, envy, and hate one another. Leaders suffer chronic fears of being demystified and assassinated. Dependents envy godlike figures yet also fear to displease them and lose their favor. At the same time competition for blessings from on high can transform followers into ruthless rivals.

The role of death-anxiety in these dynamics is clear in the way tyrants and gangsters seek to bind the group to them by escalating guilt and threats as well as greed. Once they violate taboos, followers depend on the leader to rationalize ravenous appetite and allay guilt, as Hitler and mafia bosses have done. The effect is a concentrated version of the mania in an economic bubble in which individuals feel the mood of the group giving permission—inciting them—to turn anxiety into greed and take ghastly risks. "The sky's the limit!"

The ultimate authority of the beyond lies in "God." But the lure of the beyond can sublimate abandon in an ecstasy of paradoxes, as in Romanticism. It can turn surrender into mastery and evoke a vision of the beyond at once misty and yet supercharged with meaning. E. T. A. Hoffmann envisioned Beethoven's Fifth Symphony evoking a world of "infinite yearning" charged by "awe, fear, terror, and pain."[49] F. Scott Fitzgerald's Gatsby believed in "the green light, the orgastic future that year by year recedes before us."

The "orgastic future" invites violent striving, but so does the turn, when the mirage begins to fail.

IN THE FUNHOUSE OF STYLE

Close at hand, predatory threat and heroic force appear to be distinct categories and easy to recognize. Like the hard-boiled detective, analysis should be able to follow the money, count the corpses, and hand over malefactors to the law. But in berserk style, the two categories may blur in paradox and hallucination. "What's right" becomes chimerical; idealism may reveal the fangs of fanaticism; selflessness can mask greed for transcendence. The seething worker pursues righteous indignation to a showdown and ends up on death row brooding on his criminal madness.

Mediated by style, motives can be incalculable. Threat display, for example, manipulates perceptions. It mounts a contest of illusions as adversaries face off. As a result it makes a convenient frame for a closer look at the peculiar character of berserk style. Threat display can be used to dominate others or to fend off an attack. A major theme of *New Yorker* cartoons is the boss who rules the office through ingenious threats. But the tool can serve anyone: the toddler signaling a tantrum; the terrorist and the mob extortionist; billionaires funding faux populist groups; preachers scaring up publicity by loudly praying for the death of President Obama.[50]

The berserk potential may be real but insidious and hard to grasp. The cues and interpretive categories are in motion and deform in the funhouse mirrors of cultural expectations. In a society where the once-taboo expletives "fuck" and "fuck you" may be shocking or routine, even "fighting words" can be chimerical. In his America Online profile, amid a rant about obnoxious people on the street, Eric Harris, one of the Columbine killers, snarled, "Kill 'em AALL!!!" (27). Given his slangy spelling and the permissive atmosphere online, this could be merely self-consciously comic bravado in adolescent male culture fizzing with smart-ass exaggeration. It could also be that in the tacit world of the Internet Harris was experimenting with threat display, testing limits and reactions.

Around the ninth anniversary of the World Trade Center attacks American media created a global storm over Florida Pastor Terry Jones's self-aggrandizing threat to burn copies of the Koran. Discounting its seriousness paradoxically gave it substance for hotheads around the world looking for a pretext for victimization and blazing rage—maximum threat display. At the same time media ignored reports that the military was prosecuting a few American soldiers who were allegedly killing Afghan civilians and taking body parts as trophies: classic amok atrocity turned into an apparently organized style. This story, in turn, casts the pastor's behavior in a new light, since it shows media—the public—using Jones's nasty and dangerous threats as an easily discredited aberration that distracted attention from America's extraordinary global military actions. At a time when network media treat retired generals as expert commentators, for example, motives become labyrinthine.

When coworkers give a hostile employee a nickname such as "Crazy Pat," presumably they are using humor to defuse their anxiety and preserve the group's solidarity and tolerance. In a culture with a sympathetic, medicalized view of mental illness—but inadequate health services—people may be reluctant to intervene.[51] After all, a society that tried to preempt all violence would soon be tyrannized by its own paranoia. At the same time use of the nickname "Crazy Pat" is a form of passive aggression likely to be sensed and resented by the insecure, paranoid Pat. When a Crazy Pat hears a Johnny Paycheck singing "Take this job and shove it" as a number one hit on the charts, workplace hostility acquires an eerie glow.

Berserk style, then, can distort things as in a funhouse mirror. Rampage killers invariably act out convictions of righteousness. Soldiers of secular America kill in God's name jihadi enemies who die for God. Not only does style make violence tricky to evaluate, it also may produce contrary and deceptive responses such as an aggressive overreaction. The media researcher George Gerbner has pointed out that media depict everyday life in America as an incipient rampage. A cultural environment saturated with violence creates what he calls "the mean world syndrome." "If you grow up in an atmosphere of violence, you feel at risk; you feel this is a very mean and dangerous world much more so than it really is. You are afraid to go into the streets at night; you are afraid to go into the inner cities; you are mistrustful of strangers; you are exemplifying all of the exacerbated suspicions and misanthropy that destroy the veneer of civilization."[52]

Saturation violence can spread crippling fears, but also invite overreaction: individual hair-trigger paranoia, or voter demands for authoritarian "wars" on crime, drugs, and terrorism. Like blood in the ancient amphitheater, it can pep up humdrum daily life or inure viewers to a ruthlessly competitive society. It can also contribute to the creation of a prison population that sets world records and wrecks civilized budgets, as described in a Chapter 5.

The security consultant Gavin de Becker argues that with a general theory of human needs, anyone can predict violent behavior by seeing things through the eyes of the threatening person.[53] While he overstates the possibilities of do-it-yourself psychiatry, he is encouraging the imaginative sympathy that makes critical awareness effective in the theater of social life. Yes, he says, danger can be deceptive, but people too often ignore their own self-protective anxiety and premonitions. Anxiety has evolved as a protective mechanism. But our propensity for denial keeps us from responding to the vital signals anxiety sends. What's more, he sees that culture can foster denial. Fear should be "a mere servant of intuition" and not chronic, numbing background noise (277)—Gerbner's "saturation violence." In an atmosphere of anxiety it is easy to be distracted and cowed. Fear "says something might happen. If it does happen, we stop fearing it and start to respond to it, manage it, surrender to it, whereas when real danger leaps out, fear will galvanize action" (283). By magnifying danger or reward, berserk style can move worry toward action. And the process can be self-intoxicating, gathering momentum and surpassing inhibitions as it goes.

In this psychic zone where motivation is furiously concentrated, contingency could hardly be more volatile. The heroic striving that converts death-anxiety into creative energy also makes humans spectacular predators. Ideas about abandon and the beyond are easiest to isolate when behavior is most out of control. But the behavior is incremental, and appetite is always compulsively at work, testing the varieties of civilizing taboo. "The shark does not have dexterity, guile, deceit, cleverness, or disguise," says de Becker. "It also does not have our brutality, for man does things to man that sharks could not dream of doing" (283). When imagination can use the *idea* of abandon even while acting it out, style camouflages behavior. Style may present a storm of ironies and implications. Where creaturely and cultural motives intersect in the narratives and signs around us, analysis has to look for ambivalence, conflict, and incongruity. Criticism can ask what kinds of work the ideation is doing.

As style, for example, berserk abandon can be a technique for converting flight to fight. It can be the crucial catalyst in rabble-rousing or in leadership claims. The rhetorical process of "getting psyched" or "pumping up" can itself be a kind of abandon, especially in an age of industrial entertainment, ubiquitous advertising, and spin. Since today's shocking violence is tomorrow's cliché, there is always pressure for more extreme feats of imagination. When asked about Osama Bin Laden during a debate among presidential candidates in May 2007, one senator vowed: "[W]e will do whatever is necessary. We will track him down. We will bring him to justice. We will follow him to the gates of Hell." To outdo his competitors in a show of resolve, the candidate was making a berserk vow, something like: *I will stop at nothing. My determination is cosmic.* But as his vows inflated toward their eschatological showdown at the infernal portal, the senator stopped and suddenly smiled beatifically—and sheepishly—into the camera. The incongruity stirred The Daily Show's satirical correspondent, "standing outside the gates of Hell waiting for the senator's limousine to arrive," to comment that the senator's rhetoric was "over the top," but necessarily so, since the president "has raised the bar on hollow threats" so high (May 7, 2007).[54]

In different ways the satirists' and the senator's smiles acknowledged that berserk rage can be a theatrical gesture intended to dramatize superhuman strength and reassure followers. But the smiles also conveyed an embarrassed awareness of acting out a style for strategic ends. Before the cameras the speaker tried to project and appeal to towering rage, but his sensible smile broke the spell. The question in such a situation is whether such a failed bluff will lead to greater prudence or to more brazen risk-taking.

When supercharged motives act on an overdetermined world, the signals can boggle the mind. Consider one minor yet telling example of berserk style in the prelude to the Vietnam War in the 1960s. With the Cuban missile crisis and other Cold War turbulence testing—and pumping up—the heroic identity of postwar America, the assassination of John F. Kennedy suddenly put Lyndon Johnson in the electoral spotlight. Confronted by Barry Goldwater's berserk style anti-Communism ("Extremism in defense of liberty is no vice"), Johnson countered with a now famous September 7, 1964, television spot in which a little girl counting daisy petals witnesses a nuclear fireball in the distance and LBJ's voiceover intones, "These are the stakes! To make a world in which all of God's children can live, or to go into the dark. We must either love each other, or we must die."

The "Daisy" advertisement tries to use berserk style against itself. It projects LBJ as the godlike voice of a hero who can master the cataclysmic nuclear bomb associated with his reckless (berserk) opponent, and it is widely thought to have contributed to Johnson's landslide victory. Yet despite—or because of—the triumph, the victor then felt he had to overcome charges that he was soft on Communism, and embarked on the series of tragic, futile deceptions and misjudgments that spun out of control in the Vietnam conflict. As the war and the military effort ran amok, the mushroom cloud in the ad returned to the public forum, but in Gen. Curtis LeMay's famous call to nuke Vietnam "back to the stone age."

In the storm of ironies the image of the little girl ("Daisy") eventually did work against war, but only when it returned in Nick Ut's famous news photo of nine-year-old Kim Phuc running naked in the street agonizingly burned by American napalm (1972). The symbols of superhuman ("superpower") American supremacy—the bomb and the godlike, fatherly voice in the advertisement—deformed into their opposite. The personal horror and violated tenderness of the burned child's suffering in particular exposed the way abandon had turned malevolent and undermined the noble intentions.

A quicksand of ironies can be comic, but also maddening. Nuclear weapons are real but also unimaginable, and the means to control them, at least in the political advertisement, spurious. Modernity expands the scale of things and strains the limits of imagination, but it also provides science and other tools for coping. When those tools fail or actually come to serve panic and hatred as in industrial warfare, force runs wild. Globalization is one sign of modernity's change of scale, as is globalization's handmaiden, the internet. With ubiquitous electronic communication, the intimate horrors of war in remote Afghanistan are at your fingertips. Closer to home, when a 14-year old eighth grader in Olympia Washington sent a nude cellphone photo of herself to a new boyfriend, he passed it on to her ex-girlfriend, whose jealousy sent the photo "viral" on the Internet. Petty anger ("If you think this girl is a whore, then text this to all your friends") turned into a hysterical rage for order that came to involve handcuffs and court.[55] The difficult precept to keep in mind is that the impetus to chaos is also driven by convictions of "what's right" and a rage for order.

A HISTORICAL SKETCH

Since cultures as well as individuals develop particular techniques for coping with boundary behavior, history can be seen as a succession of strategies for managing berserk style. As such, etiquette and civility are evolving technologies akin to formal institutions such as law and religion. Cross-cultural evidence shows that berserk behavior occurs around the globe. It takes a bewildering variety of forms and sometimes appears in clusters or waves.

Many groups around the world, including Native American tribes, have cultivated heroic abandon as a function of warrior morale. In the Huron and Iroquois rite described by the Jesuit Francis Parkman and others, the tribe assembled in the long house to torture to death a captive who was expected to sing warrior songs and prove his courage.[56] Killers and victim cooperated in a ritual that bonded the group and acted out the power to overcome panic and suffering. Neurologically the rite converted flight to fight, mastering death-anxiety by controlling death itself through the warrior code, up to the final blinding of the captive and ritual cannibalism.

In the New World early settlers plunged into a tantalizing, terrifying beyond, with desperate conviction and mortality to match. Many such as Ralegh were avid for treasure and glory. The first New Englanders were escaping exasperating constraints back home, absurdly conflicted in their appetite for life: self-aggrandizing and sometimes rapacious servants of God propagating a familiar Old World order and yet given to frontier improvisation and revolution. Benjamin Tompsons's two poems about King Philip's War *New-Englands Crisis* (1676) and

New-Englands Tears (1677) envision the founders' arcadia ruined by greed and barbarism. In imagery of conflagration, cannibalism, and slaughter the poems report the Great Swamp Fight against the Indians as a nightmare of psychic violence[57] that would persist in the outbreaks of witch panic to come.[58]

As expansion dismantled the Puritans' ideological stockade, the settlers found themselves not in a New Jerusalem but in a strange psychic territory, given to terror, hungry ambition, and ferocious zeal. Gradually the forerunners who labored over a divine compact transformed into merchants and helped draft a federal constitution meant to stabilize boundaries. Later generations cherished neighborliness and private property while stealing Native American lands. They worshiped liberty and fought to the death over slave-ownership. Survival rage followed the frontier, where savagery acquired mythic status that would echo through pulp novels to the obscenity and calculated mayhem of today's television serial *Deadwood*. "Pioneers" fought wild animals and "savages," ambition rushed hell-bent after gold, and Colt's "Peacemaker" regulated appetites. Meanwhile finance and industry stampeded across the continent and periodically over a cliff. The shock of the Civil War and the racial dislocation that followed created post-traumatic reverberations that contributed to lynching at home and sharpened imperial violence in Teddy Roosevelt's bigoted bully era.[59]

In 1850 *Moby Dick* set sail out of Herman Melville's inkwell, dramatizing the idea of the berserk as it modulated toward modernity. The novel is a stylized tour de force, and never had the sensational influence of, say, Buffalo Bill's or P. T. Barnum's showcases of super reality. Writing in a period of hectic expansion, the gold rush, and the hissing ideological fuses of the Civil War, Melville depicts imaginations literally "at sea." But this is not the sea of crisply limned waves in traditional oil paintings. On the contrary, Ahab famously declaims that all conventional reality is "but pasteboard masks," behind which is the "outrageous strength" and "inscrutable malice" of the white whale that has maimed him. The captain commands, begs, bribes, and seduces his crew to "strike through" the "unreasoning mask" and kill the beast. "That inscrutable thing is chiefly what I hate; and . . . I will wreak that hate upon him."[60]

To strike through the pasteboard mask can be a frantic blow but also the calculated violence of scientific dissection of nature. The obsession with penetrating the mask is a response to the realization that everything is constructed of parts—and that even selves are composed of "parts": masks and roles. The novel's sly prefatory matter satirizes natural history. Like the rendering of a whale, scientific anatomy destroys the thing it plumbs. To Ishmael the whale "shadows forth the heartless voids and immensities of the universe, and thus stabs us from behind with the thought of annihilation." Ahab expresses the shock humans feel at the discovery of the insoluble violence of the universe that lies behind the consoling masks of culture. After all, Ahab has been hunting—warring against—the beast to revenge his lost limb and the recognition of death. His howl resounds in the nineteenth century's initial reaction to Darwinism and the Social Darwinist vision of "the fittest" locked in a struggle to the death, a shock still resonating in the impassioned denial of some religious groups in the United States today. Ahab's frenzy has not dissipated. Despite growing ecological alarm, survival greed continues to dispatch fleets of factory Pequods to sweep the planet's oceans: so voraciously that once-teeming fisheries have suffered alarming depletion[61] and the idea of population crash has begun to haunt the sleep of public reason.

Ahab scans the horizon of modernity, recognizing that conventional reality is a pasteboard enabling fiction, but also locked into a traditional cosmology in which some devilish agency lurks behind appearances. The novel puts to sea, as it were, because in culture "what's right" is deceptive. Out of sight of land, fixated on a lost limb and the death-awareness it signifies, the reasoning mind may well find that symbolic immortality—and reason—is a flimsy mask. And more to the harpoon's point, as Ahab's wrath illustrates, "inscrutable malice" is a fatal, even suicidal problem in sailors, not simply in cosmic whales. Ahab recognizes creaturely motives such as survival rage but denies that they invest us—and *are* us. The outcome is the familiar cluster of berserk characteristics: the godlike and beastlike alienation ("at sea"), slaughter and cutting up of wild "enemies," and recklessness culminating in the symbolic apocalypse that tears apart the ship and leaves Ishmael clinging to a coffin on an imponderable ocean: "And I only am escaped alone to tell thee."

Victorian respectability worked to tame excess, but the malicious phantom of Ishmael's day would lead its pursuers through a civil war, a Gilded Age, industrial slaughter in two world wars, and into a militarized and corporatized empire operating on a once-unimaginable global scale. At the turn of the twentieth century, when the United States was wresting territories from Spain, there was "a sense of forces and energy running away with the world. Henry Adams felt moved to posit a 'Law of Acceleration' in history. He felt as if he could never drive down the Champs Elysees without expecting an accident or stand near an official without expecting [an anarchist] bomb. 'So long as the rate of progress held good, these bombs would double in force and number every ten years. . . . Power leaped from every atom. . . . Man could no longer hold it off. Forces grasped his wrists and flung him about as though he had hold of a live wire or a run-away automobile."[62] The exploding automobile fascinated some early filmmakers; it is a naïve forerunner of the car bomb that terrorizes the new century.

At The Hague peace conference of 1899 pressure was building for war on a new industrial scale. The US delegate Captain Mahan opposed restraints. He "made his presence felt like a voice of conscience," says Barbara Tuchman, "operating not in behalf of peace but in behalf of the unfettered exercise of belligerent power" (260). The "unfettered" idea of berserk force was in the air: for example, in the refusal to ban new, vicious dumdum bullets. "Developed by the British to stop the rush of fanatical tribesmen, the bullets were vigorously defended by Sir John Ardagh against the heated attack of all except the American military delegate . . . whose country was about to make use of them in the Philippines." Where "the civilized soldier . . . lies down on his stretcher," Ardagh scoffed, "your fanatical barbarian, similarly wounded, continues to rush on, spear or sword in hand; and before you can explain to him that his conduct is in flagrant violation of . . . the proper course for the wounded man to follow—he may have cut off your head" (262).

This thrilling sarcasm smoldered with the glow of berserk style. Ardagh makes colonized people berserk "barbarians" in order to justify more atrocious weaponry. The cool snobbery of his military fantasy would soon march Europe into cataclysmic folly in 1914. It would come back in the cold, clever rage of the September 11 terrorists and again in the colonial-scale "shock and awe" invasions of Iraq and Afghanistan. The British and American delegates saw berserk abandon as the natives' most threatening weapon: today incarnate in the suicide bomber. Their condescension would look quaint now had it not contributed to the doublethink that unleashed the horrors of poison gas, firestorm and nuclear attacks on civilians, and stockpiled today's sickening munitions. One covert premise is that the berserk fury of the weak is so dangerous that it demands "unfettered" lethal technology. Another, even more sinister, is that the strong feel victimized and therefore justly merciless.

The neocon America that adopted a policy of unilateral "preemptive" war in the twenty-first century is a late expansion of attitudes present at The Hague, where a "ban on the use of asphyxiating gas failed of unanimity by one vote—Captain Mahan's. He stubbornly refused to withdraw his negative on the ground that the United States was averse to restricting 'the inventive genius of its citizens in providing weapons of war'" (263). The "fanatical barbarian" who "may have cut off your head" became "the Hun," "Jap monkeys," "gooks," and lately the headline "hadji" terrorist beheading hostages in occupied Iraq. A century later a rhetoric of victimization rationalized a limitless, impractical, morally compromised "war on terror."

THE ITINERARY

The following chapters examine the decades between the Vietnam War and the watershed first decade of the new century. A core premise is that World War II amplified the expansiveness that has been an urgent American theme from the beginning and continues now in the resource wars and globalization that have positioned American military forces and corporations all over the planet.

Economic and military dominance made it seductively easy to maintain the momentum of wartime. The Cold War superpower invested in fantasies of heroic rescue and global policing, updating missionary zeal that looks back to Colonial preachers. But a superpower identity incurs super dangers and super stress that make it more susceptible to abandon. The Cold War made crisis a familiar style. The Union of Concerned Scientists' "Doomsday Clock" ticked the seconds to MAD (Mutual Assured Destruction), and pushed toward the nightmarish alerts satirized in *Dr. Strangelove* (1964). One outcome was the self-confounding ideology and the vast industrial arsenal that ran amok in the "pacification" of agricultural Vietnam and the literally boundless "war on terror."

As the tight-lipped terrors of World War II relaxed, deep passions found expression in the ferment of the 1960s. Between 1965 and 1968 the Senate Subcommittee on Government Operations tallied riots in over a hundred American cities. The disturbances registered the impact of change in civil rights, Great Society initiatives, and Vietnam-War-related distress. Mixing idealism and protest with sex, drugs, and rock 'n' roll, the counterculture of the Vietnam era responded to the lure of an intoxicating beyond. "Make love not war" vied with revolutionary chants to "Off the Pig" and berserk incoherence ("Let it all hang out").

After the defeat in Vietnam, recession and repression curbed aspirations. Global economies continued to rebalance and the superpower's dominance wavered. Berserk style conditioned the response. Wall Street and business culture stressed deregulation or "taking the gloves off," "creative destruction," "lean and mean" management, and entrepreneurial risk-taking. The myth took hold that President Reagan collapsed the Soviet Union by outspending the Communists in an arms race. The myth rationalized what Chalmers Johnson calls "military Keynesianism," a disguised means of pumping up a US economy still impaired by Vietnam War excesses and destined to explode in the multi-trillion-dollar wars in Iraq and Afghanistan.[63] Fascination with abandon helped to justify the bubble-and-bust cycles that climaxed in the financial mayhem of 2008.

The role of berserk style in that military and economic story is the subject of the first three chapters that follow. Business and the military cultivated tools that promised to magnify force the way that a sling-shot or a nuclear bomb magnifies the power of the human fist. Leverage can open new vistas, but it can also be perilously hypercritical. In a few dizzying decades the world's largest creditor turned into history's greatest debtor. By 2008 the global financial system was in shock. With bank failures, housing foreclosures, massive job losses, and even food supply under stress, media and the Internet hosted a new rhetoric of distress, doomsday forecasters such as James Kunstler, and familiar survivalist themes. Reporting on energy scarcity and "resource wars," Michael Klare issued a forecast titled "A Planet on the Brink: Will Economic Brushfires Prove Too Virulent to Contain?" Raising alarm-ing prospects of abandon, he observed that "continued economic decline combined with a pervasive sense that existing systems and institutions are incapable of setting things right is already producing a potentially lethal brew of anxiety, fear, and rage. Popular explosions of one sort or another are inevitable."[64] Overreactions to alarm are the focus of the chapter "Rage for Order," while the following analysis, "The Living End," considers the expansion of fear and rage to cosmic proportions in doomsday fantasies.

The pursuit of berserk style is bound to be incomplete, as I discovered when events kept outrunning drafts of this book. Too sweeping a scope yields a panoramic blur; a fine squint misses crucial connections. Criticism can no more capture the phenomenon once and for all than Ahab or Melville can make a museum trophy of the white whale. Since the berserk state itself is an elusive beast, it makes sense to follow Melville's example and explore the cultural conditions—the voyage, the pasteboard fantasies, the injuries—out of which frenzies arise. We can examine the underlying motives and enabling fictions associated with abandon, and also the resistance that gives abandon its particular shapes. Even so, criticism is bound to be tossed about like a flimsy whaleboat in pursuit of the ineffable white monster.

Culture is an elusive quarry because of course the term is a crude harpoon to be heaving at anything. What's more, much of what we see of culture takes place in the fog and squalls of public discourse, particularly media, whose appetite for berserk abandon deserves a book in its own right. Conventional wisdom is convinced that violent content on screen and in the airwaves promotes violent behavior. But diligent studies by Jonathan Friedman and others have demonstrated that the question is far more multifaceted and inconclusive than that.[65] The crucial question is whether the content or experiments trying to quantify the effects of that content actually engage the will to harm others.

Berserk style finesses the question, since it openly promotes abandon—even violent abandon—and may justify it as play. Yet play is endlessly ambiguous, and the varieties of play-aggression defy easy pigeonholes. The equivocal character of berserk motives owes much to the blurred line between violent intention and the arousal effect of furious action entertainment. As a result, play makes a mischievous defense or ground for prosecution.

Attack media, one of the landmark developments in post-Vietnam broadcasting, is a case in point. The shows saturate many markets with politically partisan rant that would have been illegal before the Reagan administration abolished the FCC's impartiality doctrine in 1987. Shock jocks are frankly vitriolic and systematically build the rhythm of their shows toward a climax of righteous invective. The host and audience implicitly take the roles of police or warriors hunting down enemies. In his August 15, 2008, show, Michael Reagan, son of the former president, called for the murder of a Muslim mother who had named her baby "Hezbollah": "You know what I would get them for a first birthday, I would put a grenade up their butts and light it. Happy birthday. Bye-Bye." He added, "What's wrong with killing the mothers and the babies?" In June 2008 he urged killing Christian antiwar activists who were trying to persuade troops in Iraq to oppose the war. "Take them out and shoot them. . . . You call them traitors, that's what they are, and you shoot them dead. I'll pay for the bullet."

In attack media as in horror movies, aggression has to keep escalating because the goal is arousal, not information. The shows consistently model victimization and survival rage. In *Liberalism Is a Mental Disorder,* Michael Savage demonizes "liberals" as "the enemy within our country;" "an enemy more dangerous than Hitler," and "traitors" who are "dangerous to your survival."

Echoing Savage, an unemployed truck driver who had read the book gunned down churchgoers at a Unitarian-Universalist service in Tennessee. Jim Adkisson had a history of threatening violence but no problem obtaining weapons. He told police "that all liberals should be killed . . . because they were . . . ruining the country, and that he felt that the Democrats had tied his country's hands in the war on terror and . . . ruined every institution in America."[66] Trying to explain himself, the man blurs unfocused rage with role-playing at heroic rescue: the stimulant that powers "entertainment"—not to mention military—budgets. Like other attackers who cite rant media to explain themselves, Adkisson may have been internalizing a powerful voice "from out of the airwaves" or using that voice as a tool—or both.

The truck driver's rampage killing touches a cluster of the themes to be explored in the pages ahead. This book is less concerned with the contest between political factions than with the relationship of cultural markers to behavior. Berserk style makes it possible for broadcasters to euphemize the manipulation of rage as entertainment, disclaiming any responsibility for the content. In the example above, the truck driver was responding to propaganda that models policy disagreements as death threats, as if "liberals" embody globalized evil that only paramilitary berserk rage—in a church—can defeat. The menace may be projected into the beyond as Satanic "liberals," immigrants, gays, and so on. But the target can be specific public figures who then receive death threats, as in the congressional effort in 2007 to pass immigration reform.[67]

The theatricalization of rage—*I'm fed up, I won't take it anymore*—creates a vicarious voice for a nation that worships freedom but in fact, like other complex cultures, demands a large degree of conformity. More specifically, the relentless outcry against despots—whether it is the catchall "socialism" or President Obama vilified as Antichrist—is a sign of the infantilization in American culture that encourages the audience to identify with victimized, angry children rather than with problem-solving adult citizens.

Once these deeper dynamics come into view, we can see that attack media often functions as a vehicle for self-medication. Broadcasters and their audience are playing at berserk fury to rouse morale, countering depressive feelings with a pick-me-up of stimulating anger like caffeine or alcohol, turning flight into fight. For an aging, unemployed truck driver facing social death, the rage in the airwaves can legitimize real grievances and extend membership in a virtual mob of angry fellow citizens bent on hunting down and figuratively lynching enemies. The host's familiar disembodied voice offers him a role of heroic indignation that can transmute helplessness and gloom into thrilling righteousness and mastery. Once in motion, the workaday nobody can be the warrior bent on closure, confirmed by the world's attention.

Still, it is useful to remember that satire—the fusion of criticism and laughter—originated as cursing: in the belief that language charged with magical power can injure or kill enemies.[68] Freud called magical thinking the omnipotence of thought: the belief that thinking can change things in the physical world—if you wish fervently enough, you can make something happen. The belief plays out in practices that concentrate will. Conjuring or ritual incantation, for example, uses devices such as repetition, rhythm, chant, vows, and imperative verbs to rouse conviction toward action. Magical imprecations, it goes without saying, depend on techniques to exacerbate rage to intoxicating extremes. If prayer attempts to compel a deity to act, it becomes magical thinking. Today the witchcraft spells and exorcisms of the early modern period are conditioned by skepticism and irony. But they are still with us in, say, the broadcaster's popular and profitable rant. For the most part they are style rather than "real" rage; threat display rather than shootouts; rhetoric rather than magical words.

But not always. It is criticism's job to sort them out.

CHAPTER 2

AT WAR WITH STYLE

Just about no mission is impossible for the United States military.

Michael Barone[1]

My rifle is human . . . We will become part of each other . . . Before God, I swear this creed. My rifle and myself are the defenders of my country. We are the masters of our enemy. WE ARE THE SAVIORS OF MY LIFE. So be it, until victory is America's and there is no enemy, but peace.

The Marine Rifle Creed

You've killed. You've taken life. What I found, though, is that you feel the shock and weight of it only when you kill an enemy for the first time, when you move from zero to one. Once you've crossed that line, there is little difference in killing 10 or 20 or 30 more after that.

Capt. Shannon R. Meehan

The proverbial berserker is the warrior. As a creaturely motive, war acts out radical appetite for more life. Although usually formulated as self-defense and a last resort, war is also a thrilling hunt for justice and trophies. Victory means more life—freedom, land, sex, slaves, and tribute—but also the joyous conviction of survival and self-worth. War is a technic for harvesting life that can be "planted"—buried in a grave but also sown like a seed—in order to produce more life, as in the Nazi philosophy of blood and soil.[2] Holding the fate of the defeated in their hands, the victors enjoy living proof that they have mastered death. War demolishes limits and burns off humdrum frustration in the fire of heroic purpose: survival registers as rebirth. But there is an unspoken, tragic volatility in this psychic economy.

The risk of course is that the harvest will be ashes. Defeat exposes the futility of war as an immortality fantasy. More than a lost contest, defeat signifies death and calls for radical survival violence. But even victory can be dangerous. Once aroused to emergency levels, appetite and fear may be self-intoxicating. Victory brings with it a fear of falling. Like alpha males among our primate cousins, a dominant nation may expend much of its energy policing real and imaginary rivals. Instead of ending, World War II actually persisted as the Cold War and the string of inclusive wars from Korea through today's open-ended "war on terror." The new "superpowers" locked horns in prodigious threat-displays featuring "mutual assured destruction" and rationalized through berserk style. Intervention could be justified in Korea and the Balkans. But extravagant military outlays and triumphalism were economically as well as psychologically heady, and with a restless peacetime army, they led to the suffering, waste, and moral damage of the Vietnam War. To this day powerful interests are trying to rewrite the history of the war and deny the allure of berserk abandon that presidential advisor McGeorge Bundy recognized too late: "Never Deploy Military Means in Pursuit of Indeterminate Ends.[3]

Every culture has to regulate the production of warfare. For victors, that means trying to freeze the moment of glory. Whoever gets enough? On Trajan's column legions march heavenward cutting down enemies in eternal triumph. After civil slaughter the massively serene Abraham Lincoln gazes out of a Greek temple at a liberated America pacified for all time. A 2006 Acorn catalog advertised a framed photograph of the B-29 Enola Gay, "hand-signed" by its pilot, whose atomic bomb "saved countless American lives." The memento turns the annihilated city into a home decoration affirming aging veterans' heroic pride and enshrining symbolic immortality bought by suffering and mass death. Compared to scalp displays and skull racks, which keep dead enemies personally embodied in the present, the photograph uses style to domesticate and abstract aggression, even as it keeps the experience of killing and survival joy ambiguously alive.

SHOCK AND AWE

In 2003, under a "Mission Accomplished" banner on a warship ironically named for Abraham Lincoln, a new president dressed in a "Top Gun" flight suit took the role of modern conqueror trying to freeze an apparent moment of triumph after the invasion of Iraq. Yet the story was couched in berserk style and already out of control. The September 11 attacks had shocked Americans into a mood of outrage and color-coded hysteria about security. The president was acting out revenge as well as the heroic rescue of "the homeland" and Iraq. Yet the carrier landing was also a public relations trick since he had actually been a passenger in the navy jet, and the carrier was about to dock anyway. Even if taken at face value, the "mission accomplished" story depended on a "magic bullet" scenario in which "the successful invasion and American-sponsored reconstruction of Iraq would lead to the collapse of all the surrounding dictatorial regimes."[4] Like Lincoln, the Top Gun president would free the slaves.

Reality did not respond to magic.[5] Saddam Hussein's threat and ties to Al Qaeda proved to be an embarrassing mirage as evidence leaked out that the administration had been looking for a pretext to attack Iraq from well before 9/11.[6] The invasion let loose a vicious insurgency checked by sometimes-vicious pacification efforts. Iraq's governance, infrastructure, economy, and invaluable oil resources remained impaired; tens if not hundreds of thousands of innocent civilians died in the crossfire; millions fled the country.[7] The new dominance of Iraq's Shiites benefited their "axis of evil" neighbor, Shiite Iran. The suffering created a more representative but also brutal regime. Beyond the torment and death of American casualties, the war has been estimated to cost 3 trillion dollars, contributing to a budget crisis that rationalized subsequent attacks on social programs at home.[8]

The near impossibility of justifying the war's outcome reinforced a cultural experience of disconfirmation and unreality itself implicated in berserk style. Yet from the start, behind a smokescreen of terms such as "surgical intervention," the planners imagined the invasion as a strategic rampage—as berserk style. The "shock and awe" theme, echoing Nazi military doctrine, presupposed that a massive threat-display would bring abject submission and spare lives. Superior technological violence and financial resources would create irresistible leverage and mastery.

But as in the Vietnam War, the planners badly misjudged. They proved to be out of touch with the inner lives of their soldiers, their enemies, and the Iraqi population. Almost from the start the occupation went awry. Looting and economic breakdown wracked Iraqi communities. Insurgents mimicked the invaders' lean-and-mean, shock-and-awe propaganda with spectacular bombings and torture. The military retaliated with escalating "collateral damage," annihilation of the town of Fallujah, and notorious torture. The official story of liberation and justice began to show the seething vengefulness characteristic of rampage killing.

In theory soldiers choose to risk death to defend the life they believe in. When home and command are incoherent, conflicted, or devious, soldiers are likely to falter or run amok. Global protests declared the rationale for the Iraq War to be faulty or cynical. From its inception the "war on terror" modeled unchecked and impulsive force. The "Bush doctrine" of preemptive war, "shock and awe" intimidation, torture, and illegal domestic surveillance resonated with the combat berserker's impulsivity, hypervigilance, and indiscriminate violence against civilians.

The analogies are more than clever abstractions. When the illicit surveillance program came to light, the editors of the *New York Times* asked, "So why break the law, again and again? Two things seem disturbingly clear. First, President Bush and his top aides panicked after the Sept. 11 attacks. And second, Mr. Cheney and his ideologues, who had long chafed at any legal constraints on executive power, preyed on that panic to advance their agenda."[9] This is the familiar berserk dynamic: panic unleashes aggressive overconfidence that defies "legal constraints." Politicized corporate media amplified the ideological violence, treating forbearance and patient problem solving as unthinkable folly.

The predisposition to panic was there from the beginning. Washington insisted that the nation faced enemies so berserk that only overwhelming preemptive force could stop them, echoing colonial attitudes toward crazed rebellious natives. Political scientist Ken Jowitt labeled them "movements of rage," and forecast "the likely proliferation of horrendous 'wildcat violence.'"[10]

These policies presented totalizing abstractions. In reality the "war on terror" and the "axis of evil" were episodes in a global struggle over energy resources and financial hegemony. With new challengers to its postwar economic preeminence and limited world oil reserves increasingly nationalized, the United States has good reason to fear a declining standard of living and the end of empire. The invasion of Iraq gave Washington an ideal opportunity to demonstrate the "global policeman's" military and economic power to the world— and to OPEC as well.

A nation that has sunk much of its wealth into history's most sophisticated and expensive corporate-military will be tempted to use it. Since World War II, US military spending has outstripped all competitors by a wide margin and now absorbs about 57 percent of the budget, though many expenses are secret and therefore incalculable. A Congressional study reported in September 2009 that "[d]espite a recession that knocked down global arms sales last year, the United

States expanded its role as the world's leading weapons supplier, increasing its share to more than two-thirds of all foreign armaments deals."[11] An arsenal of remote-controlled cybernetic weapons and an all-volunteer force encouraged leaders to overreach without fear of public protest. Peacetime interventions—demonstration wars—energize military careers just as they enrich corporate-military suppliers and boost national self-esteem.

The shock-and-awe campaign sought to minimize carnage. But threat-display is a dangerous weapon. Once adversaries see through the bluff of "controlled" abandon, they may raise the stakes. In Iraq the insurgents quickly developed their own shock-and-awe campaign of torturing and beheading victims. One result was the unforeseen chaos that frightened and humiliated the nominal victors. The policy makers escalated the threat-display—an overreaction epitomized by the annihilation of the town of Fallujah and the massacre of families in Haditha. Many soldiers were radically conflicted: asked to die for a mission they believed in only superficially. Many felt betrayed by leaders who failed to supply armor to survive roadside bombs (IEDs) and cruelly extended their tours of duty to compensate for bad planning. And the betrayal of course centered on the Iraqis. At any moment the people the troops were supposedly rescuing could suddenly try to kill them.

At the same time, as in Vietnam, many troops believed—or claimed to believe—that they were winkingly authorized and forced by necessity to skirt the rules of engagement. Although there is no delicate way to put it, "shock and awe" is, after all, the core principle of terrorism and a crucial theme in rampage killing. In practice a policy of deliberately trying to exploit boundary behaviors is bound to feel two-faced when it bridles at the obscene excesses bound to turn up from time to time.

To be sure, some American soldiers behaved with generosity and wisdom in Iraq, but that is not the subject of this book. And American soldiers were not the only source of violence. As confirmed in the military logs released by Wikileaks (October 22, 2009), Iraqi military and police also committed atrocities, and on a monstrous scale. "Trigger-happy" private security contractors killed numerous civilians as well.[12] Like their counterparts in the Vietnam War, some veterans began to recognize the dangers of traumatic stress and vicious motives. Among the moving accounts of Iraq veterans, the "winter soldier" hearings (March 13–16, 2008) stand out as a brave effort to bear witness to atrocities and to restore moral clarity and calm.[13]

A MODEL MASSACRE

US atrocities in Iraq fit the historical pattern. Under stress, predictably, some soldiers kill innocents, and nations rarely punish them. At My Lai in Vietnam (1968), US soldiers gunned down whole families, gang-raped women, and mutilated victims, leaving about five hundred dead. A participant in Operation Speedy Express in the Mekong Delta estimated that his division's atrocities "amounted to a My Lai each month for over a year."[14] By comparison, the scale of US massacres in Iraq has been small. But the killing has been chronic and distributed. Pilots bombed houses by mistake; gunfire riddled "suspicious" cars on the highway and at checkpoints; troops and CIA personnel killed prisoners. In addition, legally unaccountable private security forces cut down civilians, and preliminary evidence signals that the environmental toxicity of depleted uranium munitions may eventually prove lethal as Agent Orange did in Vietnam.

When insurgency made a mockery of the "Mission Accomplished" story, panic and revenge sent death tolls sharply higher. The Iraqi prime minister al-Maliki protested that "violence against civilians had become a 'daily phenomenon' by many troops in the American-led coalition who 'do not respect the Iraqi people.'"[15] One Iraqi Health Ministry survey estimated 151,000 violent deaths out of 400,000 war-related deaths. But these figures are speculative, and since the Pentagon declines to release civilian casualties, we cannot be sure how many of those deaths American forces caused.

We cannot do justice to the inner life of a particular soldier who has run amok. Military life is not Main Street. Conventional accounts of combat massacres focus on stress-induced personal "breakdown" and loss of control. Here is a psychiatrist's list of characteristics associated with berserk frenzy (Shay, 82):

Beastlike
Godlike
Socially disconnected
Crazy, mad, insane
Enraged
Cruel, without restraint or discrimination
Insatiable
Devoid of fear
Inattentive to [one's] own safety
Indiscriminate
Reckless, feeling invulnerable

Exalted, intoxicated, frenzied
Cold, indifferent

The list emphasizes pathology. The berserk state reflects explosive disorder in the limbic system as stress chemicals disrupt the body's regulatory systems. Numbed to pain and fear, plunging forward on a surge of strength, the berserker is apt to experience "godlike" or "beast-like" alienation akin to the cold, depersonalized aggression of science fiction cyborgs such as the Arnold Schwarzenegger Terminator (1984).

But neurophysiology is not the whole story. In the so-called fog of war, soldiers operate in a halo of motives. How individuals react to stress depends on how they are wrapped. Creaturely motives, character, and cultural themes condition strategic behavior. The men of Charlie Company who exterminated farm families at My Lai were said to be suffering traumatic stress, exhausted, fearful and vengeful, grieving for lost comrades, with no practical relief in sight. Ordered to destroy the villages, they later claimed, they spared no one. They were already adrenalized, and once inhibitions failed, violence escalated. The first assaults showed predictable creaturely motives. Rape and murder of a rival's women kills his posterity, steals his immortality, and demonstrates the victor's potency. As in branding a slave or marking a carcass in a hunt, carving initials into an enemy's flesh signifies mastery. It magically undoes the soldier's actual condition of enslavement to command. In effect, berserkers substantiate the imperiled self by "making their mark."

As the rampage at My Lai flashed into chaos, survival greed regressed to a tantrum: a wild bodily determination to annihilate everything feared and hated. While the victims cried out and floundered among the corpses in a ditch, Lt. Calley, the officer in charge, reloaded his weapon at least ten times. At such close range bodies disintegrated, yet the killers perseverated with robotic fixation. It took the intervention of a helicopter pilot and his crew to halt the frenzy at gunpoint.

Even when individuals are indisputably out of control ("crazy, mad, insane"), the boundary transition has to entail some interpretation. Stress may bring out fatalism or suicidal despair as well as rage. Not every soldier runs amok or does it in the same way. Individuals may kill for "what's right," but what's right is bound to be subjective. In a contrived war, soldiers are trapped in a fantasy system. In Iraq, for example, troops widely believed the lie that the Iraqis were behind the September 11 terrorism. As it overrides reasonable doubts, rage then becomes a useful way of compensating for hollow motivation. Under fire, it can turn paralyzing flight into fight and insure survival.

As revenge for injury and loss, it can restore a conviction of justice. It can make a battered soldier feel heroic self-worth.

Like Iraqis, the Vietnamese were a mistrusted, alien underclass, irresistibly patronized, often despised, and correspondingly resentful. The air bristled with dehumanizing epithets such as "slopes," "gooks," and "dinks." Officially troops were rescuing innocent victims of Communism, and in theory risking their lives for them. Not only could soldiers not tell friend from foe—as in Iraq—but the Vietnamese friends were strangers, and inherently tainted by death. Draftees often felt similarly ambivalent about the officers in remote, air conditioned headquarters who ordered them to risk their lives.

Since berserk mentality appears to concentrate experience into a singular fury, it is easy to simplify the motivation, including the strong element of magical thinking. "Payback," say, may feed a demand for revenge, but it may also promise to compensate for, or magically restore, a life lost. "At some deep cultural and psychological level," says Dr. Shay, "spilling enemy blood is an effort to bring the dead back to life" (89).[16] After every killing, one veteran chanted to himself, speaking to his dead comrade: "Every fucking one that died, I say, '____, here's one for you, baby. I'll take this motherfucker out and I'm going to cut his fucking heart out for you.'" He spoke to the dead friend "as if he were alive and present, psychologically bringing him back to life" (89). The hallucinatory quality of the ritual chant and the underlying psychic economy—cutting out an enemy's heart to appease and restore life—resonates with many ancient rituals such as Mesoamerican blood offerings. Sacrificial killing renews life not only for the dead, but also for the killer, whose survival makes vivid a new lease on life. The effect is similar to the gain from scapegoat murders such as lynching.

When an army is regularly amok, the term is functioning as a form of denial, classifying a cultural practice as "rogue" pathology, an accident or an inevitable outcome. The Army archive compiled by Col. Henry Tufts makes clear that atrocities in Vietnam were far more common than generally believed, and that investigations proceeded with the surreptitious aim of distracting public opinion.[17] American leaders could entertain fantasies of annihilation without censure once they were sufficiently sanitized as berserk style. Witness LBJ's quip to bring home the coonskin and hang it on the wall, as if the war were a folksy hunt with an obliging raccoon. Attacking critics of the war in 1965, implicitly countenancing extermination, Ronald Reagan scoffed that "[i]t's silly talking about how many years we will have to spend in the jungles of Vietnam when we could pave the whole country and put parking stripes on it and still be home by Christmas."[18] Such snobbish macho contempt has become a staple of right-wing media shock jocks. But berserk style can shade into action, as in President Reagan's comic opera invasion of Grenada hyped as "Operation Urgent Fury."

Suffering reverses in Vietnam and in Iraq, American leaders called for more force. Between one and two million Vietnamese died in the conflict. An industrial war machine incinerated with napalm and poisoned with Agent Orange a basically agrarian world. By the time Saigon fell, the United States had dropped more bomb tonnage on a nation of farmers than it had in World War II. Embracing what military historian Michael S. Sherry calls the "technological fanaticism" of American air power, Gen. Curtis LeMay urged bombing Vietnam "back to the stone age" (1968). This was a mindset established in his firebombing of Japan during World War II, when the American cremation of entire cities in firestorms "caused many more casualties among Japanese civilians than their armed forces suffered throughout the war."[19] Projecting the mythic awe of the atomic bombing of Hiroshima into Vietnam, berserk style made thinkable both extermi-natory ideation and the conviction of godlike power that the psychiatrist counts as a symptom.[20]

One influence on the berserk mentality was the reorganization of the US military along corporate lines. Under Secretary of Defense McNamara, a former Ford Motor president who had worked with Gen. LeMay on the bombing of Japan, the Army had instituted industrial models of efficiency and control. The premise was that the military is a machine that operates rationally at the push of a but-ton, subject to corporate cost-benefit analysis and economic logic. To maintain career momentum, officers were speeded through tours of duty in Vietnam and therefore less in touch with men at the level of Charlie Company. Trying to quantify—and advertise—progress, headquarters demanded "body counts" from troops in the field. The inflated numbers sent in quickly became suspect among journal-ists and a marker for industrial callousness.[21] This is the mentality that outraged the veteran quoted earlier, who protested that he had become "a fucking animal" because "I didn't give a fuck anymore. Y'know, I wanted—They wanted a fucking hero, so I gave it to them. They wanted fucking body count, so I gave them body count" (83). He seems to be saying, "I wanted heroism, a value to make the strug-gle meaningful, but finally I could believe in nothing anymore."

As stress intensified and rage became less unthinkable, the sense of betrayal spurred an epidemic of fragging—assassination of officers by fragmentation grenades. The attacks were akin to a workplace rampage by disenchanted employees, and like workplace rampages, as dramatized by Tim O'Brien's novel *Going after Cacciato* (1979), they escalated as anger and opposition became the norm.

THE ALLURE OF LEVERAGE

In economics, leverage is the use of borrowed money as a tool to increase financial power. But the term can also describe the use of technology as a lever to create force-multiplying effects. In warfare tools such as the sling, the club, and the nuclear warhead leverage up the force of the fist, magnifying firepower and "kill-ratios." The term is useful for this book because it calls attention to the corporate-military's use of technology to magnify the soldier's destructive force, in theory reducing casualties and even the number of soldiers needed. In World War II military-industrial leverage revived the Depression economy. For a giddy moment the atomic bomb seemed to be the ultimate leverage, promising a monopoly of force so massive that it would preclude all war. In the postwar era massive military-industrial leverage "borrowed" resources away from other sectors of the economy to project a "superpower."

Leverage is inherent in the warrior's role. Soldiers live in a state of threat-display; needing to pump up the self to face danger the way our primate cousins use threat-displays to look large and fearsome. Pyloerection, rearing up, baring teeth, thumping the chest, and screaming are all signals that warn off or overawe enemies. Military culture vividly illustrates the way physiology and ideation reinforce each other, inducing central nervous system flooding and an aggressive mindset. The paraphernalia of martial threat-display has included animal skins, war paint, armor, horses, drums, and bagpipes, not to mention tanks, cannon, and other prosthetic enhancements. In slang, "killer" can be adjectival praise, as in "killer fashions," and uneasily associated with potency, as in the term "lady-killer."

The drawback with leverage of any kind is that it increases risk as well as power and rewards. Leveraged force can go out of control so fast that panic overrides strategy. Especially when leverage is exponential, its rewards and failures are likely to seem utopian or death-tainted. To be sure, all tools magnify our capabilities: we have always been leveraged animals. But the scale of leverage has changed in recent centuries, enriching our behavior and potential for self-control while also exposing us to spectacular abandon.

In the invasion of Iraq the hawks promoted "smart" weapons and computer-assisted communications that easily overestimate executive control of the battlefield. Retired Army Col. Andrew Bacevich warned of "the OSD's [Office of Secretary of Defense] contempt for the accumulated wisdom of the military profession" and infatuation with technology, calling it "really the height of recklessness."[22] The "surgical strike" promised to pacify antiwar critics and make killing a life-saving "procedure."[23] But "smart" weapons have human operators, and they have massacred wedding parties and sleeping families.

Propaganda is a crucial form of leverage. Like the veiled interest in Iraqi oil reserves, the effort to manipulate public support kept unraveling. Dead soldiers were sent home in secrecy. Scandals broke out at Abu Ghraib and in the privatized, fabulously profitable support industry. Security mercenaries drew salaries that mocked soldiers' pay. Military recruitment dried up; reports of post-traumatic stress and atrocities multiplied. As in Vietnam, hawks blamed the problem on morale management. "We lost the war—not because we were outfought, but because we were out Psyoped," wrote Paul E. Vallely, a retired general and specialist in psychological warfare. As a Fox News "analyst" from 2001 to 2007, Vallely foregrounded his "psyops" craft: public relations, advertising, and propaganda. He "co-authored a paper in 1980 that accused American news organizations of failing to defend the nation from 'enemy' propaganda during Vietnam [and] urged a radically new approach to psychological operations in future wars—taking aim at not just foreign adversaries but domestic audiences, too." He called his approach "MindWar"—the Goebbels-like use of network TV and radio to "strengthen our national will to victory."[24]

"MindWar" seeks to get more leverage over public opinion and pump up willpower. Paradoxically Vallely is a creature of a media industry in which truth is sold to consumers. When he complains about a weak "will to victory," he is ignoring the determined soldiers who assassinated their officers in Vietnam. He typifies the way corporate-military-and-political culture sidestepped the crucial problem of principled opposition to the war. In the 1980s and 1990s, policy makers wanted to rehabilitate the military not by questioning the principles and goals of the Vietnam War, but by refining techniques. As military budgets reflated, hawks began to speak of overcoming Vietnam syndrome as if it were a mood disorder.

When jubilant Berliners tore down the Wall in 1989, Cold War domino theory toppled as well, leaving gaps in the rationale for America's corporate-military. And global predominance was costly. Though its military bases continued to proliferate, the United States was shifting from a creditor to a debtor nation, outsourcing and shuttering whole industries. Oil geologist M. King Hubbert's forecast of finite oil reserves, and memories of the Arab oil boycotts of the 1970s kept the US military policing the world's hydrocarbon belt. At a small cost the first Gulf War (1990) punished the predatory Saddam Hussein, reinforced "friendly" oil regimes, and dramatized American might.

A core motive for the war on terror was the effort to expand control over oil reserves and pipelines. The occupation of Iraq was designed to create

> an American protectorate for the next few decades—a necessary condition for the extraction of its oil wealth. If the US had managed to create a strong, democratic government in an Iraq effectively secured by its own army and police force, and had then departed, what would have stopped that government from taking control of its own oil, like every other regime in the Middle East? On the assumption that the Bush-Cheney strategy is oil-centred, the tactics—dissolving the army, de-Baathification, a final 'surge' that has hastened internal migration— could scarcely have been more effective. The costs—a few billion dollars a month plus a few dozen American fatalities—are negligible compared to $30 trillion in oil wealth, assured American geopolitical supremacy and cheap gas for voters.[25]

In theory, as Deputy Secretary of Defense Paul Wolfowitz argued, the war would pay for itself through access to Iraqi oil.[26] Such selfish aims had to be dignified for the public and the troops by an apocalyptic melodrama of "WMDs," an "Axis of Evil," and "movements of rage."[27]

Had special access to Iraqi oil fully succeeded, the United States would have vastly expanded its economic and geostrategic reach. Neoconservatives took for granted that corporate-military leverage could capture and compound that Iraqi resource leverage. The abstractions in their 1997 "Project for a New American Century" (PNAC) soared above the historical particularities of the societies they planned to convert to a US-friendly model. They stressed not diplomacy or analysis but will: "Does the United States have the resolve to shape a new century favorable to American principles and interests?"[28]

In the "war on terror," resolve was supposed to remake an ancient, tormented, utterly unfamiliar region of the earth into an oil-rich democracy friendly to multinational corporate ownership. The "American Century's" grandiosity trivialized Iraqi compliance. It perpetuated the triumphalism that has long colored American foreign policy, and unwittingly echoed millenarian themes that fueled some of the last century's ugliest ambitions.[29] Advocating military dominance of space and the doctrine of "preemptive war"—reminiscent of the Hollywood western's thrilling injunction to "shoot first and ask questions afterward"—the neocons were using berserk style to hold together thoroughly incompatible goals. Not surprisingly, the public quickly tuned out the exhortations.

The emphasis on leveraged force obscured the conflicted content. Rather than examining motives on a field in motion, the hawks construed behavior as ballistic forces, impersonal as trajectories in billiards, and controlled by executives at the center of cybernetic communications webs. Many of the core ideas derived from Reagan-era managerial models. On paper, lean and mean troop detachments would fly to a global "trouble spot" and impose order. In reality, as in Iraq, the corporate-military installed bases that were "full-scale 'American towns,' well guarded, 15–20 miles around, with multiple PXes, fitness clubs, brand fast-food outlets, traffic lights, the works." "Bumper to bumper, the tens of thousands of trucks, tanks, and humvees would stretch, from New York City to Denver."[30] Like the belated realization that lightning intervention would require forced redeployments of exhausted troops, the contradiction between bases dubbed "Camp Cupcake" and Humvees blown apart by crude roadside bombs exemplifies the conceptual conflicts that led to atrocities and abandon.

When insurgent atrocities wracked Iraq, the American reaction was sometimes brutal precisely because it had taken so little account of motives. At the top, the hawks downplayed or screened out the reality of other selves. This is not a sentimental criticism. As in Vietnam, to maximize leverage the hawks paid little attention to the inner lives, history, and contingencies of those to be rescued or their enemies. Nor were they prepared for the bystanders' condemnation of their behavior. President Bush and others were woefully uninformed about the basic sectarianism in Islam and in Iraq. On the ground in Iraq, MindWar leveraged the condescending noble abstractions of the "New American Century" into pulp fiction horrors. The invasion was pay back for the twin towers. Saddam Hussein was interchangeable with Osama bin Laden. Vietnamese "gooks" were now "hadjis." Dead hadjis were body count for troops "keeping score." In the worst months the morgues literally overflowed with corpses.

LEVERAGE AT WAR

Leveraged firepower did not work as planned. Evan Wright recounts the approach to Baghdad on April 6, 2003, when the Marines confronted "a horrorscape of human corpses and of dead cows. . . . Sergeant Espera's vehicle swerves to avoid running over a human head lying in the road. When the vehicle turns, he looks up to see a dog eating a corpse. 'Can it get any sicker than this?' he asks. Reflecting back on the battalion's performance to this point, he says, 'Do you realize the shit we've done here, the people we've killed? Back home in the civilian world, if we did this, we would go to prison.'"[31]

"Do you realize—?" Killing from behind a shield of massive firepower has the quality of half-knowledge and denial. In its way the "horrorscape" was one outcome of the furious doublethink that gripped American culture after the September 11 attacks. In the *National Review Online* (September 13, 2001), pundit Ann Coulter blustered: "We should invade [the terrorists' Islamic] countries, kill their leaders and convert them to Christianity." With blithe, sadistic illogic she switched from Christianity to genocide: "We weren't punctilious about locating and punishing only Hitler and his top officers. We carpet-bombed German cities; we killed civilians. That's war. And this is war."[32]

The sergeant's anxiety about punishment ("we would go to prison") anticipated what would turn out to be insurgent mania for revenge. Exemplary violence—teaching "a lesson"—always risks inciting retaliation.[33] "At least some of the initial impetus for Iraq's insurgency came in the spring of 2003, when American troops in Fallujah shot and killed seventeen demonstrators, and kinsmen of the dead sought revenge by killing Americans."[34] Unlike many animals hard-wired to signal submission and halt a conflict, human cycles of revenge have no natural upper limit.

Economic leverage also backfired in the occupation. Staggering infusions of taxpayer money went to privatized military support and to outside contractors rehabilitating Iraqi infrastructure. But the work was plagued by ineptitude and waste. When L. Paul Bremer's Coalition Provisional Authority (the CPA) disbanded the Iraqi army to purge all Baathists, the decree spawned mass unemployment, hardship, and fears of social death. In an absurd failure of imagination the CPA never disarmed the soldiers. Like terminated employees, many joined the insurgency, with suicidal attacks akin to workplace rampages.[35]

The immediate response to the "liberation" of Iraq was the looting rampage that plundered government offices, utilities, and national treasures, crippling Baghdad. Many accounts blamed the disorder on troop shortages—the Pentagon's "lean and mean" leverage. "Stuff happens," Secretary Rumsfeld quipped, playing on a bumper sticker associated with pickup trucks, rednecks, and cool toughness. As berserk style, however, his joke masks an assumption that social disintegration would make Iraqis more compliant. Critics contrasted the tolerance of the urban looting to the forceful occupation of the oilfields. Klein argues that the strategists tacitly used the rampage as a deliberate application of "shock doctrine," since it weakened the Iraqis' powers of self-governance, strengthening the hand of the occupiers.[36] Yet the rampage unexpectedly helped ignite the insurgency—another instance of the blowback that has jolted American policy since the Cold War.[37] Retired Maj. Gen. John Batiste, an Iraq veteran, openly accused Sec. Rumsfeld of causing "uncontrollable chaos" in Iraq, and eventually Rumsfeld was forced to resign.[38]

Financial leverage was supposed to generate model prosperity through free markets, yet the nation that put a man on the moon proved unable to fully restore electricity in Iraq. Ideally Iraq was to be converted to a "free market" open to multinational corporate penetration.[39] Complicating this vision, however, were tropes of colonial warfare and exploitation guaranteed to alienate Iraqis. "Getting the rights to distribute Procter & Gamble products would be a gold mine," one corporate warrior vowed. "One well-stocked 7-Eleven could knock out 30 Iraqi stores; a Wal-Mart could take over the country."[40] "Free market" breakup of state-owned enterprises exacerbated unemployment. In the event, infuriated insurgents threatened to take over the country, and corporate money fled.

In the CPA's freewheeling efforts to jumpstart the economy, Washington dispatched billions of taxpayers' dollars to Baghdad from US repositories in shrink-wrapped bundles, many of which unaccountably vanished.[41] Some of the money apparently bought off warring groups. Incalculable sums went to "privatized" contractors despite a parade of scandals. No bid profits poured into corporations such as Halliburton that were closely connected to Vice President Cheney and his circle. During the Vietnam War the construction company Brown and Root—a Halliburton subsidiary, now KBR—had been known as "Burn and Loot."[42] Privatization encouraged short-term thinking that was bound to be more impulsive and opportunistic than a long-range government strategy. An exasperated Rep. Henry Waxman protested that the privatized contracts "may well turn out to be the largest war profiteering in history."[43]

Berserk style was both a cause and an effect of the chaotic occupation. Regional tribes and religious sects were embroiled, as well as some foreign jihadis and opportunists such as Abu Musab al-Zarqawi, not to mention predatory militias and police death squads as well as criminal gangs. Disoriented American troops and their leaders were unable even to name all the shadowy actors or their motives.

As casualties rose and control failed, commanders retaliated as they had in Vietnam with ferocious force. When a mob in Sunni Fallujah killed four Blackwater mercenaries in March 2004, media branded the town a "hotbed of hatred" and the mob criminals to be "hunted down" with a "precise," "deliberate," and "overwhelming" response.[44] The military obliterated the city. "US soldiers opened fire on houses, and US helicopters fired on and killed women, old men and young children, according to Associated Press photographer Bilal Hussein."[45] The Italian documentary "Fallujah: The Hidden Massacre" includes interviews with witnesses who report that the military used the banned chemical white phosphorus. "'Phosphorus burns bodies, melting the flesh right down to the bone,' says one former US soldier, interviewed by the documentary's director, Sigfrido Ranucci."[46] After a year of denials the Army acknowledged use of the banned munitions, but only against enemy combatants—a claim disputed by eyewitnesses.[47]

In Fallujah as in Vietnam, the determination to crush all resistance led to a "free fire zone" policy. By 2005, "faced with intractable and growing armed resistance in Iraq, the Pentagon has drafted plans for the organization of death squads to assassinate political opponents of the US military occupation and terrorize the civilian population. The plan . . . has been dubbed by Pentagon planners as 'the Salvador option.' It was a measure of the leadership's growing desperation over the deteriorating situation in Iraq. 'We have to find a way to take the offensive against the insurgents,' a senior US military officer told *Newsweek*. 'Right now, we are playing defense and we are losing.'"[48]

LEVERAGE AMOK

Beginning in the Vietnam War, American soldiers carried more ammunition and were trained to achieve a strikingly higher "kill ratio" than in previous wars. The success in overcoming inhibitions registers tragically when soldiers commit murder on or off the battlefield without compunction, as in the premeditated "kill team" slaying of civilians "out of pure bloodlust" in Afghanistan.[49] For a military culture striving to maximize its lethality, particular individuals with a heightened potential for violence are attractive but risky prospects.

From the start American troops in Iraq showed confusion about their motives. A February 28, 2006, poll showed that 58% said "the U.S. mission in Iraq is clear in their minds, while 42% said it is either somewhat or very unclear to them, that they have no understanding of it at all, or are unsure. While 85% said the U.S. mission is mainly 'to retaliate for Saddam's role in the 9–11 attacks,' 77% said they also believe the main or a major reason for the war was 'to stop Saddam from protecting al Qaeda in Iraq.'"[50] While the poll reports that most troops didn't "blame [the] Iraqi public for insurgent attacks," they were operating on discredited, unrealistic beliefs that would polarize their feelings about the Iraqis. It is logical that vulnerable soldiers in morally queasy operations needed to believe the MindWar canard that Saddam Hussein was behind the terrorism.

In a combat emergency, experience sharpens beliefs and prejudices. "They're all guilty," former Pvt. Kenneth Eastridge told an interviewer, "all hadjis. They're not human like us."[51] In places such as Ramadi soldiers felt hated and futile. When terror flared into panic and rage, their killing became indiscriminate and, as in the Bush doctrine, preemptive. Ramadi, said Marcus Mifflin, "was just a free-for-all,"[52] a term reminiscent of "free-fire zones" such as My Lai. Yet berserk style conditions such sweeping explanations.

One of the first massacres to come to light took place in Haditha after a roadside bomb killed a Marine on November 19, 2005. Lance Cpl. Roel Briones reported that "[a] lot of people were mad. Everyone had just a [terrible] feeling about what had happened to TJ," their dead friend.[53] It was a classic scenario: shocked, terrified, grieving men, and a highly aggressive sergeant leading the way to further killing by allegedly shooting dead a taxi driver and his four student passengers. They felt hate and hated; they wanted revenge. The ensuing slaughter left 19 people in two families dead in adjacent houses, including mothers and children and a wheelchair-bound grandfather.

The official reaction medicalized the rampage as a symptom of traumatic stress. "'Many of our Marines have been involved in life or death combat or have witnessed the loss of their fellow Marines, and the effects of these events can be numbing,' said General Hagee. 'There is the risk of becoming indifferent to the loss of a human life, as well as bringing dishonour upon ourselves.'"[54] Trying for balance, the general warned about "indifference to the loss of human life" and "dishonor." Despite humane intentions, these euphemisms distort the reality of atrocity. After all, the problem at Haditha was not an isolated slip; not indifference but rage and chaos; not "loss of human life" but the murder of innocent families; not just dishonor but the risk of war crimes prosecution and disgrace to a nation waging an unprovoked war.

The core dilemma is that trauma is an injury that entails interpretation of the injury. Shock and exhaustion may seriously disturb body and mind; but much depends on the way you understand the experience. How you—and those around you—are wrapped determines how you will respond to traumatic stress. In turn, how you interpret is part of how you are wrapped. US Army Field Manual 22–51 acknowledges in bureaucratic jargon that "misconduct combat stress behavior" is likely in guerrilla warfare. The manual notes that "even though we may pity the overstressed soldier as well as the victims," such cases "must be punished." What the manual cannot acknowledge is that the rules themselves exist in a cultural environment that may be profoundly compromised by conflict and denial. In actual combat soldiers develop styles of thinking and acting that try to match rules of engagement to real world exigencies. Style mediates between an idealized blueprint and the "fog" of war. Berserk style, whether in General Hagee's euphemisms or in the decision to kill "suspect" Iraqis, preserves possibilities of empowering violence that otherwise might be ruled out. And in the end, as the Marines in Haditha knew, the murder of civilians is rarely punished.

To be sure, war attracts aggressive personalities. And an Army short of manpower has been known to wink at recruits with criminal records.[55] Yet even antisocial personalities will be affected by living in a fractured environment that fears, condemns, but also surreptitiously praises berserk behavior. Occupation soldiers experienced a fractured reality every time they left familiar American bases to patrol a world in which strangers could be suicide bombers. The reality of the streets, that is, was always potentially berserk. At once the selves in view were "just like you and me" and yet also specters of death. They were familiar parents and children, but also predatory animals, invisible demons, and contemptible losers.

At home reality was fractured as well. The American public was torn between yellow ribbons and antiwar banners, sympathy for Iraqis and masked rage. These Marines "suffered a total breakdown in morality and leadership, with tragic results," an unnamed "US official" told the *Los Angeles Times* (Cohn), as if the atrocities could be an isolated anomaly. Right-wing media, by contrast, vociferously defended the Marines, and shock jock Michael Savage ranted that the Marines arrested for the massacre in Haditha were being treated even more harshly than the Afghan War prisoners that the United States was holding—over a hundred of whom had died in American custody by 2008.

None of the Marines in the Haditha massacre were charged with murder. Staff Sgt. Frank D. Wuterich faced nine counts of voluntary manslaughter, "with the charges alleging that he had an intent to kill and that his actions inside a residential home and on a residential street in November 2005 amounted to unlawful killing 'in the heat of sudden passion caused by adequate provocation.' Charging documents released this week say he killed at least nine people without properly obtaining positive identification that they were the enemy in the midst of an attack." In accounts such as this, "complexity" and bureaucratic terminology sanitized the killings: "Initially called a massacre by Iraqi residents of Haditha and later characterized as coldblooded murder by a U.S. congressman, the case has turned not on an alleged rampage but on a far more complex analysis of how U.S. troops fight an insurgency in the midst of a population they seek to protect."[56]

Loss of Self

When boundaries are violated, it can feel like ecstatic freedom or insane chaos. Empowered to kill with impunity, soldiers can feel godlike. But the experience is treacherously unstable. The excitement is, literally, like nothing else in life. Without boundaries the self threatens to come apart. In the wisdom of slang, you "lose it." After the Haditha massacre, Lance Cpl. Briones felt himself eaten alive. In Marjorie Cohn's account, "he was ordered to take photographs of the victims and help carry their bodies out of their homes. He is still haunted by what he had to do that day. Briones picked up a young girl who was shot in the head. 'I held her out like this,' he said, extending his arms, 'but her head was bobbing up and down and the insides fell on my legs. I used to be one of those Marines who said that post-traumatic stress is a bunch of bull,' said Briones, who has gotten into serious trouble since he returned home. 'But all this stuff that keeps going through my head is eating me up. I need immediate help.'"

His metaphor says he feels that a predator is consuming his identity, as if he has fallen victim to cannibals or to the hunter he was. But the predators, unthinkably, are his own country and his buddies who have destroyed a child and exposed him to guilt, grief, disgust, terror, and alienation. Behind them is the most terrifying predator, death, which reveals life as nothingness: a smear of brains on a pant leg.

Psychic defenses usually keep the ephemeral nature—the nothingness—of the self hidden from us. To "lose it" is to lose self-control and in turn, self. Even in the face of actual death, that terrifying abyss is likely to remain disguised or denied. Consider the way berserkers may mutilate enemies. John Needham, who tried to commit suicide in Iraq, reported that Iraqis were shot for invented reasons, then mutilated. "The sergeants particularly liked removing victims' brains, Needham said, and had photographs to prove it."[57] Whatever they thought they were doing, the sergeants were unwittingly emulating American culture's focus on the evil "mastermind" Saddam Hussein (or Osama bin Laden). After all, the war opened with a missile bombardment specifically targeting Saddam's palaces, hoping to "behead" the enemy.

But the behavior has a deeper dimension too. By carving out an enemy's brain you take apart his personality as if to discover a core self, even as you annihilate him. In this way the sergeants were doing to enemies what the war—the enemy—was doing to the Americans' inner lives. They were acting out their distress. John Needham's father, a retired Army officer, recognized the fragmentation when his son was on trial for murdering a girlfriend after his discharge: "He was a good soldier, and his group was doing things he knew was wrong. And he was in this prolonged combat situation where they have all this armor and life-saving technology to keep them alive, but mentally, they are in pieces." On his MySpace page the young soldier had written: "I'm falling apart by the seams it seems the days here bleed into each other I have to find the will to live man I miss my brothers. These walls are caving in my despair wraps me in its web, I feel I'm sinking in, throw me a lifesaver throw me a life worth living. I'm a part of death I am death this is hard to admit but this shits getting old."

To feel yourself "a part of death" is to experience the annihilation of meaning, which is the nothingness of the self. As Ernest Becker says, we depend on heroic purpose—a sense that our lives have some sort of enduring significance—to manage the terror of death that is built into us.

In this context atrocious aggression acts out a struggle not simply to avoid death but to substantiate the self. This helps to explain the otherwise pointlessly cruel hazing Marines inflicted on "weaker" comrades. Domination of a "bitch" creates a conviction of alpha mastery as slavery does. In crushing the will of the victim, the master not only appropriates it to build himself up, but does so with a special surge of righteousness—"I'm doing this for your own good." When soldiers committed suicide, turning aggression against the tormented self, their suicide notes "almost always cited hazing."[58]

As a ferocious and fearless gunner, Kenneth Eastridge was decorated and praised. He was important to others. He was somebody. His tattoos boasted of his power as a killer. Yet one tattoo, an SS insignia, revealed an awareness of evil: a devil's pact. And as combat stress wore him down, Eastridge began to "lose it." Once while his platoon searched a house in Ramadi and he covered the street,

Eastridge began firing as Lt. Calley did at My Lai. "Families were out playing soccer and barbecuing," and fled when the gunfire erupted. "Orders came over the radio to cease fire, he said, but he kept yelling, 'Negative! Negative!' Eastridge said he shot more than 1,700 rounds. When asked how many people he killed, he said, 'Not that many. Maybe a dozen.'"

Eventually Eastridge was court-martialed for "sex and drugs," but not for "things that can never be told, but that everybody knew about and approved of—basically war crimes." On his return home Eastridge was convicted in the murder of another soldier and sentenced to prison. "I had no job training," he explained. "All I know how to do is kill people."[59] On the brink of nothingness, emergency physiology and the illusion of godlike power can be self-intoxicating even as it overrides the governing limits that define personality and puts you—as slang has it—"out of it."

Looking back, combat berserkers and rampage killers may describe a feeling of blackout or dissociation. "Did I do that? Was that me?" At the court-martial of a sniper accused of murder, another sniper, Sgt. Evan Vela, "all but broke down as he described firing two bullets into an unarmed Iraqi man [that] his unit arrested last May." After his squad leader, Sgt. Hensley, cut off the prisoner's handcuffs, "I heard the word 'Shoot,'" Sgt. Vela recalled. "I don't remember pulling the trigger," he said. "I just came through and the guy was dead, and it just took me a second to realize the shot had come from the pistol." As the suspected insurgent convulsed on the ground, "Sergeant Hensley kicked him in the throat and told Sergeant Vela to shoot him again. Sergeant Vela, who is not on trial but faces murder charges in connection with the killing, said he fired a second time."[60]

In Iraq troops were often exhausted because of extended tours, insomnia, and unrelieved nervous system arousal. In addition, they personally or officially treated exhaustion and post-traumatic stress disorder (PTSD) with drugs and alcohol that affected judgment. Mentally they lived out impossible conflicts of right and wrong, sympathy and hate, trigger-finger omnipotence and relentless terror. Not least of all, they struggled with conflicts over nervous system fight or flight. Escape into drugs, distraction, or depression can try to leave the troubled self behind. But flight may explode into fight, and fight may plunge into depression.

Military culture and militarized American culture are complicit in the problem. Military obsession with obedience and threat constricts awareness and intensifies the explosive potential of stress. Armies have routinely used berserk style to harden recruits. The Japanese military in the 1930s engrained in recruits the Three Alls Policy: kill all, burn all, and loot all. The temptation to reduce the soldier to an insensate weapon is strong. The power of technological leverage promises to bypass or overcome the psychic conflicts that can torment soldiers, but it can also make them expendable and literalize their enslavement to command. The frightening possibilities register in popular fantasies such as James Cameron's *Terminator* (1984). Michael Belfiore describes military research in which machines coopt the human bodies with which they merge, given so much autonomy that they run amok when subject to hacking or malfunction.[61] Americans are horrified by terrorist fanatics, yet such fanatics are a version of "smart" weapons and proof that people can be trained to self-destruct.

This is no academic cavil. Perhaps the cruelest use of leverage by the corporate-military is its new reliance on psychiatric drugs to get more fight out of soldiers who are coming undone from combat stress. The soldiers quoted above showed severe symptoms of PTSD. Yet in case after case they were treated as high-tech machines to be lubricated with prescription drugs and returned to battle. Worn out and badly shaken, they kept going with antidepressants such as Celexa and the mitrazapines, Valium, Ambien for insomnia, antipsychotics, plus alcohol, marijuana, and other drugs. Often they combined official prescriptions and self-medication, with perilous side effects. Coming home they faced withdrawal and an appalling void. In Eastridge's words, "All I know how to do is kill people."

Doublethink haunts the problem of combat stress. Since berserk frenzy can make soldiers exceptional fighters if it doesn't destroy them, it is tempting to tolerate or even wink at the role of trauma. In *Shock and Awe* (1996), Harlan K. Ullman and James P. Wade enthused about the use of trauma as a weapon against enemies without acknowledging its paradoxical effects. They adduced "the comatose and glazed expressions of survivors of the great bombardments of World War I" as proof of the power of shock to immobilize enemies. Ullman defended the "life-saving" annihilation of Hiroshima as a model. Yet despite "great bombardments," Germans and Vietnamese fought on for years.

While everyone deplores traumatic injury in soldiers, military thinking also allows for or even sustains PTSD when it leverages up ferocity and daring in combat, or unless it cripples operations. The ambiguities of the syndrome make it possible to rationalize injury. Military psychiatry treats PTSD with a mix of talk therapy and drugs, but help is not always available. A Rand study estimated that nearly one in five veterans of the Afghanistan and Iraq wars suffered symptoms of PTSD or depression, though many avoid seeking help for fear that the stigma of weakness will hurt their military careers.[62] Researchers are currently testing drugs that may block overreaction to traumatic memories rather as ice applied after a burn prevents the body's emergency response from causing more serious harm.[63] One concern would be that efficient relief of symptoms could support the dream of cyber soldiers who could be more deliberately driven to frenzied aggression and then pharmaceutically disarmed and restored to civilian life—a version of the *Terminator* scenario.

AT WAR WITH STYLE

As havoc overtook the occupation, the berserk trope began to surface in accounts such as Pepe Escobar's "Counterinsurgency run amok" (*Asia Times*, November 18, 2004). The Internet and even embedded journalists began to recognize berserk style at work. The psychiatrist's category "beastlike" found euphemistic expression in a few instances such as Oliver Poole's description of "feral" Marines on their third tour of duty in Iraq who had been involved in the mayhem at Fallujah and Haditha.

At Kilo Company's encampment at a dam on the outskirts of Haditha, Poole observed that "institutional discipline had frayed and was even approaching breakdown." As a rule, "American camps in Iraq are almost suburban, with their coffee shops and polite soldiers who idle away their rest hours playing computer games and discussing girls back home." By contrast, these Marines had set up a separate camp that was "a feral place [and] resembled something from *Lord of the Flies* . . . and on the day before my arrival one soldier had shot himself in the head with his M16. No one would discuss why."[64] The group had withdrawn to an emergency culture signposted with death's heads to warn off strangers. Their fears showed in the stereotyped bravado of their skull-and-crossbones threat-displays. They were encamped at a massive dam that was a constant reminder of their precarious situation. With its chronic alarms and broken machinery, the dam was under terrific strain, holding back a flood as the troops were tenuously holding in check a lethal insurgency, every Marine casualty another crack in the structure.

The "feral" metaphor evokes the berserk style fantasy that by shedding civilized restraints we can access extraordinary instinctual resources. It also picks up on the idea of war as predation. An article in the *Marine Corps Times* quotes Col. Clarke Lethin: commanders "believe that if we create a mentality in our Marines that they are hunters and they take on some of those skills, then we'll be able to increase our combat effectiveness." He adds: "The Corps hopes to tap into skills certain Marines may already have learned growing up in rural hunting areas and in urban areas, such as inner cities." Nick Turse points out that the colonel's language implicitly compared "enemies in urban warfare, today largely Iraqis and Afghans, to animals that are hunted and killed as quarry. As Lethin had unabashedly noted, 'We identified a need to ensure our Marines were being the hunters. Hunting is more than just the shooting. It's finding your game.'"[65] Just this idea turned up in the prosecution of snipers allegedly authorized to operate as "death squads," using "bait" such as fake explosives and spools of wire to lure Iraqis into shooting range.

As a style of organizing aggression, the trope reaches from firefights in Iraq through US inner cities to the leaders dictating policy. President Bush outdid LBJ in faux-heroic references to "hunting" the enemy. Of Al Qaeda terrorists he liked to say, "We're hunting them down, one at a time," or as he put it in November 2001, "we're smoking them out." The president "talked incessantly of hunting humans—in speeches to American troops, at photo ops with foreign leaders, at family fundraisers, even in the midst of remarks about homeownership."[66]

To recognize what Robert J. Lifton calls "atrocity-producing situations," we need to see more clearly the deep tropes such as hunting and predation that shape them, even when they are transparently packaged. A style preconditions a behavior so that it can be put on like a costume off the cultural rack. What begins as style can trigger actions, but the reverse is also true. For example, in the Iraq War ubiquitous digital cameras have filmed actual killing. On the Internet the photos are equivocal: they can be taken as trophies that prove heroism, but they could also enhance legal and moral oversight, as did a video clip released by the whistleblower website Wikileaks of two US helicopter mistakenly or wantonly slaughtering two journalists and six other people on a street corner in New Baghdad on July 12, 2007.[67] Similarly, displayed death may produce opposite reactions. Killings may arouse abhorrence yet in time, with familiarity, become desensitized in the manner of "reality show" entertainment or war porn.

In style, tropes may insidiously combine. The camera, say, can also be a weapon, seeming to tame the killing it witnesses or even enables. Sniping and photographing from cover are kinds of ambush, a predatory strategy. The implicit breakdown of cultural categories and rules that protect our sense of human rightness is evident in the prominent symptoms of godlike (spying on quarry from an invisible, commanding blind) and beastlike behavior. A Marine blog called Slaglerock

Slaughterhouse[68] posted a photo of a large-caliber automatic weapon
behind an armored housing with the hand-painted sign:

Iraqi photo's [*sic*]
Look here
Smile
Wait for
Flash

The macabre joke is a threat-display to intimidate Iraqis and to
advertise alpha male confidence to other Marines and, on the web, to
the world. The intuitive nature of the wit is striking, since the joke
parodies a photo studio but turns the portrait's substantiation of
identity into a threat of annihilation in a "flash" of gunfire. Further,
the joke associates military conquest with the photo studio "business,"
the more disturbingly conflicted since the business of rescuing and
rebuilding Iraqi identity in reality means the "flash" of death. The
blog's title, "Slaglerock Slaughterhouse," implies rampage killing
while the joke daydreams about total Iraqi compliance. The instructions - "Look here and smile"—evoke a carnival shooting gallery with
passive targets, even as it commands the victim's smiling assent to
murder. In this way the joke shares in the dynamics of hazing.

This cluster of tropes can be seen extending to wartime rape. Like
killing at will, rape promises godlike mastery over life and death. The
rapist acts out mind and body's appetite for more life: but evil in its
destruction of the love that nurtures new life. Like war, it is a fantasy
of putting in seed to overcome death. In his rape of Europa and Leda,
Zeus acts out the clinical qualities of the berserk state, at once god
and beast, forcing life into being. In wartime rape victims take on the
soldier's enslavement to command, his terror, his threatened loss
of self. Their suffering and abjection confirms his being.

Rape, then, merges the physiology and ideation of taking and
giving life: of killing and fucking as a means to survival ecstasy. Shay
points out that some people experience the "adrenaline rush" of the
berserk state "as immensely pleasurable and willingly refer to [it] as
exaltation or intoxication. Some combat veterans speak of it as 'better
than sex'" (92).

This is the psychic economy underlying one of the war's most
appalling atrocities: the gang rape and murder of fourteen-year-old
Abeer Qassim Hamza al-Janabi following the slaughter of her parents
and five-year-old sister.[69] Berserk style influenced the crime from the
moment the girl caught the attention of four soldiers from Bravo

Company in a town southwest of Baghdad at a time when insurgents had killed seventeen from their battalion in four months. The four men stalked the girl and searched her family's isolated farmhouse as a pretext to make advances toward her. The alarmed family allowed the girl to sleep at a neighbor's house for safety, but on the afternoon of March 12, 2006, after drinking and hatching plans, the soldiers acted.[70] Subsequently insurgents abducted and beheaded two of their fellow soldiers in revenge.

All of the accused invoked traumatic stress in their defense. Before the rampage came to light, Pfc. Stephen D. Green was discharged for a personality disorder that according to an Army spokesman "does not necessarily indicate a mental disorder. Such a notation can be used to document willful disobedience or a personality that does not mesh well with military life."[71] Yet Green had been welcomed into the army despite a criminal background, and had boasted to a neighbor that he was "gonna go over there and kill 'em all."

To appreciate the role of style in the "atrocity-producing situation," recall the joke about photographing Iraqis to death. As Brian Nicol observes about paparazzi who stalk celebrities using the language of hunting and prey, "The camera 'shoots', it *takes* (i.e. steals) pictures." In the soldiers' photo the gun "shoots" people and "takes" their lives. Nicol cautions that "[i]t would be a mistake to overstate the links between photography and serial murder, but there is a similar logic at work in both, which revolves around the 'capturing' of a targeted individual (often for the image they represent) and involves a similar dynamic of power and control."[72] The ambivalence implicit in the relationship of stalker and prey also resonates with the soldiers' role as would-be liberators of Iraqis. Instead of being greeted with kisses and adulation, the invaders meet ambush and death and feel enraged at what seems to be a betrayal.

The stalking soldiers pumped up sexual excitement and rage, as in sadistic pornography, and echoing the "war porn" photos of Iraqi deaths on the Internet. A sublimated echo of these themes captured media attention in mid-2006 and resonates with the rape and murder of Abeer.[73] At his base Cpl. Joshua Belile performed an original folksong called "Hadji Girl" for an audience of laughing, applauding fellow Marines. The song is about erotic attraction to an Iraqi girl that leads to a Marine's slaughter of her family. Videotaped, the song appeared on the Internet, where it was officially censored. The performer apologized that it was only a joke, and some soldiers vehemently justified it. In the lyrics the speaker is under fire in Iraq. Facing death, he "looked up and I saw her eyes / And I knew it was love at first sight."

And she said . . .
"Dirka Dirka Mohammed Jihad
Sherpa Sherpa Bak Allah."
Hadji girl, I can't understand what you're saying.

Invited "to meet her family," unable to "figure out
how to say no. / Cause I don't speak Arabic," the
soldier goes home with her to a "side shanty." There,

Her brother and her father shouted. . .
"Dirka Dirka Mohammed Jihad
Sherpa Sherpa Bak Allah."

They pulled out their AKs so I could see. . . .
So I grabbed her little sister and pulled her in front of me.

As the bullets began to fly
The blood sprayed from between her eyes
And then I laughed maniacally

Then I hid behind the TV
And I locked and loaded my M-16
And I blew those little fuckers to eternity.

And I said . . .
"Dirka Dirka Mohammed Jihad
Sherpa Sherpa Bak Allah."
They should have known they were fucking with a Marine.

A theatrical occasion can accommodate scathing satire, and in its origins satire is a form of cursing,[74] so the murder of the "little sister" could be taken as gruesome gallows humor about insurgent treachery. But the same text is also projecting aggression onto the Iraqi father and brother in order to enable the Marines onstage and in the audience to fantasize about romance, sex, fertility, and an orgasmic rampage that could discharge tremendous internal stress and reinforce a conviction of godlike inviolability. The enemy males are rivals for the "Hadji girl," and the song substitutes the "Hadji girl's" alter ego, the little sister, in order to kill the rivals and take the girl.

Style conditions the psychic *stage* on which life stories play out. Just as the gunner in the photo imagines manning a machine gun and a camera, using witty condescension to manage his own psychic turmoil, so the song acts out an inner storm of conflicts in a "safe" play space.

In the videotaped performance at his base in the war zone, Cpl. Belile is actually on a stage with a microphone and his guitar before an audience of buddies, behind him a set of drums, and trained on him a "TV" camera. His "act" emulates American industrial entertainment: talent shows, American Idol, pop protest music, and the television cartoon satire "South Park," from which he took the mock-Arabic phrases in his lyrics. At the same time his audience applauded the sadistic fantasy they shared, either blowing off steam—or tragically reinforcing—the group's urge to "blow those little fuckers to eternity."

In the song the soldier hides behind the TV set. As a style, television provides a shield. It stands for home: it literally contains familiar icons and values that can make a soldier's sacrifices meaningful. To the extent that television style shapes the warrior's actions, it is formative. For the self under stress, TV-as-style provides a platform like the machine gun "camera" from which to kill the hostile, alien Iraqi family. In the pervasive idea of performance the unthinkable becomes thinkable, and an "act" may also be an action, ambiguously scripted and visceral. Stylized, violence masters death by dispatching enemies who represent death, even as its element of play and controlled unreality tames—or promises to tame—death's terror.

THE ECONOMY OF TORTURE

Though torture inflicts pain, it is at bottom, like war, an economy of creaturely motives. The ultimate leverage in torture is the threat of death, just as the ultimate prize is supposed to be life-saving information. The torturer seeks to break the will of the victim. The term "brainwashing" points to the underlying idea of a conversion experience in which the prisoner's will is "washed" away and replaced by the will of the torturer. The torturer consumes the victim's will and life-giving secrets. Bureaucracy may disguise it, but torture acts out the creaturely drive to consume the vitality of others evident in slavery, vampire fantasies, and in the cannibalistic obsessions of a Jeffrey Dahmer or the berserk sergeant's scooping out of an enemy's brain. At Abu Ghraib the motive crystallized in the bared fangs of guard dogs attacking prisoners.

In these terms torture is a form of virtual killing. Carried to its conclusion, as in lynching, it shares the dynamics of human sacrifice, epitomized in the interrogation and ritual burning of witches. In witchcraft prosecutions and show trials, for example, a vicious feedback loop of pain, paranoia, and panic reliably extorted confessions that rationalized judicial murder. Torture by the Argentine and Chilean juntas in the 1970s regularly led to murder.

In the "war on terror" an unknown number of prisoners have died in American custody.[75] At Abu Ghraib, a badly beaten prisoner kept shackled in a "stress position" suffocated as in crucifixion. His CIA interrogator allegedly expressed surprise at the outcome. By contrast, berserk rage is unequivocal when guards have literally beaten a prisoner to a pulp, as in the death of an Afghan civilian recounted in Alex Gibney's documentary *Taxi to the Dark Side* (2007).

Viewed in terms of berserk style, torture grades by degrees toward atrocity. In the Bush administration's justifications of "harsh interrogation," jargon sanitized the cold rage. The practice of "waterboarding," which fascinated the media, is not "simulated" drowning regulated by legalistic adjectives, but actual drowning carried to the brink of death. The suffering comes not merely from pain but from the terror of knowing that someone is killing you.

Torture is always latently berserk because it is a self-fulfilling and self-intoxicating system. Operating to revenge or prevent injury, it is incipiently paranoid, driven by suspicion and anxiety. As in witchcraft interrogations, innocence is virtually impossible to prove. If a victim has some information, it raises the possibility that pain will force out more. Likewise, the proximity to pain and death may excite in the perpetrator fear, guilt, frustration, and survival rage that only the victim's guilt can relieve, so the process feeds on itself. The victim's helplessness invites the sadistic total control that Erich Fromm linked to authoritarian fantasies of invulnerability and immortality.

The Geneva Conventions and habeas corpus in American jurisprudence developed for good reason. The Senate Armed Services Committee report on torture (2008–09) shows that when President Bush stripped suspects of those protections (February 7, 2002), his inner circle sprang into action. The principals were "obeying orders" but also licensing aggression.[76] The administration's hair-splitting embrace of torture cost the nation so much prestige and moral authority that its motives remain puzzling. Since evidence shows that torture produces unreliable information, it is unclear how fully Vice President Cheney, his legal advisors, and the CIA believed in its efficacy. One answer is that conspicuous torture is berserk style threat-display, exaggerating the "tough cop" face of the global policeman in hopes of intimidating adversaries. In addition, since the administration was defying international law, possible prosecution for war crimes, as in the belated arrest of Chile's Gen. Pinochet in 2000, gave policy makers reason to defend their decisions aggressively.

The improvised and incoherent policies at the top played out in the Abu Ghraib scandal. The Army's initial investigation recorded that

"Numerous incidents of sadistic, blatant, and wanton criminal abuses were inflicted on several detainees . . . systemic and illegal abuse."[77] A former intelligence official told Seymour Hersh that the photos of torture "turned out to be the result of the [approved 'special-access'] program run amok."[78] Conditions at Abu Ghraib were chaotic. "As mortar attacks rained down on the overcrowded prison—at one point there were only 450 guards for 7,000 prisoners—its command structure broke down. At the same time, the pressure from the Pentagon and the White House for "actionable intelligence" was intense. . . . Intelligence agencies such as the CIA were apparently given the green light to operate by their own set of secret rules."[79] With the arrival of Maj. Gen. Geoffrey Miller, the former Guantánamo interrogation commander who allegedly brought tougher intelligence tactics to Abu Ghraib, the confusing and sometimes disingenuous orders to "soften up" prisoners intensified pressure on the blundering young military police staff in the prison.

On March 15, 2006, Salon.com published extensive official documentation of the abuse. In a report written by Special Agent Seigmund for CID (June 6, 2004), "A review of all the computer media submitted to this office revealed a total of 1,325 images of suspected detainee abuse, 93 video files of suspected detainee abuse, 660 images of adult pornography, 546 images of suspected dead Iraqi detainees, 29 images of soldiers in simulated sexual acts, 20 images of a soldier with a Swastika drawn between his eyes, 37 images of Military working dogs being used in abuse of detainees and 125 images of questionable acts."

Sensationalized in global media, torture in the prison was a sinister, squalid carnival. In much of the low-level abuse the low-ranking young soldiers attempted to humiliate Iraqi men with infantile sexual aggression and violated cultural taboos. Abuses included urinating on detainees, sodomizing with a baton or possibly a broomstick, smearing them with excrement, putting women's underwear on them, forcing them to masturbate, riding naked prisoners like donkeys, and "Tying ropes to the detainees' legs or penises and dragging them across the floor."[80]

The obtuse rationale for such practices—that they would distress macho Iraqi men, for instance—says much more about the psychology of their tormenters than about the detainees. The aggression shows immature young people under stress and taking shelter in fantasies of humiliation and mastery. By posing for photos gleefully showing off their socially dead "trophies" for the camera, soldiers could play heroic warrior to support shaken self-esteem. At the same time the infantile sexual themes expressed childish rebellion against the authority that, after all, had the soldiers imprisoned along with the Iraqis.

Two of the young women soldiers were drawn into charged sexual relationships with Cpl. Charles A. Graner, Jr., who also directed most of their abuse of prisoners.[81] Given the atmosphere of death-anxiety and caged rage, it is not difficult to understand the fantasies of intimacy and fertility that seduced the trio. For the alpha male Graner and his small harem, the social and sexual humiliation of Iraqi prisoners on display in the famous photographs confirmed their superior status. Dominating frightened and angry Iraqi men, Graner could act the protector to the younger women.

In "Iraq for Sale" Michael Greenwald shows CACI personnel, deployed as "expert" interrogators, tying men together with cords looped around their penises and then pushing them over, symbolically castrating them. Castration of rival males is a feature of ancient warfare. Likewise, anal rape is a marker for male dominance, just as confining prisoners in their excrement literalizes the verbal assault in slang insults such as "asshole" and "shit," or the hazing term "shit-bag." The taboo is especially sensitive in the military, where soldiers are nominally heroes yet enslaved by command, and in recent years homophobia has protested attempts to legitimize gay enlistment. When Gen. Taguba reported to Sec. Rumsfeld about the Abu Ghraib scandal, someone asked, "Is it abuse or torture?" As Taguba recalled, "I described a naked detainee lying on the wet floor, handcuffed, with an interrogator shoving things up his rectum, and said, 'That's not abuse. That's torture.' There was quiet."[82]

When berserk style goes amok, humiliation and social death turn into real death. In the military, brutality against prisoners is common enough to have its own slang term, "to fuck up PUCs" (= Persons Under Control). At Abu Ghraib, where outnumbered guards were always potentially in danger, some beatings expressed retaliatory rage. More difficult to sort out is the influence of the secret CIA task-force teams on the young military subordinates. A CIA source told Seymour Hersh that "the task-force teams 'had full authority to whack"—to go in and conduct 'executive action'"—meaning assassination. 'It was surrealistic what these guys were doing,' the retired operative added. 'They were running around the world without clearing their operations with the ambassador or the chief of station.'" Cpl. Graner confirmed that CIA interrogators operated outside the law. "You know these guys can kill people," Graner said in an April 2005 statement to the Army Criminal Investigation Command (CID). "The OGA guys do whatever they want. They don't exist."[83]

Like secret police the world over, clandestine OGA or "other government agency" operatives were unaccountable. By cooperating with vicious regimes, the CIA maintains a screen of deniability for policy makers. When the mayhem at Abu Ghraib became public, sophistry and denial echoed up the chain of command. The president and vice president confronted allegations with a campaign to sanitize torture as "enhanced interrogation"—a term echoing the Gestapo's "Verschaerfte Vernehmung," going on the offensive to justify their involvement.[84]

This boldness about torture is the more puzzling because the risks of injustice and inefficacy could scarcely be more obvious. Without access to courts, prisoners were subject to suspicions that could be neither proved nor disproved. In her memoir Brig. Gen. (now Col.) Janis Karpinski, the prison commander, estimates that 90 percent of detainees in the prison were innocent. However, when military intelligence ordered the release of all but a few detainees, Gen. Wodjakowski summarily overrode the decision. In one exchange he vowed, "I don't care if we're holding 15,000 innocent Iraqis, we're winning the war." And I [Karpinski] said to him, "No, sir, not inside the wire you're not, because every one of those detainees becomes our enemy when they're released, and they will be released one day."[85]

Gen. Wodjakowski's tough-guy reflex trivializes the suffering and deaths at Abu Ghraib as mere detention ("holding"). Yet his response dimly recognizes that cruelty is supporting or feeding his triumphant conviction. The acute excitement of a contest ("we're winning"), the impatience with systematic interrogation, and the self-defeating creation of more enemies suggest the berserker's godlike indifference to risk and pain. The problem is not simply that the general ignored justice and truth, but that style overwrote the motives he needed to manage. The core conflict is the old colonial conundrum, the need to dominate yet win the cooperation of a subjugated people.

Trying to manage with incoherent policies, the Guantánamo lawyers charged with devising interrogation techniques found inspiration in the television series "24."[86] As Jane Mayer has reported, the show's producer, Joel Surnow, systematically uses the unspoken premise that the show's antiterrorism agents, especially their leader Jack Bauer, are actually in emergency-panic mode.[87] During the Iraq War a delegation from the military academies complained to Surnow that the show's sensational treatment of torture was encouraging young officers to disregard legal codes and the inefficacy of torture. In reply, echoing debates over violence in children's programming, Surnow scoffed that the show was "only fantasy."

Surnow systematically uses Orwellian doublethink to rationalize Jack Bauer's viciousness. In Jane Mayer's account he claims the show is "all just fantasy." Letting down the mask of facetious dismissiveness, however, he can comment "in a more sober tone" that

> We've had all of these torture experts come by recently, and they say, 'You don't realize how many people are affected by this. Be careful.' They say torture doesn't work. But I don't believe that. I don't think it's honest to say that if someone you love was being held, and you had five minutes to save them, you wouldn't do it. Tell me, what would you do? If someone had one of my children, or my wife, I would hope I'd do it. There is nothing—nothing—I wouldn't do." He went on, "Young interrogators don't need our show. What the human mind can imagine is so much greater than what we show on TV. No one needs us to tell them what to do. It's not like somebody goes, 'Oh, look what they're doing, I'll do that.' Is it?"

This argument turns on non sequiturs. But its core is pure berserk style in the service of self-abandon: "There is nothing—nothing—I wouldn't do."

Significantly, Surnow's fantasy of abandon is psychologically blind or dishonest. He gives no hint that authority might take out its rage and fear on an innocent victim. His language is deviously indirect: if someone you love "was being held" [by whom?]; "if someone [who?] had one of my children." Thinking himself a self-made Hollywood success, he imagines that all behavior comes from within: "No one needs us to tell them what to do."

Ironically, Surnow's prosperous connections to the right-wing media establishment and to the White House dramatize precisely the sort of social influence on individual thinking that he denies, since they are rewarding him for his show. "'It's been very heady,' [lead writer Howard] Gordon said of Washington's enthusiasm for the show. Roger Director, Surnow's friend, joked that the conservative writers at '24' have become 'like a Hollywood television annex to the White House. It's like an auxiliary wing'" (Mayer). The fantasy explicitly makes broadcast fantasy a function of government.

Style mediates creaturely motives but cannot entirely dispel them. Laura Ingraham, the talk-radio host, has cited the popularity of "24" "as proof that Americans favor brutality. "'They love Jack Bauer,' she noted on Fox News. 'In my mind, that's as close to a national referendum that it's O.K. to use tough tactics against high-level Al Qaeda operatives as we're going to get.'" So far Ingraham's plug for the series is merely intellectually dishonest: euphemistic ("tough tactics" not torture) and demonizing ("high-level Al Qaeda" instead of possibly innocent suspects). But then come some unwitting revelations: "Surnow once appeared as a guest on Ingraham's show; she told him that, while she was undergoing chemotherapy for breast cancer, 'it was soothing to see Jack Bauer torture these terrorists, and I felt better.' Surnow joked, 'We love to torture terrorists—it's good for you!'" (Mayer). Vicariously inflicting pain and death on an "enemy," the cancer sufferer relieves her death-anxiety and enjoys a boost to morale.

Throughout history the sacrifice of enemies and scapegoats has been a common practice to generate exaltation. Style can help to dissolve taboos and makes the psychic economy of killing available for vicarious mass consumption. Laura Ingraham is "fighting" her illness, but in her radio broadcast she is also propagating berserk style, modeling aggression, for a mass audience. The style may be ceremonial, even festive, as in the Roman amphitheater's choreographed torture and death, which took place in a holiday atmosphere, with the crowd excitedly participating in the coup de grace, and prostitutes at the exits to fulfill the creaturely drives excited by the show. The Aztecs invited foreign dignitaries to be impressed by their periodic ritual slaughter of captives. Photographs of American lynch mobs commonly capture signs of expansiveness and glee. When the sadistic exhilaration includes a conviction of heroism and righteousness, it can be irresistible.

The abuse of captives in modern warfare perpetuates a kind of ecstasy common in history. The Iraq War began with the usual sanitized, hallucinatory belief in "surgical"—that is, healing—intervention. Any savagery in the combat "theater" must be an aberration: a failure or tragic mishap befalling "our" good intentions. In practice it is nearly impossible to determine exactly the extent and nature of the self-deception: the *quality* of the belief. In *Fiasco,* Thomas Ricks describes US troops taking turns assaulting prisoners, as in one unit where a cook took part, breaking a captive's legs with a Louisville slugger.[88] The baseball bat evokes fantasies of sports heroism, but also the war club and its euphemistic offspring, the royal scepter. As a prop of berserk style, the bat stands for play, the pieties of home and childhood that armies fight for, and the thrilling exertions of the playing field. Above all, like the machine gun jokingly analogized to a camera, the baseball bat dispels guilt and horror. When a prisoner screamed "Allah" at each blow to his solar plexus, personnel took turns making him cry out until he died.

While individuals act out deep creaturely motives in such aggression, cultural or organizational style shapes the outcome. Ricks titles his chapter "The Descent into Abuse," as if the invasion might have avoided the usual viciousness if warfare had all gone according to plan. But one reason to explore berserk style is to bring into focus the preconditions for violence that are already latent in policy makers' tidy filing cabinets and in the magic circle of everyday civilian life.

The contrast between the unreported testimony of experts opposed to torture and the "speculative defense of waterboarding offered by semiofficial advocates," says David Bromwich, "has been among the most disquieting revelations of these years. A group of men who think what they want to think and pay little attention to evidence have been running things, and they are guided not by experience but by words that were constructed for the purpose of deception."[89] The shock goes even deeper than this. The magical thinking of putting shimmering words before all else harks back to the ambiguity of Norse berserking, in which the axe-wielding raiders are simultaneously fighting for their lives and dreaming of booty.

Ironically, when Laura Ingraham fantasized on the air about torture as therapy, her guest Joel Surnow applauded with a chuckle, sounding like an infomercial for a health product: "'We love to torture terrorists—it's good for you!'" His smart-aleck quip reflected not only his position as a businessman in Hollywood making a profit from representations of torture, but also another facet of the privatization of torture, removed from and yet not unrelated to the private security agents hired to conduct torture at Abu Ghraib.

The businessman's sinister quip points investigation toward the following chapter, which examines berserk style in American economic life.

THE PEAK OF THE PEAK

American culture in the new century moved through a series of peaks, nominally—but only nominally—beginning with the September 11 terrorism. Thereafter the nation undertook confrontations with one enemy after another. As Iraq became calmer in 2007, sirens were already whining for a renewal of hostilities in Afghanistan and a battle with Iran. An October 21, 2007, editorial the *Los Angeles Times* captured the operation of berserk style in US policy:

> The war of words against Iran grew scorching this week when President Bush declared that "avoiding World War III" requires preventing that country from developing nuclear weapons. . . . [T]he escalation of American threats against Iran is unwise. It is grossly premature. It is dangerous, as it greatly increases the likelihood of accidental escalation into a preventable war. It is alarmingly ill-timed, as an isolated United States wages simultaneous ground wars in Iraq and Afghanistan, and both conflicts are going badly. . . .

So why rattle the sabers now, at a moment of US military weakness? In 1969, with the Vietnam War going badly, President Nixon devised a plan to spook the Soviets and the North Vietnamese into making concessions by making them think that he was just crazy enough to use nuclear weapons. Nixon called it the "madman theory." There is speculation that the Bush administration could be trying out its version of the madman gambit by advertising Vice President Dick Cheney's alleged desire to bomb Iranian nuclear sites and Revolutionary Guard targets, in hopes of scaring Tehran into submission. . . . But who wants to stake U.S. foreign policy on the wisdom of Iran's mullahs and its titular head, President Mahmoud Ahmadinejad, a paranoid who can beat us at the madman game any day of his choosing?

The editorial rightly sees that berserk threat-display invites escalation. But it is not only supposed enemies that may misjudge the "madman's" intentions and limits. In press conferences the same president who conducted a "scorching war of words" also lightly denied knowing that his administration had given legal immunity to Blackwater security forces accused of berserk slayings in Iraq.[90] Parrying questions about his policy on torture, Mr. Bush invoked the "ticking time bomb" scenario that justifies torture in Joel Surnow's "24." In seeming unaware and unconcerned, the president implicitly rationalized excessive or "crazy" violence, potentially alienating anyone not party to the ruse—if it was a ruse.

What makes the "madman gambit" especially trenchant here is that its use against Iran coincided with the first rumblings of collapse on Wall Street. President Bush, the secretary of the treasury, and the Federal Reserve head warned that the American-led global financial system was about to implode. Financier Warren Buffet had dubbed the Wall Street derivatives "weapons of mass destruction," patently criticizing the spurious rationale for the Iraq War. Since the rationale had included guns and butter enticements as in the Vietnam era, the post-9/11 wars opened a massive hemorrhage in the national budget, so that in effect the United States did go to war with the self-destructive financial "weapons of mass destruction" that Buffet skewered.

Naomi Klein has summed up the intersection of the Pentagon, Wall Street, and the federal government as a central feature of the "Disaster Capitalism Complex":

The stats on this new disaster economy are incredible: Counterintelligence Field Activity, a new intelligence agency created under Rumsfeld that is independent of the CIA, outsources 70 percent of its budget to private contractors. . . . The global "homeland security industry"—economically insignificant before 2001—is now a $200 billion sector, bigger than Hollywood or the music industry. And the private companies performing these functions are a kind of shadow state, with extraordinary power and very little oversight, since the details of most of these contracts are completely obscured under the blanket of "classified" intelligence. In other words, extraordinarily sensitive state functions are being privatized—but we can't know about it because they are too sensitive.[91]

This sort of "privatization" means lack of accountability and promotion of external threats in the competition for funding. It is only one face of the postwar corporate state. Symptomatic are the administration's lavish sweetheart contracts that pay businesses to do tasks that armies have always done in a war zone. The results have been marred by malfeasance, spotty performance, and waste. Large sums also went to tribal sheiks, giving some of them the status of mafia godfathers. The Office of the Special Inspector General for Iraq Reconstruction, led by Stuart W. Bowen Jr., reported a damning inventory of incompetence, incoherence, and corruption in the reconstruction regime.

On September 16, 2007, the Iraqi government protested bitterly against security contractors after hair-trigger Blackwater mercenaries cut down 27 civilians at a Baghdad intersection. Like the massacre, which exposed the unregulated extralegal status of the mercenaries, the policy of privatizing torture and detention called attention to the cluster of themes shared by "free market" visions of military and economic force. The US policy of dispatching suspects to be tortured by security forces in countries such as Egypt and Syria in effect employed private contractors to evade accountability.[92] Like Wall Street investment banks setting up an off-market private exchange in Canada for their shadowy derivative instruments, the CIA was able to sidestep Constitutional oversight and pursue windfall information with a free hand. For both, the cost would prove to be a critical loss of trust.

By the summer of 2008 conditions in Afghanistan were once more deteriorating. Iraq's oil resources were still crippled, hardship widespread, and the region still expensively insecure. Agreements were in force authorizing indefinite American military and corporate ("market") involvement in Iraq. Meanwhile years of financial abandon were bringing the United States itself to an economic crisis—the subject of the next chapter. When General Motors Corp. announced thirty thousand job cuts, the head of an autoworkers union local in Lansing, Michigan, said of his members, "It's kind of a used term, but they're calling it 'shock and awe.'"[93] Cold War historian Chalmers Johnson was "convinced that the U.S. Empire of Bases will soon enough bankrupt our country, and so—on the analogy of a financial bubble or a pyramid scheme—if you're an investor, it's better to get your money out while you still can."[94]

With the all-in costs of the post-9/11 wars projected to be in the trillions, the nation's financial health required reining in military spending. The Defense Business Board, which includes corporate executives, concluded that the spending binge was no longer tenable. But like Wall Street banks grown "too big to fail," the corporate-military boldly counterattacks. The berserk dynamics surface in the analysis of Winslow Wheeler, director of the Straus Military Reform Project at the Center for Defense Information in Washington, who presents congressional efforts to confront the corporate-military as a suicidal assault: "The forces arrayed against terminating defense programs are today so powerful that if you try to do that it will be like the British Army at the Somme in World War I. . . . You will just get mowed down by the defense industry and military services' machine guns."[95]

The corporate-military economy, that is, fights Americans at the cash register as well as distant enemies. But then, in the 1980s, as the post-Vietnam military was rebuilding, a new economic doctrine began praising the free market as a free-for-all in which the survival of the fittest would be good for everybody. At least that was the theory. In the midst of the global crisis that flashed warnings of another Great Depression around the world in 2008, *The Economist* magazine put on its October 4 cover a silhouetted figure on a precipice staring into an abyss—the "abyss" by now a routine trope in gloomy financial reporting, The magazine titled the issue, *World on the Edge*.

Six months after this appeal for desperate action, April 8, 2009, the *Washington Post* was running a story by Philip Rucker, "Some Link Economy with Spate of Killings: In One Month 57 Die in Eight Mass Murders," followed two months later by the assassinations of an abortion doctor in his Kansas church and a security guard at the Holocaust museum in Washington.

CHAPTER 3

MAKING A KILLING

The massive global pool of speculative finance has run amuck.

Doug Noland, *"Riddle of the Burst Bubble"*

In the wake of the financial crisis of 2007–2008, a Google search for "economy amok" turned up 595,000 hits, one sign of the role berserk style played in the mayhem. In Joseph Stigitz's summary, "No democratic government . . . has ever wasted resources outside of war on the scale which our private sector misallocated capital . . . a massive, massive failure [*sic*]. But after the crisis the consequences are even larger, the gap between full employment, potential output and actual output, is trillions of dollars and mounting."[1]

Comparisons abounded to the 1929 "crash," to the recurring bank panics of the nineteenth century: to the Mississippi Bubble, the Dutch tulip mania, and the 1720 British South Sea bubble, which climaxed in daily suicides, expulsion of the Chancellor of the Exchequer, mob demands for vengeance, and reading of the Riot Act—that is, in rampage. Critics routinely described the speculative bubbles and the "meltdown" as berserk—meaning out of control. But speculative mania is a familiar facet of capitalism and the business cycle. What's more, it has many features of the berserk state, in particular the sense of godlike, do-or-die recklessness that goes with trying to "make a killing."

In the wreckage of the 2008 crash investigators found evidence of complex structural failures and operators amok. Media and the Internet effervesced with explanations, from partisan boilerplate and placative euphemisms to frankly mystified mathematical analyses. The contradictions and incompleteness attested to the magnitude of the crisis. The following two chapters are less concerned to sort out the competing, now-familiar explanations than to investigate forms of berserk style that contributed to the rampage.

The idiom "making a killing" preserves the ancestral relationship of prosperity to hunting and warfare. Bull and bear markets take the names of awe-inspiring totem animals that humans have hunted, fought, and tamed. In a *New Yorker* cartoon a businessman queasily notices that the Wall Street statue of a bull has been marked out in choice cuts for butchering.[2] In business slang, competition is "cutthroat." Buying a stock you "pull the trigger." A small, quick profit is "scalping." When markets fall, there is "blood in the streets" and "carnage"; equities may be "slaughtered" or rally in a "dead cat bounce."

Where tribal societies valued equilibrium, capitalism stresses dynamism and growth. In the *Grundrisse*, Marx held that the circulation and accumulation of capital cannot abide limits. It creates barriers and strives to overcome them. Cartoonists satirize obsessive concerns for growth and profit by associating business life with charts whose trends point up toward prosperous abandon ("off the charts") or downward, toward doom. Fear and greed drive markets. A "bull" market gives off potency: a "bear" will devour you. Investors have or lose an "appetite for risk." The feeding frenzy of "dog-eat-dog" competition is implicitly cannibalistic. Matt Taibbi named the taboo oft talked about yet ever struggling to be heard when he described Goldman Sachs as a "great vampire squid wrapped around the face of humanity, relentlessly jamming its blood funnel into anything that smells like money."[3] The trope struck a nerve, and in no time vampire squid were swarming in financial journalism.

The aggression and death-anxiety in this market glossary help to explain why berserk style figures so strikingly in economic relationships—and why cultures have always had to regulate market behavior. Charles Mackay's *Extraordinary Delusions and the Madness of Crowds* (1841) and Keynes's "animal spirits," for example, recognized creaturely motives as an economic force, and today the term has entered into mainstream economic thinking. "Irrational exuberance" inflates bubbles; survival panic—hoarding, paralysis, and paranoia—drives a depression.[4] Setbacks have an apocalyptic quality when described as an economic "blow off," "tsunami," or a "meltdown." As creaturely motives, "animal spirits" are built into us as appetite for more life. But language such as Alan Greenspan's merry coinage "irrational exuberance" shouldn't blind us to the role of survival greed in economic behavior.

Still, we are social animals. Traders have to be able to see that there are at least two sides to every transaction, and that all the parties have to satisfy their needs. Business requires imaginative sympathy in order to understand what others want and to determine the value of things. Traders need psychological and diplomatic skills. The problem is that these qualities are richly ambivalent, since the trader's imaginative sympathy can foster mutuality, but it can also be the weapon of a sociopath seeking advantage. And in the real world, though the balance scale symbolizes objectivity, economic behavior is almost always conditioned by scheming and social relationships, including the enduring childhood urge to grab what we want.

Since people are so often irrational, unaware, or mistaken, economic thinkers usually schematize or exclude unruly motives. Modern economies have invented the corporation to juggle this problem. With double vision the law treats corporations as persons, with the right to free speech, even the right to influence elections. Yet by design, corporations exist to shield their owners from liability. In simple markets owners are responsible for the debts and liabilities of their business. But by permitting so much risk, a simple market limits economic activity. By allowing corporations to declare bankruptcy, diluting the risk, the political system shields the owners, and business can go on.

As corporations become multinational and "too big to fail," a culture of impunity develops. Government guarantees emerge, operations can be moved beyond any strict jurisdiction, and accountability becomes difficult. Like Wall Street banks, the petroleum giant BP grew to global stature through manic acquisitions and reckless practices. The explosion of its Deepwater Horizon platform in the Gulf of Mexico (2010) capped BP's gruesome record of fatal disasters. As in the Iraq War, the scale of profits made any particular loss appear to be cost-effective. In the post-Vietnam era corporate culture rewards executives who operate "on the edge," and shields them when they fail.

When corporations run amok, who or what is making—or doing—the killing? Officers? Investors? Company policy? "Corporate culture?" If taxpayers are silently guaranteeing corporate risk-taking, socializing risk and privatizing reward, whose motives are in play? The question keeps courtrooms bustling and makes the idea of the corporation one of the most elegantly useful and pernicious forms of berserk style.

THE BUBBLE BEYOND

As the world rebalanced after World War II, American dominance diluted. In the decades after the Vietnam War the nation began to face global competition of a sort it had never seen before. "Since the 1970s . . . the US economy has grown more slowly than in the thirty-year period after the end of World War II, but also very likely more slowly than in any other period in the nation's history."[5] In these years Detroit shrank its hourly workforce by nearly half a million employees; the "heartland" became a "rustbelt." In the 1980s the world's largest creditor became history's greatest debtor. Outsourcing shifted jobs and capital abroad. Day trading epitomized a shift in mentality away from long-term investment. As factories closed, ambitions shifted to finance, technology, and a housing boom. As the American-led global economy adapted to new realities with frenzied zeal, the mirage of a "new economy" spawned dotcom delirium and market bubbles.

New vigor in Asia and the European Union was bound to qualify America's postwar wealth and power.[6] For too long the dollar was overvalued, making for binge consumption, hobbled exports, and trade deficits. In the post-Vietnam period the unwelcome question was how the pain of adjustment would be distributed. Who would survive and prosper? In 1976 the trend toward increased economic equality reversed. In 2008 real wages were still lower than in 1972.[7] The forces that favor extreme concentration of wealth and power made most Americans less secure. By 2009, the 74 wealthiest people in the nation "made as much as the 19 million lowest-paid people in America, who constitute one in every eight workers."[8] This is a severe distortion last seen in 1928, the trigger point of the Great Depression. In different ways those at the top and those below were both susceptible to fantasies of abandon.

Berserk style resounded in business culture. Instead of collaboration and trust, the Harvard Business School promoted the Business Process Movement and the magic bullet of relentless competition. In the technology boom of the 1990s, belief that "the sky's the limit" because "it's different this time" rationalized abandon and a massive capture of wealth and power in fewer and fewer hands. Critics harped on the dangers of inebriation, yet the Federal Reserve's Alan Greenspan refused "to take away the punch bowl." Hedge funds, easy credit, and ungrounded valuations made for "casino" markets.[9] After the collapse of the tech bubble, Wall Street fashioned ingenious devices that promised to expand leverage for bankers and the poorest homebuyers without limits or risk. The atmosphere was self-intoxicating. As late as 2007 one wishful critic was still vowing that "[t]he conditions that allowed [Federal Reserve Chair] Greenspan and [Treasury Secretary] Rubin to run amuck with their bailouts in the 1990s are no longer present today."[10] A year later massive bailouts were underway to avert an international banking panic. Hedge funds bled to death. Lehman Brothers vanished in the largest bankruptcy filing in the nation's history, and some in Congress were speaking as if Wall Street banks were rampage killers holding the government hostage. Some critics saw it as a coup d'etat: "the finance industry has essentially captured our government."[11]

The epic proportions of this crisis invited melodrama. Alarms had sounded repeatedly, even as the rising tension and giddy profits spurred more participants to get in on the action before it peaked. Their conflicting stories disguised the allure of abandon. Much of the financial sector developed the double-or-nothing mania familiar in binge gambling and combat recklessness. As in post-invasion Iraq, panic took hold on the highest levels: "The Bush administration and Congress discussed the possibility of a breakdown in law and order and the logistics of feeding US citizens if commerce and banking collapsed as a result of last autumn's financial panic. . . . [The] former Treasury secretary Hank Paulson said it was important at the time not to reveal the extent of officials' concerns, for fear it would "terrify the American people and lead to an even bigger problem."[12]

Anyone attuned to berserk style could have seen that the 2008 collapse was only the latest in a cycle of increasing perturbations. The first economic rampage of the postwar years was the guns and butter binge of the Vietnam War era. In the decade that followed, the careening dollar had to be cut loose from its gold moorings, and the Federal Reserve grappled with inflation by taking interest rates to 20 percent. To overcome stagflation President Reagan began to reflate the economy through conventional pump-priming methods, generating an epic peacetime military-industrial budget and cutting regulations and taxes—especially taxes on the highest personal incomes, which shrank dramatically. The national debt tripled and real wages stalled, but business picked up and those at the top had more money for global investment and speculation. A new emphasis favored entrepreneurial daring and genius more typical of the 1920s than the gray flannel postwar era. And like the flurry of popular new business books on the shelves, the ideology linked making a killing to daredevil command.

President Reagan established the basic contradiction of the decades to come. While stressing "conservative" responsibility, he worked to undermine regulations and oversight. He called for revolt against "big government" and yet overspent. The corporate-military resumed its worldwide expansion, while in the new go-go atmosphere over a thousand deregulated savings and loan institutions self-destructed in "the largest and costliest venture in public misfeasance, malfeasance and larceny of all time."[13] To be fair, Reagan was less a cause than a facilitator of this doublethink: his rhetoric and his avuncular image helped to rationalize an appetite for excess that in coming decades would remind critics of the "roaring" twenties and the Gilded Age.

As berserk style crept into business news in the 1980s, metaphors of piracy invaded boardrooms: corporate "raiders" and "buccaneers" used overpowering leverage to "loot" companies.[14] To be sure, some of the restructuring led to needed innovation and efficiencies, and the myths of the day celebrated the wholesome birth of Apple Computer on a shoestring in a California garage. But management training also stressed "lean and mean" toughness and led to the "millions of casualties" that the *New York Times* reported in the workforce, and the liquidation or monetization of productive assets for windfall gains.[15]

Global competition excited a decade-long "golden age of junk financing [that] built to a virtual frenzy." Even some partisans of creative finance acknowledge the berserk dynamics that in 1989 and 1990 resulted "in an unprecedented number of defaults by junk bond issuers and the bankruptcy of Drexel Burnham."[16] The new leverage provided much-needed capital and flexibility, but with dubious transparency, creating corporate agglomerations on a scale that recalled the trusts of the pre-Depression era, and the sort of speculative overreach evident in the Black Monday (1987) stock market swoon.

Junk finance aroused familiar ambivalence. When abandon worked magic, the magicians were celebrities; when it failed, they faced prosecution. In Oliver Stone's *Wall Street* (1987) the speculator Gordon Gecko (Michael Douglass) was partly modeled on Ivan Boesky, one of the few junk bond desperados jailed for trading violations. Gecko made famous the battle cry of berserk finance: "Greed is good." In his survival greed he spares no one. For him Wall Street is a battlefield, and his concentration and rage epitomize the berserker's godlike and beastlike cruelty. The screenwriter, Stanley Weiser, grumbled that audiences overlooked Gecko's pending prison sentence, but then Weiser was overlooking the ambivalent fascination that berserk power arouses: "Gordon Gekko has been mythologised and elevated from the role of villain to that of hero."[17]

In the following decades financial culture legitimized and emulated Gecko's aggressiveness. To some extent the bravado came from the Federal Reserve's punch bowl and monetary policies that earned Alan Greenspan the nickname "Easy Al."[18] "Deregulation" became catchall jargon for corporate efforts to disarm "watchdog" accountability. With Glass-Steagal and other Depression-era firewalls dismantled in the 1990s, banks invaded territories once restricted to brokers and speculators.

When the tech bubble popped, the finance industry turned to mortgages. Selling and reselling derivative instruments with chimerical insurance guarantees or "securitization," bankers collected stupefying fees and paid themselves piratical bonuses. Since housing prices seemed destined to soar forever, the prosperous beyond lured many borrowers, lenders, and home builders into risk-taking at a time when wages were stagnant, consumer credit already overextended, and savings rates negligible.[19]

As the gap widened between "big money" and ordinary wage earners, day traders and new state lotteries acted out a growing assumption that speculation paid off. Striving to discredit government and regulation, "conservative" business culture implicitly attacked the principle of lawful oversight. The conceptual shifts supposed that deregulation freed up minds as well as institutions, and that uninhibited will to win would free up intuitive cunning. The buzzwords "innovation" and "daring" sizzled with assumptions about intelligence and novelty. But they also privileged gaming skills that could outwit competition. Business culture enjoyed gala dramas of executive genius with subplots linking star CEOs, compensation committees, and accounting and ratings agencies in sly cronyism. A few sirens sounded but no detectives flashed their badges until Enron's edifice of fraud crumbled.

Suddenly some of the cognitive confusion, collusion, and deception in the new business culture revealed features of classic bubbles. But still no systematic reality testing was able to halt the feeding frenzy in housing and finance. Finally, faced with collapse in 2008, fuddled Wall Street "masters of the universe" naively lived out the cliché by claiming to see the colossal folly as a "Tsunami"—in effect an "act of God"—the excuse Donald Trump actually tried to apply to his ungainly debt in 2009.

Like nervous system flooding under stress, gambling feeds on itself and becomes addictive. Nick Paumgarten tuned in to the behavior when he described one of 28 million pens given away by New Jersey's failed, flashy Commerce Bank, which aimed for "a unique brand of WOW." "The pens were, in a way, a souvenir of the shadow banking system, a by-product of securitization. Finding one was a little like stumbling on an empty crack vial in the public park."[20] Some personalities were more susceptible than others, but addiction was also a cultural predilection, a structural compulsion, as if a force of nature was directing the participants: "The price of things came to be determined largely by how easily they could be financed. A long-term decline in interest rates, promoted and abetted by the Federal

Reserve, helped create a perpetual motion machine that encouraged people to borrow, buy, and borrow some more" (48). Paumgarten quotes a business professor who regards securitization and its fabulous fees for banks as "a machine that said, 'Feed me.'" And so "debt was created to sate the machine" (49). An inexorable machine demanding to be fed is akin to an addiction. But a "perpetual motion" machine represents addiction's deathless intoxicating promise—the bliss of the beyond. Perpetual motion appears to be free, bountiful, unforced, like the early stages of a Ponzi scheme, when the transactions seem magically self-sustaining.[21] And as a belief system, perpetual motion can live up to its name. By 2011, Wall Street was again awash in profits, derivatives, and absurd compensation, and Alan Greenspan was once more attacking efforts to supervise the financial sector: "With notably rare exceptions (2008, for example), the global 'invisible hand' has created [relative stability]." Floyd Norris spotted the deep reliance on berserk style in this nostrum: "I really like that part about 'notably rare exceptions.' It reminds me of a defense lawyer arguing that while his client may have committed a few murders on one particular day, his conduct on all the other days of his life had been exemplary."[22]

One addictive property of the securitization machine was the illusion that it guaranteed against risk. Hedge funds similarly relied on machines in computer programs whose arcane formulas promised to guarantee profits by detecting the subtlest market signals and responding faster than a live trader. The computer revolution promised new controls over price discovery and risk, even at giddy levels of abstraction. Algorithms (in Wall Street jargon "Algos") acquired the magical aura of alchemy.[23] Like military drones, the computer programs were designed to see over the horizon and make a killing while safeguarding the operators. And like other strategies, hedging—combining long and short positions to offset risk—is more reliable when markets are bubbling upward and nearly every investor is a genius. The relentless rise in house prices since World War II convinced many in real estate that it was an unshakable formula. Hence the unrealistic mortgages, the purchase of houses "on spec" to "flip" them—as in judo's cunning leverage—at a higher price. And hence the loans subsequently drawn against home equity that could transform the house into a cash machine.

All sorts of personalities participated in the financial addiction. Almost all accounts stress their greed. Some were hustlers, some naïve believers in the "new economy" or brilliant algorithms that could outsmart traditional market behavior. Some were overstretched executives fatally out of touch and eager to believe upbeat subordinates who were, after all, sharing in bonuses that defied belief. Many were employees of public companies, with no personal stake in the firm's future. The atmosphere was feverish with possibility. More money. More prestige. More autonomy. More future. More life. According to critics such as Jonathan Walton, a professor of religious studies, the growth of the popular Christian "prosperity gospel"—that God wants everyone to be wealthy—"tracks fairly closely to the pattern of hotspots" for house foreclosures as mortgage lenders teamed up with pastors and blind faith overrode financial caution.[24]

When the crisis finally broke, the distress rumbled across the globe. "U.S. credibility and the credibility of U.S. financial markets is zero everywhere in the world," the Nobel economist Joseph E. Stiglitz warned."[25] Analysis of the chaos tried to sort out villains, and the business press turned to the idea of abandon in reports such as "Berserker Funds in Commodities."[26] As political power shifted in the 2008 elections, images of civil insurrection and rage boiled up. The Internet and the Fox network buzzed with survivalist alarm. Partisans spawned rumors that the new "fascist" president would confiscate all guns. Like an unemployed worker on a crime spree, "Wall Street put a gun to the head of the politicians and said, 'Give us the money [for a bailout]—right now—or take the blame for whatever follows.'"[27] On October 2, 2008, Rep. Brad Sherman reported that members of Congress faced threats of "martial law in America if we voted no."

The rage was not all just journalistic spice. Caught up in the derivatives fever, Richard Fuld, CEO of Lehman Brothers, had turned a deaf ear to warnings from his subordinates. On the afternoon he announced the firm's bankruptcy to shocked employees, Fuld—once known as "the Gorilla"—was on a treadmill in the company gym wearing a heart monitor when someone "pumping iron . . . walked over and . . . knocked him out cold."[28]

LIFE AS LEVERAGE

A club, a slingshot, a cannon, and a nuclear missile all magnify the impact of a fist. Similarly financial instruments such as bonds, options, derivatives, margin, and other instruments magnify the impact of capital. They are all force-multipliers. Like signs, writing, even memory itself, they are means of expanding our control over reality. Financial leverage maximizes force by borrowing against the future and the beyond. But it also magnifies risk, not only because accidents may disrupt repayment, but also because leverage may distort creaturely motives such as greed and fear of exposure. Shakespeare's *Merchant of Venice* still excites audiences with the association of usury with cannibalism implied in the demand for a pound of flesh. Every school child knows that leverage "wiped out" many in the 1929 market crash.

Berserk style expresses the creaturely motives that link financial leverage to other forms. In the military, leverage is technological firepower. But in wartime the military also "borrows" the autonomy and savings of citizens to maximize its force for the projected gains of victory. It hopes to pay back the "loan" through glory, loot, veterans' benefits, and other rewards. The factory borrows the autonomy of its "hands" to magnify productivity till payday pays it back with—in theory—the means to a better life. In the cosmic scheme of things all lives are on loan. As Hal says to Falstaff before battle, "thou owest God a death" (5.1.126).

Leverage opens toward the beyond. If borrowed money can be used as collateral to borrow more money, and the process is repeated, the gains are potentially infinite, As the scale of the lender's loans and the debtor's debt increases, however, so does contingency. When sums borrowed exceed collateral or bank reserves, the sum becomes hyper-critical, since a failure can destroy both parties. When Warren Buffett deems derivatives weapons of mass destruction, he means that the multi-trillion-dollar obligations created by derivatives could blow up the financial world. Should a borrower or a lender be considered "too big to fail" and therefore always implicitly supported by a government, "moral hazard" can moot inhibitions and send leverage to extremes.

In the pre-2008 bubble, easy money, lax regulation, and the cult of innovation lubricated speculative mania. The tech boom and the history of rising postwar real estate prices seemed to justify maximum leverage for borrowers and lenders. As in the 1980s, when tradition-ally constrained Savings & Loan banks were allowed to be friskier and riskier, overextended parties kept parlaying gains from the prolonged economic bubble or, if poor, stretching budgets. With regulatory "firewalls" coming down, Wall Street banks began acting like brokers and hedge funds, devising and repackaging derivatives so complex that rating agencies—hired by the banks—later confessed to vetting them more or less on faith.

As it became clear that the banks were leveraging their reserves at three to four times customary ratios, many critics warned against the excesses. In *The New Paradigm for Financial Markets* (2008), George Soros warned that feedback loops (reflexivity) were self-reinforcing and eventually self-defeating. Nouriel Roubini described the effects of abandon: "The crisis was caused by the largest leveraged asset bubble and credit bubble in the history of humanity where excessive leveraging and bubbles were not limited to housing in the US but also to housing in many other countries and excessive borrowing by financial institutions and some segments of the corporate sector and of the public sector in many and different economies: a housing bubble, a mortgage bubble, an equity bubble, a bond bubble, a credit bubble, a commodity bubble, a private equity bubble, a hedge funds bubble are all now bursting at once in the biggest real estate sector and financial sector deleveraging since the Great Depression."[29]

In 2006 it was still possible to marvel at the "Mind-boggling growth in derivatives."[30] Simple derivatives can be a practical commitment to a future act: say, to buy or sell a crop at an agreed price. The contract in effect uses leverage to "buy" time and stability. The new generation of "high-tech" derivatives used complex mathematical formulas to justify greatly expanded leverage by creating networks of counterparties that would insure the values in a given deal. This made it possible for banks and shadow banks to bundle and resell through tax-exempt conduits contracts of perilously untested soundness involving a multitude of participants. Collecting rich fees and bonuses at every step, the banks mixed dubious mortgage debt into sanitary packages for global resale.[31] So fatally opaque and feverish was the repackaging process that incompetent or dodgy records eventually made put many failed mortgages in limbo. By 2010 the uncollectible debt precipitated yet another crisis, called "foreclosuregate."

The scale of the derivatives bubble defied ordinary analysis. As in a Ponzi scheme, the expanding pyramids of counterparties seemed to guarantee ever-enlarging hypothetical value in the rosy beyond. With only $1.2 billion in equity J. P. Morgan controlled $91 trillion in derivatives.[32] As in junk finance, the parties kept transactions private— Over the Counter or OTC—creating their own clearing agent so that the products and their web of derivative formulas bypassed market corroboration. In 2008 the Bank for International Settlements [BIS] estimated that the global Over the Counter [OTC] derivatives market had grown almost 65 percent from $414.8 trillion (December 2006) to $683.7 trillion (June of 2008).

The new instruments promised to magnify the safety as well as the velocity and impact of credit. Lenders could "securitize" risk by arranging for counterparties to guarantee loans, then repackaging and reinsuring them, distributing risk over the horizon. "By appearing to provide an interlocking safety net, derivatives had the unintended effect of encouraging more risk-taking. Investors loaded up on the mortgage-based investments, then bought 'credit-default swaps' to protect themselves against losses rather than putting aside large cash reserves." When real estate valuations slumped, the guarantors were caught up in a dizzying web of obligations magnified by feedback loops. The result was a whirlwind of losses. "Instead of dispersing risk, derivatives had amplified it."[33] Nominal wealth vaporized overnight. By the summer of 2008 the insurers and ratings agencies were struggling. Yet two years later Bank of America and others were still trying to finesse adequate capital reserves by repackaging mortgage bonds, a strategy now dubbed "re-remics."

The prestige of computer technology and mathematical models conditioned risk-analysis. And technologies have always been susceptible to magical thinking and cheating, as Mickey Mouse, the sorcerer's apprentice, discovered. All such machinery depends on the quality of the data fed into it, and the questions being asked. Wall Street's ratings agencies proved treacherously inept not because risk-analysis was impossible—if it was, they had a fiduciary obligation to sound a warning—but because they were swept up in, or played along with, the Street's profitable delirium.

Mystification penetrated to the world's central banks. The master of "masters of the universe," Federal Reserve Chair Alan Greenspan, was renowned for his ambiguity. Markets danced to his gnomic utterances. "As far back as November 1998, only weeks after the near-meltdown of the global financial system through the collapse of the LTCM hedge fund, Greenspan had assured an annual meeting of the US Securities Industry Association that 'Dramatic advances in computer and telecommunications technologies in recent years have enabled a broad unbundling of risks through innovative financial engineering. The financial instruments of a bygone era, common stocks and debt obligations, have been augmented by a vast array of complex hybrid financial products, which allow risks to be isolated, but which, in many cases, seemingly challenge human understanding.'"[34]

This admission of cognitive overload recalls the gnomic utterances of Defense Secretary Rumsfeld. In the diplomatic shadow play before the invasion of Iraq, about to make more literal killings, Rumsfeld famously intoned: "Reports that say that something hasn't happened are always interesting to me, because as we know, there are known knowns; there are things we know we know. We also know there are known unknowns; that is to say we know there are some things we do not know. But there are also unknown unknowns—the ones we don't know we don't know."[35]

The link between the financial world and the Pentagon is psychological but also structural. Both take in investments and promise forms of insurance or "securitization." Their stupendous budgets calculate risk to turn the threat of "unknown unknowns" into the riches of the beyond. As historians of empire remind us, sooner or later wealth and superpower dominance lead to the overconfidence that this book associates with the berserker's godlike conviction. As with financial leverage, a drive for peak power can become over-extended and hypercritical, with panic on the downside.

In a bank run or a market crash or a battlefield rout, panic is contagious. The "unknown unknowns" show in feedback dynamics that overwhelm everyday expectations. For example, Wall Street devised "dynamic portfolio insurance" to preempt severe losses in investor portfolios. The scheme laid out a series of "stop loss" orders based on algorithms that would progressively sell off shares in a portfolio if the market declined, limiting the investor's losses. But this proved to be a two-dimensional map of a three-dimensional world in the Black Monday crash of 1987, when feedback loops spawned a cascade of selling. The cascade is a metaphor for the nervous system flooding in panic. And the creaturely motive involved is fear of being wiped out: the terror of death.

In this root fear, financial leverage reveals its kinship to the leverage of weapons. When crisis struck in 2008, some commentators invoked berserk combat as an explanation. There were analogies to General Custer and to Victory Culture: "With its decision last week to pump an additional $1 trillion into the financial crisis, the government eliminated any doubt that the nation is on a wartime footing in the battle to shore up the economy. The strategy now . . . is essentially the win-at-any-cost approach previously adopted only to wage a major war. And that means no hesitation in pledging to spend previously almost unimaginable sums of money and running up federal budget deficits on a scale not seen since World War II."[36] A "win-at-any-cost" battle on an "almost unimaginable" scale: this is berserk style's familiar edge of abandon. The next paragraph shudders with survival panic: "analysts warn that the nation's next financial crisis could come from the staggering cost of battling the current one."

When the tech bubble sagged, Greenspan's Fed encouraged the real estate binge to sustain the economy. When a given war ends, the corporate-military follows a parallel track, pumping up new threats and new weapons systems to sustain its economy. Like the fatal arsenal of derivatives, the scale of nuclear weapons, for example, makes them imponderable and impractical.[37] The weaponization of space through "Star Wars" is practically infinite. Describing "mind-boggling" ("unthinkable," "superhuman") financial aggregates, critics invoked nuclear war. For Warren Buffett derivatives are financial weapons of mass destruction; for former Federal Reserve Chair Paul Volcker, they are hydrogen bombs. Two of the wiser heads in finance recognized the link between the signature atom bomb of victory culture and the financial devices magnifying American capital to epochal ends at a time when American hegemony was under severe stress and the Bush administration was hyping nuclear peril to justify its futile multiple wars.

In combat berserk frenzy is the ultimate gamble: suicidal failure or survival. In economic life do-or-die risk-taking opens windfall riches or the prospect of being "wiped out." The casino is only the most obvious financial battlefield. In the service of consumer utopia, advertising pumps up desire in order to sell not only products but also the idea of leverage—buying on "easy terms," with repayment in a blue sky beyond. Critics recognized the self-intoxicating character of advertising culture and sanitized gambling. "Everybody wanted to bet," said Bill Bonner. "The track takes about 20%. In the financial races, Wall Street took 50% to 80% of all the profits." Financial sector growth was a bubble promoting bubbles. "Before 1987, only about one of every 10 dollars of corporate profits made its way to the financial industry—in payment for arranging financing, banking and other services. By the end of the bubble years, the cost of 'finance' had grown to more than 3 out of every 10 dollars. Total profits in the United States reached about $6 trillion [in 2007]; about $2 trillion was Wall Street's share. What happened to this money? Other industries use profits to build factors and create jobs. But the financial industry paid it out in salaries and bonuses—as much as $10 trillion during the whole Bubble Period."[38]

As in warfare, strategy emphasized exploiting an opponent's weaknesses—and it needs to be said that creditor-debtor relationships are always potentially adversarial. There was a killing to be made in the rentier farming of interest and fees. Credit card interest caps rose while lending standards declined. The changes "had a bad effect on the moral character of the nation. Because interest rates were so high, the banks no longer *wanted* borrowers with good moral character."[39] In James Scurlock's documentary *Maxed Out* (2007), Harvard law professor Elizabeth Warren quotes a loan industry executive who objects that "[i]f you cut out the [customers] who are most in trouble, least likely to pay—that's where we make most of our money." That is, they sought out weakness to be exploited.

With house prices exploding beyond the reach of ordinary salaries, mortgage originators and buyers moved with berserk daring. The mortgage company HCE, for example, touted "Ninja" loans—No income, no job (and) no assets. The name attributes magical force to the lender, but also tries to allay the fears of borrowers too. One mortgage company commercial crowed that "if you own a home, and have a pulse you can get a home equity loan." In the frenzy some banks fudged legal documentation, precipitating an echo bust when they tried to foreclose on distressed properties in 2010. The *Chicago Tribune*'s Mary Umberger warned that "[r]eal-estate insanity is becoming the norm in Florida" (June 15, 2005). But of course if everyone is insane, then nobody is. And in any event, "insanity" here is a euphemism for predatory behavior. The outcome was an epic wave of foreclosures, with berserk style sure to follow. One headline asked, "As Foreclosure Nightmares Increase, Will More Homeowners Pay Off Their Bankers in Violence?" The news story itself opened with a form of threat-display: "The economic crisis revealed late-capitalism's central offense: Human beings are being transparently treated if they were mere transactions. And they're going postal over it."[40]

MAKING A KILLING

The term "Ninja loan" conflates economic aggressiveness with combat and imagines leverage as an unorthodox heroic weapon. As berserk style, the term manages to be witty, satirical, and yet serious too. In one direction the ninja fantasy looks to the culture of aggressive, underhanded entrepreneurs such as the junk finance buccaneers jailed in the 1980s or the Ponzi swindler Bernard Madoff. In the opposite direction the fantasy evokes the alienated employees, usually armed like Rambo, who have carried out the rash of workplace rampages that began in the 1980s.

The workplace rampages roared into the news just as the *New York Times* was openly deploring the "battlefield of business" strewn with "millions of casualties."[41] The journalists' trope was an echo of the Vietnam War, which had left the nation in a decade-long slump after "capitalism's" costly clash with "Communism." The ideology that accompanied economic recovery celebrated combative "lean and mean" competition, creative destruction, and workforce triage. Manufacturing jobs and plants went overseas. By the 1990s the labor force faced relentless rustbelt triage and serious loss of union protection, while "captains of industry" were beginning to command record-breaking wealth. As Steven Greenhouse has shown, to reduce labor costs, more than a few businesses brazenly abused employees, deliberately subverting New Deal labor guarantees while shrinking health and retirement benefits.[42] By 2011, the campaign to maximize control over labor reached an unexpectedly heated showdown in Wisconsin when massive crowds protested Republican legislation designed to strip public workers of their historic right to a union.

On the "battlefield of business" stress began running amok as the new ideology took command in the 1980s. The Vietnam vet John Rambo (Sylvester Stallone) naively dramatized the transition to the new era in 1982 by grieving that "Back there [in Vietnam] I could fly a gunship. I could drive a tank. I was in charge of million-dollar equipment. Back here I can't even hold a job parkin' cars."[43] In Ted Kotcheff's *First Blood* the unemployed warrior and parking lot attendant faces social death. His best friend's death from the effects of Agent Orange leaves him the sole survivor of his unit. When local police bully him, Rambo resists with a sensational one-man guerrilla war against the town authorities, anticipating the fired workers and unemployed vets who made headlines in the 1980s and 90s by "going postal."[44] His grief, alienation, and subjugation reproduced in civilian life the explosive disturbance that sent soldiers amok in Vietnam, and especially in attacks on their own officers (fragging). The screenwriters give Rambo posttraumatic flashbacks that continue the war on the American home front and limit his responsibility.

The film equivocates in typical Hollywood fashion. Rambo's rampage is a criminal rebellion and yet also justified by the Reagan ideology that "big government" has betrayed citizens like him. The public's trust in government never fully recovered from the strain of the Vietnam War and the deceit revealed in the *Pentagon Papers.* Rambo enjoys a spectacular purgative revenge yet he kills no one. He is a nobody, yet also a berserker with virtually superhuman powers who forces the authorities to respect and fear him. In the real world a succession of rampage killers acted out similar guerrilla-warrior fantasies.

The *New York Times* study of rampage killing (April 8, 2000) found that while 26 percent of typical murderers were unemployed, the number rises to 57 percent among rampage killers.[45] In a culture that organizes identity around work and equates success with heroism, this is no surprise. Like Rambo, 30 percent of rampage killers in the United States have had military training. As in warfare, to be a loser means to face a form of death. Hence the pattern of wearing fatigues and hefting an arsenal of military-style weapons, as if anticipating the usual climactic battle with paramilitary SWAT police. Like a large percentage of killers in the *Times* database, Rambo suffers symptoms of mental illness: intrusive flashbacks to his torture in the war.

The film appeared as Washington was trying to rehabilitate the military and cure "Vietnam syndrome." In 1979–1980 the Iranian hostage crisis had crystallized the unresolved fear, anger, and humiliation of the lost war and its domestic aftermath. For months the media bellowed that the nation was "held hostage" like the imprisoned Rambo. The media campaign helped to force the berserk Rambo-like rescue mission that crashed in the Iranian desert.

In George Cosmatos's sequel to *First Blood* (1985) Rambo is sent to rescue American POWs treacherously "left behind" in Vietnam.[46] In this fantasy the unemployed vet and berserker finds "America [still] held hostage" by the defeat in Vietnam. Courage redeems the American hero's manhood, though treacherous officials thwart his triumphant rescue. The outcome reinforces "stab in the back" excuses for the failed war, which in turn suggests that a soldier such as Rambo survived only through his capacity for special fury. Rambo manages to be both a loyal hero and a renegade. He confirms President Reagan's claim that "we" would have won the war if allowed to "take the gloves off," even as Rambo thrusts his menacing phallic knife in the face of his cynical government handler and heads for the wilderness in disgust.

In that disgust berserk style registers the ongoing manipulation and incoherence plaguing the cultural moment. The tough ideology that President Reagan popularized folded military pride into sunny pep talks, combining ideas of fitness and diet with "lean and mean" policies intended to shrink government "fat," organized labor, and "welfare queens." In practice Reagan genially expanded government, military Keynesianism, and the national debt while enabling business to toughen up the workplace. The rehabilitated military advertised the new program of toughness in comic opera military missions such as the invasion of Grenada, which advertised force but also advanced careers.[47]

As John Kenneth Galbraith once remarked, American CEOs see themselves as generals commanding armies on the battlefield of business. In the 1980s business culture emphasized berserk style to repudiate postwar softness and glorify an uncompromising will to win. Management shelves featured books with titles such as *Leadership Secrets of Attila the Hun* (1987) and Robert Ringer's *Winning through Intimidation* (1973), which made threat-display central in business and urged a gladiatorial recognition of "the certainty that you will die . . . so you might as well make the most of your one shot at life." Ringer formulated a classic berserk principle, his "Ice Ball Theory," according to which "it is ridiculous to take yourself too seriously because in the long run, nothing makes any difference; one day, the earth will be a lifeless ice ball."

The new generation of MBA slogans such as "no pain, no gain" and "lean and mean" fused martial ideas of purifying discipline, sacrifice, and rousing death-anxiety with the implicit violence of "cutting," "shedding," "burning fat," or "downsizing" a bloated body. Just as eating disorders became a preoccupation in the 1980s and 90s, so downsizing became a form of corporate anorexia. In both behaviors, sacrifice and pain fuel convictions of perfectibility. Implicit is the economy of sacrificial killing, as in the Chicago School adage that "you can't make an omelet without breaking eggs." The complementary trope was bodybuilding and the luxury fitness gym to service executive and corporate muscle. Business and the Pentagon shrank the workforce while looking to technology, rapid response, and pumped up morale to achieve exceptional results.

In squeezing labor through triage and givebacks, management was maximizing leverage to "get the most out of" workers. The core idea, as in berserk abandon, is that people have a reservoir of extra energy that can be tapped. Labor experienced the squeeze as stress. Like the speeded-up assembly line in Chaplin's *Modern Times* (1936), which leads the Tramp to run amok and shoot the boss with squirts of oil, the new workplace began to suffer episodes of rampage killing.

In ratcheting up survival anxiety to motivate the workforce in the 1980s, business culture praised Social Darwinism. In a glossy pamphlet called *New Work Habits for a Radically Changing World,* for example, the aptly named business guru Price Pritchett argues that business is war. "Examine the corporate body count over the last dozen years or so," he commands. "What you'll find is that 'slow' kills companies. And that, of course, means the death of many careers." Presumably including yours and mine. Mr. Pritchett tries to soften this death-threat by explaining that organizations *must* "travel light" and sacrifice anyone who can't keep up. "These are not casual moves or random acts dreamed up by bored or heartless top executives. What you're witnessing are raw survival instincts at work. Organizations *must* accelerate, or they will die" (p. 10).

Pritchett's pamphlet honors violence—"raw survival instincts"—and a hierarchy with the fittest—the most violent—at the top. There is no social contract in this business culture. The "bottom line" can take you out at any time, for any reason, with no recourse. If you can never feel safe and never trust others to behave in a rationally predictable way, then you are likely to experience what John Bowlby calls "disconfirmation" of your feelings, and to suffer symptoms that Bowlby associates with trauma.

As a trope, the battlefield of business established an atmosphere in which thwarted expectations of security created stress. If disconfirmation becomes too severe, the effect is alienation. To feel hopelessly misunderstood is to feel crazy as well as socially dead. The classic modern trope for this is the revolt of cyborgs. The speeded-up assembly line, for instance, reduces Chaplin's tramp to a spastic mechanism: a robot. As the soldier is enslaved in the "war machine," so laborers are tacitly—and in American history literally—enslaved on the battlefield of business.[48] Today the cyborg mutiny is a staple of futuristic fiction. But in the nineteenth century Populists and others protested against wage slavery, and in "The Bell Tower," Melville for one combined the tropes of slavery and mechanism. The story imagines an automaton fabricated to strike a bell but instead kills the inventor: "So the blind slave obeyed its blinder lord, but, in obedience, slew him. So the creator was killed by the creature." Robot or cyborg revolts routinely storm across the mental landscape of modernity. Masters aggrandize themselves by consuming the slave's will and vitality, as in the related trope of vampirism.

President Reagan's dissolution of the air traffic controllers' union (PATCO) in 1981 was the opening salvo in a new campaign to subdue labor. Forty-eight hours after issuing an ultimatum, he fired 11,350 controllers. AFL-CIO President Lane Kirkland saw berserk style in this "harsh and brutal overkill."[49] For 15 years after the union was wiped out, "employers all across the country cut jobs, cut pensions, cut health coverage, and stepped on workers' rights."[50] The financial press praised the waves of terminations and the liquidation of traditional "lazy" businesses. For a time *New Yorker* cartoons regularly satirized bosses who, like Sunbeam's "Chainsaw Al" Dunlap, "slashed" payrolls. The deep metaphor is eugenics: culling the weak from the herd. Often it has sadistic, paramilitary overtones, as in this analysis of "What Went Wrong with the Business-Process Reengineering Fad," which evokes a death march: "In re-engineering, we carry the wounded and shoot the stragglers."[51]

This is the atmosphere in which "going postal" became a recognizable syndrome. In one *New Yorker* cartoon (January 27, 1997), an executive says to a manager: "We've got to get rid of some people, Cosgrove. Who are the least likely to come back and shoot us?" The cartoon's language ("get rid of some people") has mafia echoes, and the fear of retaliation implies gang warfare. While executive culture praised strategy and planning, the deep trope of survival violence colored responses to the specter of rising global competition. To maintain its standard of living, a typical US household now required two wage earners, even as income at the top soared, sharpening discontent over "what is right."

"Making a killing" began to look like a killing spree at the top, since income increased from 1997 to 2007, but mostly for corporations and the very rich. For the average family, income stagnated and insecurity about health care, unemployment, and retirement, intensified.[52]

FREE FALL

In October 2008, the financial system's shock-and-awe policies finally provoked massive blowback. Alan Greenspan told Congress that he was in a state of "shocked disbelief" and that the "whole intellectual edifice [had] collapsed." Chicago school theorists such as Milton Friedman had preached a faith in self-correcting markets that Ronald Reagan hallowed as the "magic of the marketplace." Freedom from regulation is supposed to insure maximum productivity and efficiency. In its popular forms the ideology shares berserk style's assumption that by overthrowing restraints we unleash special powers. Like the theory behind derivatives, that is, "free market" theory is open to abandon even as it promises self-correcting stability. But free market models "were never based on solid empirical and theoretical foundations."[53]

The term "freedom" can be sticky and amorphous. It can mean creative liberation but also lawlessness and anarchy. It can license malign as well as virtuous motives. In practice freedom makes an opportunistic slogan, since no system or person in the real world can be wholly free. Every economy mixes freedom and control. The United States celebrates laissez faire capitalism but relies on the Federal Reserve and other tools of central planning. The corporate-military enjoys a command economy that fosters oligopoly. While trumpeting free market principles, conglomerates have swallowed up competitors, creating monopolies enjoying with implicit government backing.

Like any other form of bad government, bad market regulation can be pernicious. But instead of evaluating the *quality* of governance or freedom, vernacular free market ideology advances a melodrama in which freedom is the gratuitously heroic adversary of governance. Like all forms of chauvinism, this melodrama invites doublethink. Borrowing selectively from Adam Smith, the theorists have implied that self-interest is naturally harmonized by market forces if not by natural benevolence, and that markets naturally tend toward equilibrium. But whether nomads are bargaining over salt or futures traders are punching into a computer, trade necessarily entails rules and rites to control volatile emotions, misperception, and trickery. In boom times the assumption that individuals can know their own best interest is beguiling but sentimental, and it is easy to forget that death-anxiety, crime, and tragedy are also "natural."

In its most militant forms free market theory is a romance of the beyond. It attributes superhuman guidance to "the invisible hand of the market" or in financial jargon "Mr. Market," a tutelary spirit who stands in for God. In effect, it mystifies regulation by locating it in the beyond. Likewise, it mystifies creaturely motives, sublimating death-anxiety in the consoling, schematic triumphalism of Social Darwinism, or denying it outright in assumptions about benevolent appetites and limitless expansion. In free market fundamentalism, utopian tropes glimmer alongside dog-eat-dog competition, and competition can be muscle-building sport yet also a war of deceit, suspicion, and triage.

These contradictions are problematical because they screen out problems of failure and death that can undermine a society. Personal endowments and power are never fairly distributed. Information and advantage are usually asymmetrical, and economic success is hardly the only value worth pursuing. "Survival of the fittest" sentences "losers" to suffering and death—not an attractive basis for corporate public relations. Worse, the same threat can also spur the successful to survival greed. Friedman wanted to believe that players would always do the right thing in order to protect their reputations. But when death looms, "reputation" may be less potent than rage for life. When berserk style prevails in markets, "private market discipline" not only fails to protect integrity and trust, it can foster a climate of criminal aggression. "Me first" has its organizational counterpart in the drive toward monopoly, which at bottom is the drive to subsume or exterminate all competitors.

In practice, the theorists were revealingly contradictory. While he espoused freedom, for example, Friedman was drawn to repressive regimes such as Pinochet's Chile, and was friendlier to multinational corporate lions than to entrepreneurial church mice that need protection from predators to thrive. Naomi Klein pinpoints the berserk dynamic in Friedman's contention that "only a crisis—actual or perceived—produces real change": that is, the elimination of allegedly inefficient regulations. Once a crisis has struck, Friedman "was convinced that it was crucial to act swiftly to impose rapid and irreversible change before the crisis-wracked society slipped back into the 'tyranny of the status quo.'" The strategy is "a variation on Machiavelli's advice that injustice should be inflicted 'all at once.'"[54]

Klein sets out to "show that this fundamentalist form of capitalism has consistently been midwifed by brutal forms of coercion, inflicted on the collective body politic as well as on countless individual bodies. The history of the contemporary free market—better understood as the rise of corporatism—was written in shocks" (18–19). Shock-and-awe, to recall, was in part an effort to remake the Iraqi economy by overwhelming the status quo. What "has animated Friedman's counterrevolution," says Klein, "is an attraction to a kind of freedom and possibility available only in times of cataclysmic change—when people, with their stubborn habits and impatient demands, are blasted out of the way. . . . It is in these malleable moments, when we are psychologically unmoored and physically uprooted, that these artists of the real plunge in their hands and begin their work of remaking the world" (20–21).

To be "psychologically unmoored and physically uprooted" in crisis is trauma. Shock can make people more compliant but also more violent. Free to shock, the capitalist may act out the berserker's "godlike powers" as "creative destruction" in which destruction may prevail over creativity. The behavior may be self-serving, but the fantasy is that the shock restores what is right. The basic conundrum is that people uprooted from the life they've known may be too stunned to build anew. In that event, the designers of the new free market become leaders or executives with advantages that contradict the idea of free interplay. Friedman's experiment in Chile, for example, produced better outcomes for certain multinational corporations than for ordinary Chileans.

Because control is never equally distributed, a free market is a utopian scheme. The cliché of "belt-tightening" associates deprivation with dieting and self-discipline. But in history the conviction that less is more, and that pain builds character, is applied most often to the weak and the poor. Shock and coercion are practical weapons that juntas and their corporate sponsors used in countries such as Chile to force down labor costs and acquire stripped-out national infrastructure and raw materials. In theory, authoritarian freedom imposed sacrifice for longer-term benefit. But the results proved to be ambiguous at best, usually incurring prolonged unemployment and a weak wage structure.

Friedman himself was willing to work for General Pinochet's notorious Chilean junta in the 1970s. A decade later free market doctrine rationalized the use of death squads and "Contras" in Central America, for a time making Guatemala, in Amnesty International's account, the most violent nation on earth. To be sure, motives were complex. The doctrine shimmered with special promise at a time when the failures of Communist economies were self-evident. The capitalism it served was charged with ambivalence. It seemed inexorably triumphant on the stage of history, yet after the debacle in Vietnam and the prolonged slump at home, "the pitiful helpless giant"[55] America was looking to "the magic of the marketplace" to recover lost vitality.

The theorists sidestepped these troubling realities. In an echo of American military planning, they imagined behavior in terms of impersonal trajectories, with benevolent self-interest akin to a law of physics. While identified with conservatism, free market themes were actually working like motivational speakers to excite ambition and appetite for risk, minimizing human complexity, frailty, and perversity.

Like Alan Greenspan, whose policies contributed to the financial debacle of 2008, Friedman advocated conservatism but relished radical heroic intervention in the name of growth. The free hand they prescribed suited the titans of the Gilded Age. Both men were acolytes of Ayn Rand and youthfully enthralled by her didactic account of the indispensable leader—cf. the indispensable super-power—the "Atlas" who holds up the world. When beset by a world of parasitical dependents, her Atlas (cf. "masters of the universe") must "shrug" them off.

The acolytes seemed to share the psychological myopia in Rand's premise. Behind the self-made mastermind is the fantasy of self-creation that Ernest Becker called the "narcissistic project": a belief in "mastery and possession of the world through self-control."[56] As history's tyrants remind us, rather than invest in steady state or sustainable systems, the indispensable Atlas frequently prefers self-aggrandizement bolstered by the exploitation or extermination of scapegoat dependents. Sooner or later the great one's death-anxiety arouses predatory greed for life, making the leader an epic killer. The self-righteous architect Roark in *The Fountainhead* dynamites "his" housing complex after its owners add some unwanted ornament to his design. Rand's fiction barely hides the vindictiveness of the lordly "shrug." The destruction of habitat when there is never enough shelter for everyone has the coloration of terrorism. In practice, her acolytes banded together to relish their individuality even as the hero-worship in her system flattered their self regard and groupthink.[57]

A conviction of godlike impunity is the berserker's oxygen. This is what credit analyst Christopher Whalen meant when he concluded that the traders peddling catastrophic credit default swaps at insurance giant AIG were "deluded." The CDS "phenomenon [was] dreamt up by those whose obsession with the free market has caused them to lose their grip on reality. 'In a world where people believe in market efficiency, in total market completion, things like CDSs make sense. It goes back to Milton Friedman.'"[58]

As deregulation gathered force in the 1980s, among the Atlases who shrugged were the Bernard Ebbers and Ken Lays whose criminal monkeyshines made a mockery of "market discipline." In his October 2008 congressional testimony Alan Greenspan confessed: "I made a mistake in presuming that the self-interests of organizations, specifically banks and others, were such as that they were best capable of protecting their own shareholders and their equity in the firms." But Greenspan hedged: the instruments were too complex for even the most capable regulators to control. And he saw no harmful motives in the perpetrators of the disaster. By contrast in 1963, writing in Rand's "Objectivist" newsletter, he had warned that regulation was a murder or holdup weapon. "Self-governance by choice," he said, "would be more effective than governance through government. Regulation, Greenspan maintained, was the enemy of freedom: 'At the bottom of the endless pile of paper work which characterizes all regulation lies a gun.'"[59]

To hammer home this doctrine, the proponents turned explicitly to berserk style. The claims advanced were often hyperbolic articles of faith, dramatized with Madison Avenue overstatement, effectively putting them in a rhetorical beyond where practical criticism was irrelevant. "The first head of the Office of Thrift Supervision in the George W. Bush administration came to a press conference on one occasion with a stack of copies of the Federal Register and a chainsaw. A chainsaw. The message was clear. And it led to the explosion of liars' loans, neutron loans (which destroy people but leave buildings intact), and toxic waste. That these were terms of art in finance tells you what you need to know."[60] With its allusion to the famous slasher film (Tobe Hooper's *Texas Chainsaw Massacre*), the chainsaw flaunted a determination not to reform but to demolish restraints.

To describe the Enron and subsequent crises, critics have pointed to berserk abandon at the top, as in Ben Stein's "Executives Gone Wild: It's Not a Pretty Sight" (*New York Times*, December 16, 2005). Paul Craig Roberts summed up: "According to Forbes magazine, the top 20 earners among private equity and hedge fund managers are earning average yearly compensation of $657,500,000, with four actually earning more than $1 billion annually. The otherwise excessive $36,400,000 average annual pay of the 20 top earners among CEOs of publicly-held companies looks paltry by comparison. The careers and financial prospects of many Americans were destroyed to achieve these lofty earnings for the few."[61]

With free markets celebrating rougher competition, business culture played up hypermasculine warrior-aristocrat tropes. With tabloid breathlessness *Wall Street Journal* editorialist Holman W. Jenkins Jr. claimed that "a company like General Electric . . . is alive today to brag about its pedigree because its last chief, Jack Welch, a self-proclaimed radical from the 'lunatic fringe,' questioned every assumption, tore down every wall, and waged guerilla war against his own company's bureaucracy." While the guerilla war might recall the dangerous Rambo,

Jenkins believed that increased "risk appetite, taken to a logical conclusion, helped produce the quicksilver corporate order that characterized the late 1990s. Companies came to be judged more on their opportunities than their past performance. This is especially true of the companies that typified the opportunities afforded by technology and intellectual capital, or those that reflected innately speculative ventures like entertainment, fashion, or radically innovative new consumer-business models." He did wonder about "the several trillion dollars in wealth destroyed in the market correction that followed the dotcom bubble. Can we really afford such 'dynamism' if the cost is so devastating to so many investors?" Well, yes. "Indeed, for all the surface turmoil, the high-risk economy has a subterranean stability that must surprise anyone who remembers the stagflationary 1970s." Jenkins drily winked that "[a] replay of the 1929 crash . . . has not materialized."[62]

Four years later the crash roared in with a vengeance and GE's finance division was gasping for air. "Subterranean stability" gave way to F. Scott Fitzgerald's elegiac anthem of the 1920s: "Gatsby believed in the green light, the orgiastic future that year by year recedes before us." The orgiastic beyond is what the psychiatrist Peter C. Whybrow sees as the cause of *American Mania: When More Is Not Enough*.[63] He holds that in the turbocharged 1990s Americans launched into a full-blown pathological episode of mania, pursuing status and possessions, in an outbreak of addictive greed, especially in business. In a compulsive drive for more, we were making ourselves sick.

FEED THEM OR SHOOT THEM

As the nation deindustrialized in the 1980s, business culture fetishized magic bullets, from Japanese management models to the latest incarnations of Taylorism. Total Quality Management (TQM) dressed up the older factory mentality while locking workers into a script the way command subsumes the combat soldier. While efficiency demands discipline and order, TQM dressed up venerable ideas such as interchangeable parts, making the controlling script more important than the individual worker. Despite its scathing mockery of Soviet-style central planning, autocratic capitalism shared some of the same dynamics. In Warren Bennis's quip, "The factory of the future will have only two employees, a man and a dog. The man will be there to feed the dog. The dog will be there to keep the man from touching the equipment."

This factory is striking not for its automation, but as an elite immortality fantasy—a self-contained, bountiful entity with no human limitations. Yet the fantasy also embodies the seeds of workplace rampage. The working "man" exists only to serve the dog, who polices the man to prevent him from touching—taking a share in, or lashing out at—the exquisite machine. For management and owner this is an Atlas fantasy of total self-creation. No regulations, labor demands, or competition mar the dream. It is timely, too, since it reflects the sudden preeminence of the private security sector, and has an eerie echo in the famous Abu Ghraib photos of guard dogs baring fangs at prisoners locked out of jobs and family.

Granted, Bennis's model is supposed to be witty, and most businesses do not station fangs at the office watercooler. Even so, the model takes for granted that a hostile, invisible autocracy owns and runs things. But after the meltdown of 2008, it can be applied to the "financialization" of the American economy. The factory that once relied on a workforce to manufacture goods such as cars became the unaccountable banking machine taking 40 percent of all profits. The banking machine facilitated the transfer of production to low-wage countries, the consumption of cheap imports, and the indebtedness of now-underemployed workers struggling with usurious credit card debt. Like Bennis's machine, the financial complex is perversely autonomous insofar as it feeds on the resources that pass through it. The American worker is "there to feed the dog"—guarding the inaccessible machinery. In real life the dog is the hugely hungry corporate-military and private security industry that protects the American financial factory around the world. The system that Bennis describes is "autocyclic" in economic terms: it feeds on itself, without oversight. In social terms it relies on threat (the dog) to subdue challenges. In Bennis's witticism what looks like a model of invincible stability is powered by berserk style.

America's great mythic factories rolled out cars. When Chrysler and General Motors suffered bankruptcy in 2009, it shook the nation's self-image. Critics blamed globalization, unionized labor and its benefits, stultified planning, and out-of-touch executives who arrived in private jets to ask Congress for bailouts. Less often noted were characteristics of berserk style. In a parody of the Bennis factory, Detroit had long fixated on the beyond: on more cars, bigger cars, with grandiose tailfins and incalculable prestige. Ads placed the cars on a vast mesa, at a swanky resort, among the stars. The industry moved toward the model of a self-contained machine. When fuel prices spiked and the economy slumped in 2008, GM was still fixated on producing inappropriate new SUVs, the most profitable product in company history. As the industry sent production abroad, it shifted to finance. As the joke has it, Detroit only produced cars in order to collect interest on their sales.[64]

These are intractable systemic problems. In the Great Depression, Chaplin satirized them in *Modern Times* (1936), which defines the corporation as a machine amok. In the film the factory is always pushing the limits of control, striving for more product even as hunger oppresses the city outside. The Tramp is virtually enslaved on the job, and in one iconic scene devoured by the machinery. His boss is a Henry Ford look-alike who polices workers through an Orwellian telescreen, evoking Ford's company police spies and also the enthusiasm of American industrialists in the 1930s for Nazi controls on labor. The boss personifies the corporation, but in the telescreen he is part of the machine, the more unaccountable because—like advertisements showing Henry Ford's face hovering in a sunburst above his plant—he is also godlike. Spying on the Tramp in the bathroom, the boss intrudes on his inner life like the voice of God, as if the Tramp has no control over his own mind—a precondition of the berserk state and akin to the intrusive flashbacks that overtake Rambo.

The point is, the system is amok. When the boss has a machine feed the Tramp on the job, the robot arm runs wild, a crazed parent cramming bolts down the throat of a helpless man. As the assembly line accelerates, the Tramp's body goes into autonomic rebellion, perseverating as in the tics of shellshock. In his subsequent rampage the Tramp travesties beastlike and godlike fury as he swings over everyone's head like a monkey, "kills" the plant's power, and "shoots" fellow workers and the boss with squirts from an oilcan. With bitter memories of the four demonstrators gunned down at the Ford Rouge plant several years before in 1932, played out in the clash of police and the unemployed in the film, the satire seethes with injustice. At one point during the Depression, Henry Ford's mansion had a machine gun emplacement for security. Then in 1937, following a riot described as "the Battle of the Running Bulls," autoworkers occupied the GM factory in Flint Michigan and forced the negotiations that established the United Auto Workers.

Modern Times disenchants the self-serving assumption that the berserker goes crazy while the reasonable world looks on. As a factory, society itself is the "battlefield of business." Although elite management and workers are in conflict, they share a common fear of the ultimate enemy—deprivation, emptiness, and death—which fuels the frenzy of manufacture and policing in the first place. As Chaplin's plot illustrates, the chronic stress in society keeps the individual childlike and marginally competent, with unresolved symptoms. The tramp caroms from one disaster to another, with no time to recover his equilibrium.

The Tramp's ordeal in the factory in 1936 anticipates the dystopian cyber-state in films such as the *Terminator* and Robert Longo's *Johnny Mnemonic* (1995), and *The Matrix* (1991). There is a revealing counterpart in a General Motors advertising film of 1936 entitled "Precisely So," which depicts the factory as a seemingly autonomous machine. At its climax a formation of animated tools marches into the camera. The tools—calipers, slide rules, and the like—are robots, more efficient and disciplined than human craftsmen. Precisely so. The tools replace human workers, anticipating the automation to come. The boss is a gauge that commands the march from an elevated dais like Hitler at the Nuremburg rally filmed in Leni Reifenstahl's *Triumph of the Will* (1935). The tools parade to the triumphal march from Tchaikovsky's *Pathetique* Symphony, that most tragic—and inappropriate—of laments. The conversion of despair to a triumphal march is the 1930s fascist solution to the Depression. In its final moments the march cuts to an endless stream of identical new cars that rush out of the factory and at the consumer-viewer, cycled by trick photography in an endless, accelerating loop. As if self-created, the cars assault the viewer like robots, coming faster and faster, with berserk, orgasmic force.

Even as it pumped up morale during the Depression, promising greater personal freedom, the onslaught of cars in the advertisement signals an alarming loss of autonomy. The incarnations of consumer desire look and behave like military machines in a frontal assault. The factory shoves cars into the viewer's face like the feeding machine assaulting the Tramp.

Paradoxically, the production mania was self-defeating insofar as overproduction and underconsumption helped to bring on the Great Depression in the first place. With incomes skewed to the top, wages sinking, and consumers unable to buy the goods pouring into a glutted marketplace, the economy deflated. Henry Ford was able to give his son Edsel a million dollars in gold for a birthday present even as he was forcing down wages.

Under stress in the Depression, that is, the dream of the autonomous machine rigidified as bosses such as Ford demanded more control. By 1936 the editors of *Consumer Reports* were criticizing American business leaders for their Nazi sympathies. "Nazi pile-drivers [are] pounding the German workers into serfdom," while "in some of the large corporations of this country the techniques of Der Fuehrer and his cohorts are followed with avidity and approval and a feeling of 'why can't we get away with that too.'"[65]

During World War II the automakers prospered as defense contractors. And the ties persisted, as in Ford CEO Robert McNamara's service as secretary of defense during the Vietnam War. Thereafter, confronted by foreign competition, Detroit joined in the frenzy of deindustrialization: outsourcing, downsizing, and concentrating on product lines such as the burly SUV. The strategy was corporate streamlining but also a kind of survival rage, and after the misery chronicled in Michael Moore's *Roger and Me* (1989), it climaxed in bankruptcy.

Moore's film opens with archival footage of postwar parades and advertising that defined General Motors as a family. In effect, CEO Roger Smith is the absentee father of the corporate "family." Downsizing the company, he made many destitute orphans of GM's "children," shrugged off corporate responsibility, and rebuffed pleas for help. Unemployed workers suddenly found themselves infantilized and helpless. Like Chaplin's Tramp, Moore's friend Ben suffers a breakdown in the factory and takes refuge in a mental health center. In search of work families migrated—fled—as they did during the Dust Bowl crisis and as the Tramp and the girl do at the close of *Modern Times*.

The corporation cultivated doublethink, exuding executive calm yet acting out survival panic, with minimal safeguards for the casualties. In the early stages the mass layoffs had the impact of a massacre. As Flint Michigan reeled in shock, squalor crippled the city. Abandoned housing fell to ruin. Sanitation and public services failed. Crime set records, and in a familiar mix of profit and panic, scarce resources went into a new high-tech prison in which former autoworkers would guard their former line mates. In a telling incident a mentally disturbed black man in a Superman cape squats in the street with a shotgun, bent on rescuing the city until police marksmen shoot to disable him. He uses the form of a workplace rampage in a futile effort at heroism. Hauled off to an ambulance like the Tramp in *Modern Times*, his weapon and cape reminiscent of Rambo's revolt, the deranged Superman acts out the communal loss of control.

The counterattack against decay centered on public relations: psywar. Paternalistic government sponsored discount entertainment, celebrity pep talks, and consoling nostalgia. On camera the singer Anita Bryant gushes Reagan and Thatcher nostrums about "a great new day" until she abruptly runs out of clichés, stammers, and the interview collapses. In time the city tried to rebrand itself as a tourist destination, featuring a glitzy but doomed high-rise hotel and a new mall with a nostalgic museum depicting Flint in its automotive heyday and a GM version of Disneyworld featuring an animated mannequin autoworker singing "Me and my buddy" to the robot replacing him on the assembly line. The propaganda sought to manage morale, converting fight to flight—to migration and escapism.

For many audiences the definitive berserk trope in *Roger and Me* is the behavior of the unemployed Rhonda Britton, who sells rabbits for "pets or meat," and on camera kills one of the animals for sale by bludgeoning it with a pipe. "I was raised to be a survivor," she explains. The rabbits have to be slaughtered early in life, before overcrowding leads the males to gnaw one another's genitals. The animals' castrating survival competition and the woman's planned triage are a parable of the local effects of global capitalism. The trapped, determined survivor skins the rabbit before the camera, emptying out its organs as houses are being gutted, children evicted, and lives consumed around her.

The film's conclusion recapitulates the symbolic logic. As Roger Smith broadcasts a Christmas message to GM employees "around the world," a fatherly figure at a pulpit-like lectern, supported by a choir of children, the film cuts back and forth to an eviction in Flint in which bewildered toddlers watch their panicky young mother rage at Deputy Sheriff Fred Ross. Death-anxiety is in the air. The sheriff instructs a prison trusty moving out the family's belongings to lay the family Christmas tree down in the snow "or else the wind gon' blow it away." The soundtrack plays a novelty version of "Jingle Bells" featuring barking dogs that might evoke the guard dog policing the worker in Bennis's idea factory.

Then Roger Smith recites a line from Dickens about Christmas as a time of unqualified generosity and love. Then with bizarre, unwitting irony the choir sings "Here Comes Santa Claus," whose lyrics depict menacing paternalism:

> You better watch out, you better not cry,
> You better not pout, I'm telling you why:
> Santa Claus is coming to town.
> He knows when you are sleeping,
> He knows when you're awake
> He knows when you are bad or good,
> So be good for goodness' sake.

The choral arrangement ends with a witty warning, a shouted "Watch out!" By association Santa Claus is the callous father Roger Smith and the kindly Deputy Sheriff Fred who executes evictions.[66] Spying on the sleeping and waking, Santa is also the all-seeing factory boss, the Big Brother who polices the Tramp via the telescreen as he sneaks a break in the men's room. The song reinforces the infantilization of those dependent on the company with a warning not to complain or misbehave. To be "good," the displaced workforce needed to abandon Flint and reinvent itself elsewhere; to be "bad," radically bad, would be to storm murderously through the workplace.

Santa Claus never reached Flint in the 1980s, but the automakers did recover for a time. They took advantage of a Reagan-era loophole in fuel-efficiency standards to sell the mock-military Hummer and monster SUVs. They thrived on ads touting the berserk freedom to go "off road" and enjoy crash "survivability," as if driving is combat or the hunt. In the new century some Chrysler models sported oversized chrome grilles like huge devouring mouths, evoking dog-eat-dog appetite. But by then, the energy costs driving America's resource wars were also demanding more efficient vehicles.

Jim Kingsdale highlights the almost unfathomable centrality in American fantasies: "Cars cause America's 'oil addiction' which in turn has caused so much of America's balance of payments and foreign policy and military pains—with no end in sight." To think about the baffling scale of the problem he imagines, he turns to berserk style. Any government help would be a do-or-die gamble: "There's no currently discernable [sic] path to profitability for G.M. and Chrysler and thus no exit strategy for the bailout funds they need." Then he calls up rampage killing and the interminable "war on terror." "So G.M. and Chrysler are like suicide terrorists wandering around the business community threatening to blow up both themselves and everyone else in the room. Nobody knows whether to feed them or shoot them."[67] Or their workers.

DENIAL, DECEPTION, AND DELUSION

As the financial crisis deepened in 2008–2009, alarmed economists and critics began construing Washington's open-ended bailouts, secrecy, and employment of Wall Street insiders as signs that the finance industry now controlled the US Government. Anxiety about bankers as puppet masters looks back through the Great Depression to the Founders' quarrels in the early days of the Republic. The global scale of the crisis created an air of panic. By the spring of 2009 the Chinese and others were openly strategizing to displace the compromised US dollar as the world's reserve currency. Critics struggled to sort out the mix of denial, delusion, and deception in the financial system.

The trope of combat troops amok shadowed the crisis. Treasury Secretary Paulson, said William Greider, "gets to decide who lives and who dies. The former investment banker from Goldman Sachs would be empowered as treasury secretary to be savior or grim reaper, the liquidator who essentially pulls the plug on some banks and financial firms or the man who rescues them from ruin."[68] Said Anatole Kaletsky: "Mr Paulson fired what he himself described as his financial 'bazooka'—and vaporised the shareholders of Fannie Mae."[69]

This imagery associates the treasury secretary with a berserk soldier or a mafia contract killer. It prepares the way for the next chapter's use of mafia as a window on the cultural fantasies behind the economic emergency. Here is a particularly trenchant indictment: "Psychologists concluded that, for a variety of reasons, the larger the number of observing bystanders, the lower the chances that the crime may be averted. We have just witnessed a similar phenomenon in the financial markets. A crime has been committed. Yes, we insist, a crime. There is a victim (the helpless retirees, taxpayers funding losses, perhaps even capitalism and free society). There were plenty of bystanders. And there was a robbery (overcompensated bankers who got fat bonuses hiding risks; overpaid quantitative risk managers selling patently bogus methods)."[70]

"A crime has been committed." There were individual criminals such as Attorney Marc S. Dreier and former Nasdaq Chair Bernard Madoff, whose Ponzi scheme fleeced investors of $50 billion or so. But the indictment above faces up to the crime's social and cultural frame. Although they never anticipated a Ponzi scheme, many of Madoff's more astute victims suspected him of crooked insider trading since his inexplicably superior returns implied something fishy.

But that's why they trusted their money to him.

CHAPTER 4

BOOTY AND THE BEAST

[The] American capital markets are a crime in progress.

Matt Taibi, *Rolling Stone*, October 14, 2009

Drugs money worth billions of dollars kept the financial system afloat at the height of the global crisis, the United Nations' drugs and crime tsar has told The Observer.

The Observer, December 13, 2009

The hidden hand of the market will never work without a hidden fist.

Thomas Friedman

The Enron collapse in 2001 betrayed what critics would come to call a "criminogenic environment" in business culture. Before long the FBI was warning of an "epidemic of mortgage fraud" (December 14, 2005). The metaphor picked up on concurrent fears of a flu pandemic and suited the global scope of rogue economic behavior that was about to break the banking system. "Major Wall Street Firms Face Criminal Probe," headlined Reuters (May 13, 2010). This chapter examines that criminal contagion as an expression of cultural fantasies shaping behavior in and beyond the boardroom. Specifically, it reconsiders the antisocial character of some powerful post-Vietnam economic motives.

In boom times it is easy to overlook the role of survival concerns in economic behavior. But greed is greed for life, and can infect even euphoric success. The underlying survival rage stands out more clearly when prosperity falters, as in the violence that accompanied the banking crisis of 2008. "More and more experts attribute the rise in crime in recent months to the dire state of the economy. "I've never seen such a large number [of killings] over such a short period of time involving so many victims," Jack Levin, a professor of criminology at Northeastern University in Boston, told the *Washington Post*.[1] The number of stress-related workplace suicides also jumped.[2] As awareness of the downturn took hold, media shock jocks played up frightening stories about social unrest featuring stockpiled canned goods and guns.

In times of plenty we are disposed to see a naturally stable social order punctuated by crime. Yet given survival physiology and competition, who can be surprised that around the globe audiences are fascinated by con games, tycoons, and gangsters? In a bubble economy berserk style naturalizes dark motives in everyday transactions. In 2008, according to the Treasury Department's Financial Crimes Enforcement Network, over 730,000 "suspicious-activity reports" were recorded in America, roughly a tenfold increase from 1997.

The new scale, pace, and complexity of financial activity make it difficult to detect and prosecute criminal behavior even as they make it easier to run amok. Since the brain copes with this unprecedented cognitive stress by plugging in computers and esoteric math—who would have predicted that algorithms or "algos" would become routine jargon?—decision makers operate at a technological remove from their actions. A quality of mystification complicates and dilutes responsibility.

In *Kapital* (1853) Marx likened capitalism to a vampire. But the association of blood and money is more than a rhetorical conceit, since vampires may dramatize compulsive consumption and debt. They borrow the blood of others to renew their own lives, and repay it by offering victims vampire immortality. As in a bubble economy or a Ponzi scheme, their legions multiply until sooner or later daylight returns and the feeding frenzy goes bust. Vampirism acts out the economic violence of expropriation and subordination. Like Viking raiders, who commonly captured and traded in slaves or thralls, vampires enthrall victims. Bram Stoker's predatory Dracula is bestial and yet also elite, hiring lawyers to acquire London real estate. Slashed by a knife during a confrontation, the Count's clothes disgorge a stream of gold coins—a bubble punctured—that epitomizes the predator's stealth and greed, but also his fascination. In this cluster of metaphors grasping at money acts out hunger for more life and in turn death-anxiety, since vampires must have blood or die. Like the vampire in his coffin, suspended between life and death, the medieval miser is depicted quaking on his deathbed with wealth withheld from others and in effect passively stolen.

The miser's sin can be understood as a stealth crime, akin to the tax avoidance of a billionaire who refuses to share with a community. Stealth only masks aggression. William Black argues that the financial sector deliberately creates recurrent financial bubbles. The bubbles make possible what he calls accounting "control frauds," which "are seemingly-legitimate entities used by the people that control them as fraud 'weapons.' In the financial sector, accounting frauds are the weapons of choice. The financial industry's power and progressive corruption combined to produce the perfect white-collar crimes."[3]

Stealth diffuses the drama of berserk crisis. In the housing "flu" the FBI was trying to cope with a "decentralized criminal conspiracy" that implicated "many with actual criminal records, whose entry into the mortgage industry was in no way hindered by the state regulatory agencies. They proceeded to amass fortunes large and small, using the same techniques familiar from previous financial scandals—pressurized sales techniques; targeting of the weak, elderly and insecure; outright fraud, forgery and deception."[4] In Florida, according to the Miami *Herald*, more than ten thousand convicted criminals entered the mortgage business, roughly four thousand of them as licensed brokers. "According to law enforcement experts, drug dealers often became [house] flippers, in order to launder money."[5] The subculture of cooperative deception is nicely exemplified by the mortgage industry's "liar loans."

In vain critics railed against "the unprecedented bingeing of the financial markets." They warned that "the global credit boom was nothing more than a massive pyramid scheme that is now toppling like a house of cards in a stiff breeze," outraged that profits "are being disgorged in a violently abrupt fashion [that] threatens the financial system as we know it" with "financial Armageddon."[6]

Decades of complaints reached a crescendo. As savings, pensions, and job security shriveled, public voices reached for images of radical violence. David Walker, the US comptroller general, saw terrorism in the nation's financial abandon: "I would argue that the most serious threat to the United States is not someone hiding in a cave in Afghanistan or Pakistan but our own fiscal irresponsibility."[7] He could have pointed out that just before the 9/11 attack unnamed players made a killing in options that bet the airlines' stocks would fall. Terrorists use fear to leverage their power as mafia does. The deep trope is risk-taking for gain—gambling—which mafia promotes and exploits.

MAFIA BUSINESS

This chapter uses mafia with a lower case "m" to investigate ways in which berserk style shapes American fantasies about criminal business. Mafia is a particular historical entity, but also shorthand for the tendency of economic units to coalesce in gangs that use coercion and deception to do business. Used as a thought experiment, mafia foregrounds the atavistic roles of family, tribe, and warrior band that persist in modern business organization.

Mafia shows up regularly in business writing to indict shady behavior, as in this complaint: "The SEC has forgotten its investigation role, ever since ex-Wall Street heads have been in control of the commission. That is like hiring ex-Mafia dons to run a police force."[8] One journalist compared Wall Street's connivance at government bailouts in 2008 to the mafia practice of torching an asset for the insurance money.[9]

As loan sharks and surreptitious investors, mafias function as banks. Credit card issuers are infamous for usurious interest rates and their pressure on government to close off debtors' relief through bankruptcy. It could be argued that the speculative banking system and the Federal Reserve's nominal godfather "Easy Al" Greenspan invited the nation to go for broke with borrowed money. When the loans went bad, the broken bones and murders that mafia usually inflicts took the form of unemployment, bankruptcies, foreclosures, and social death. At the same time the bankers' collusion with government recouped the lost money from taxpayers in so-called bailouts, even as godfather CEOs scooped up obscene "bonuses."[10]

Before he was routed from office in a prostitution scandal reminiscent of a Hollywood gangster movie, New York Governor Eliot Spitzer attacked "predatory lending" whose scale was "widely understood to present a looming national crisis" in which the Bush administration was allegedly colluding with the crooks.[11] Documents eventually revealed that the banks were not merely wrong in their housing market forecast, "they intentionally ignored critical information given to them by the very people who were supposed to perform due diligence. And then they apparently withheld from investors that critical information about the quality of the bonds they were selling."[12] So many mortgages and bond packages were legally defective that futile attempts to foreclose when they failed resulted in a scandal dubbed "Foreclosuregate" after President ("I am not a crook") Nixon.

In a lawsuit against major banks the mayor of Cleveland contended that "the companies irresponsibly bought and sold high-interest home loans to people who had "no realistic means of keeping up with their loan payments," resulting in defaults that depleted the city's tax base and left entire neighborhoods in ruins, the *Cleveland Plain-Dealer* reported. The mayor compared the lenders' behavior to "organized crime. . . . It has the same effect as drug activity in neighborhoods."[13]

The mayor sees the finance industry as a mode of organized crime enticing victims to gamble. Exorbitant rates allowed credit card companies to target customers whose interest charges kept them in debt peonage. In James Scurlock's documentary film *Maxed Out,* the manager of a debt collection agency brags that he "like[s] to make the analogy that you're like this pirate on this pirate ship, right? And you got this person and you're walking them out on the plank, and you walk them as far out as you can go without pushing them off. And then you bring them back to get what you want." This is classic mafia use of berserk style intimidation.

Operating on the edge, mafias are able to exploit creaturely ambivalence. Society's respectable Dr. Jekylls prowl the night as Edward Hyde. Mafias exploit that doublethink by devising an underworld whose drugs, sex, and gambling invert the virtues of Main Street. In effect, they market berserk play as a commodity, selling an experience of desperate conviction, making illicit ecstasy and rage available to customers toiling in the workaday grind. Mob playgrounds such as old Havana or Las Vegas mimic Cony Island or Disneyland.

"International affairs," says Noam Chomsky, "is very much run like the mafia. The godfather does not accept disobedience, even from a small storekeeper who doesn't pay his protection money. You have to have obedience otherwise the idea can spread that you don't have to listen to the orders and it can spread to important places."[14] After Venezuela nationalized assets of Exxon Mobil in 2007, President Hugo Chavez bristled. "The outlaws of Exxon Mobil will never again rob us," he vowed, claiming that the oil major colludes with "the imperialist government of the United States" as part of "worldwide mafias."[15] Similarly, Vice President Cheney asserted that control over energy pipelines is a mafia-style "tool of intimidation and blackmail"—benevolent when the tool is ours, malevolent in the control of others.

Globalization moves business offshore, beyond national laws, into the traditional zone of piracy. Sociologist Zygmunt Bauman deems this an outbreak of berserking: "A most spectacular and potentially sinister consequence of the erratic globalizing processes, uncontrolled and running wild as they have been thus far, is . . . the progressive 'criminalization of the globe and globalization of crime. . . . Never before were the mafias so numerous, powerful, well-armed, and prosperous.'"[16] The central fact of globalization, says Richard Rorty, is that "[t]he economic situation of the citizens of a nation state has passed beyond the control of the laws of the state." No country's laws can any longer govern money flows because "we now have a global overclass which makes all the major economic decisions," beyond the reach of legislatures and voters. "The absence of a global polity means that the super-rich can operate without any thought of any interests save their own."[17] To this Bauman adds: "If this is . . . the 'central fact of globalization,' then the genuine issue is not so much the 'globalization of crime,' as deBernard says, but the annulment of the distinction between 'legal and illegal' which only an abiding and enforceable law may draw. There is no such global law to violate. There is no global law in operation that could permit the setting apart of mafia-style criminal pursuits from 'normal business activity'" (64–65).

Like the berserk state, then, mafia can be viewed as a trope for processes that annul the distinction between legal and illegal. From fraudulent contracts to money laundering involving major banks, mafia dissolves conventional boundaries or "firewalls." A federal prosecutor summed up a case involving Wachovia the bank's "blatant disregard for our banking laws gave international cocaine cartels a virtual carte blanche to finance their operations." Yet the bank was allowed to settle out of court for a total fine of less than 2 percent of the bank's $12.3bn profit for 2009.[18] According to the *State of the Future* survey by the World Federation of United Nations Associations, international organized crime is a "$2 trillion threat to the world's security" since "Billions of dollars worth of bribes paid each year go into the pockets of public officials in rich countries."[19] Says the *Guardian*, "The annual taking of criminal gangs around the world are roughly equivalent to Britain's GDP, or twice the world's combined defence budgets. Half of that amount is paid as bribes, which tend to make the rich and powerful even wealthier. The 225 richest people on the planet now earn the same as the poorest 2.7bn, equivalent to 40% of humankind."[20]

Globalized scale, secrecy, and corporate penetration of government erode distinctions and frustrate accountability. What emerges is the hybrid corporate state and corporate military. As whistle-blowers keep signaling, revolving doors and collusion are everywhere in Washington. Intensifying J. P. Morgan's incestuous role in government, Goldman Sachs executives such as Robert Rubin and Hank Paulson have run the US Treasury for many years.[21] Military officers routinely retire to the executive suites of defense contractors and hire out as commentators on television news shows, while defense contractors operate as government policy advisors. Journalist Bill Moyers, among others, has worried about a "Secret Government"—a tacit mafia— within the constitutional government in Washington.[22] With the help of the "Citizens United" Supreme Court decision (2009), today's equivalent of Gilded Age robber barons can use unlimited money to influence elections in perfect secrecy.

Berserk style naturalizes the criminal coloration of society. As in an optical illusion, it makes figure-ground relationships unstable. In movies the bumpkin who blunders into crime and miraculously triumphs is a heroic stereotype. A number of cable television series present sympathetic ordinary folks pushed by circumstances into crime. In "Weeds" a widowed suburban soccer mom deals pot to make ends meet; in "Breaking Bad" a chemistry teacher cooks methamphetamine to pay for his cancer treatment and his family's security; in "Dexter" a police lab specialist moonlights as a homicidal vigilante; and "Nurse Jackie" steals drugs from the hospital pharmacy to get through her heroic work day. The premise is that the stress of American life demands a touch of crime if underdogs are to maintain a decent life.

As a rule, mafia excess is background to "real" life. But let the mood change slightly, and crime appears dominant. As economies contracted in 2008 and Mexican drug cartels—classic mafia—escalated their chronic violence, US media suddenly saw a nation consumed by crime. *Newsweek* gasped that Juarez Mexico was a "slaughterhouse." The magazine quoted "an acting special agent" who claimed that "the United States faced another lawless Waziristan—except this one happens to be right at the nation's doorstep."[23] To audiences resentful about immigration, broadcast media hyped the "nightmare scenario" of US troops mobilized to defend the border against drug-crazed invaders.

BOOTY AND THE BEAST

There is more to the mafia analogy than the axiom that everybody has a touch of larceny. David Chase's HBO mafia epic (83 episodes) *The Sopranos*[24] opens a particular local window on fantasies of abandon and fears of cultural exhaustion in post-Vietnam America. The series ran from January 1999 to June 2007, the period that careened toward the crash of 2008.

"Sopranos" became shorthand for business crime on a personal scale. A Reuters story titled "Insider Trading Case As Much Sopranos as Wall Street" begins: "Zvi Goffer could have passed for Tony Soprano when he warned confederates in his alleged insider-trading ring that 'someone's going to jail.'"[25] In a familiar feedback loop screenwriters mimic criminals, who in turn emulate the models. In the insider trading case, "A criminal complaint naming Goffer [and others] . . . reads like a script for TV dramas like 'The Wire' or 'The Sopranos,' in which drug and Mafia criminals try to stay one step ahead of the law." Investigators had to use wiretaps and other methods "'traditionally reserved for the mob and narcotics traffickers' when the accused began 'taking a page from the drug dealers' playbook (and) deliberately used anonymous, hard-to-trace, pre-paid cellphones in order to avoid detection.' Calls recorded by law enforcement officials were littered with nicknames like 'the Greek' and 'the Rat.'" In making a killing Wall Street wise guys goosed up their morale by ripping off the prime example of berserk style on television.

The appetites and survival rage shaping the Soprano family and mafia "family" give distinctive, garish immediacy to inner life that helps to account for the show's power. In the opening episode Tony Soprano (James Gandolfini) worries that he "came in at the end. The best is over." Postwar America is vanishing; his father, the old boss, is dead; and his nominal successor, Tony's Uncle Junior (Dominic Chianese), is senile. Like the younger President Bush, Tony is a son trying to prove himself in a gap between the worlds of an iconic "greatest generation" and his own children, who want to be comfortably assimilated in respectable American life. For the family "business," reliable contracts and boundaries are fading, and rival families are a relentless menace. New immigrants and blacks have taken over old neighborhoods and the drug trade is flourishing where ethnic solidarity once prevailed. Meanwhile crime is sloppy, opportunistic, and shameful. Dogged by the FBI and paranoia, the mobsters are susceptible to panic and rage, and lamed by denial and regret.

In this environment the Soprano mafia family is an outmoded, failing local business. As scrappy underdogs, they attract audience sympathy. At one point Tony tries to adapt to the global scale by conspiring with Neapolitan mafia to smuggle a few luxury cars. But the tide is against him, and Tony the ostensible waste manager increasingly fears slipping into another sort of mob: the masses of wasted lives—to use Zygmundt Bauman's term—marginalized by globalization. To be sure, some new supermafias such as Enron, with its dummy global subsidiaries and price-fixing, may also die. Yet their impersonality and flimsiness only intensify the sense of instability and mistrust in business life. And on Tony's level, far down the food chain, stress leads to "wasting" lives as in killing.[26] But the problems are systemic: "Bankers and investors, especially global investors, abhor uncertainty in financial assets they hold. They treat it like toxic waste."[27]

The Sopranos and the series are spellbinding because they play to the insoluble ambivalence in us, by turns predator and underdog, infantile in appetite and desperate for self-disciplined honor. In a world fuddled by denial Tony can be bravely realistic. Yet the family spins self-serving myths as politicians do, so that it can play Santa Claus once a year. As in Wes Anderson's popular film *Fantastic Mr. Fox* (2009), in a tradition going back to peasant tales in re-revolutionary Europe,[28] a Robin Hood archetype justifies the outlaw life of the underdogs as a response to oppressive monopoly. The godfather fox and his extended family raid food stashes and narrowly escape to their underworld of burrows.

Behind the opening credits in each episode, Tony Soprano drives up to his McMansion like one of the affluent hosts of a "Great Gatsby party" in Flint Michigan. But Tony really is a crooked Gatsby. He suffers from affluenza: anxiety that in the midst of plenty, nothing has lasting value. "Civilian" life is a grind. Making a killing gives survival appetite ecstatic urgency but has poisonous, addictive side effects. Like other executives living on the edge such as Enron's drug-bedeviled Andy Fastow, Tony combats harrowing competition crippled by panic attacks and alcohol, drug, and gambling binges. He is fitfully honest enough to be a sympathetic character, but cannot get free of toxic lies. Like top American CEOs who have raised their pay from about 39 times that of the average employee in 1970 to nearly 1,000 times more in 2008, he skims everyone's earnings.

Unlike Fitzgerald's mournful criminal romance, Chase's mafia is at once surreally violent and implacably banal. Where Gatsby is expansive, the Soprano families are defensively clannish. Unlike the deliriously monogamous Gatsby, Tony pursues insatiable love affairs with opportunistic *comares*. Where sadistic rage is sublimated in Meyer Wolfsheim's cufflinks—"the finest specimens of human molars"—Tony's life abounds in raw, frenzied atrocity massively denied. Gatsby has Nick to make his story meaningful, whereas Tony uneasily confides in, and deceives, a therapist—and has to hide even that feint at authenticity from other mobsters. Fitzgerald gives Gatsby's life elegiac closure, whereas Tony's story ceases in a moment of humdrum randomness in the final episode, as the screen goes abruptly, unsatisfyingly, frighteningly blank. Rhapsodic desire and jeweled prose console for doom in *Gatsby*. Raw death-anxiety pervades Tony's milieu. The local godfather is not protected from turmoil below as executives are in *Roger and Me*. Making a killing leaves fingerprints on the psyche. Because Tony faces vertiginous change, with old blueprints in tatters and old leaders senile or dead, he makes an apt vehicle to explore the beyond in recent American culture.

The profundity of the series lies in its atmosphere of complex cultural exhaustion. Tony's nominal business is "waste management." Mob rackets are decaying, yet insatiable expectations and exasperated discontent keep goading imagination to violence. Tony misses the ruthless conviction of his gangster father despite his crippling, half-conscious fear of him. Like his wife Carmela (Edie Falco) and their friends, he wants to believe in the American dream, yet they all fear, despise, and cheat on "big government." They watch their kids struggle for meaning, unable to accept that heroic values have hardened into consumer glitz—rings, watches, swanky cars—and stale rituals in church and on television.

Tony feels the exhaustion acutely because he is caught in the coils of a larger cultural transition. He sends his daughter to an overpriced prestige university to become a modern professional, yet mafia is atavistic. The godfather puts a plausible suburban face on a warlord subculture. He is the warrior-protector: priest, judge, and teacher. The poet Tasso trusted in his patron "as we trust in God. It appeared to me that, so long as I was under his protection, fortune and death had no power over me." As cruel and remote as his father was, Tony nevertheless mourns for that heroic faith.

This transference helps to explain audience fascination with the fantasy of the godfather. The Sopranos' post-Vietnam America celebrated individualism and weakened government guarantees while vastly enriching celebrity insiders. After 9/11, White House publicity tried to fashion a warrior president. Corporate CEOs make absurdly inflated incomes while commanding their underlings to be aggressive and to mistrust the "delusions" of loyalty and cooperation: "Don't fall into the trap of assuming that you're automatically 'entitled' to pay increases, promotions, or even your job . . . even if you perform well. [Never] con yourself into thinking that your employer is supposed to protect your future."[29] To expect a reasonable reward, personal loyalty, or "a future" is to "fall into the trap" or to "con yourself." Like marriage, mafia's oath of do-or-die loyalty is supposed to transcend that dog-eat-dog mentality, but mafia history shows otherwise. Overtaken by anxiety, individuals resort to berserk aggression—ultimately the cannibalism evoked when the mobsters cut up a corpse to dispose of it. In the large arc of the saga the family eventually consumes itself.

As a tribal or clan system, mafia generosity and rage are personal, grounded in kinship or tacit family, with little or no loyalty to abstractions such as the nation state or the human condition. Tony's New Jersey gang is closer to the social organization of Iraq than to modern democracy. As in Iraq, the propensity for dog-eat-dog violence increases when change undermines boundaries and hierarchies. After the American invasion Iraqi mafia gangs were quick to exploit an orgy of looting and kidnapping, while sectarian militias and government agencies have conducted ongoing turf wars against religious and tribal rivals. The comparison could be extended in many directions, including the flood of money pumped into Iraq the way the banking system was pumping up the US economy—paper money that would vanish in a squall of misallocation and malfeasance.

On a tribal scale Tony's mafia family is at once predatory and defensive—the ultimate guarantor of security. Tony considers himself a provider, an enforcer of local values, a protector, just as the United States appoints itself the global policeman. Yet the protection racket is elemental human behavior and can corrupt police as it does mafia. The high-minded global policeman does after all bomb civilians and force protection on some clients who happen to have valuable natural resources. In the process the world policeman takes advantage of his special leverage to speculate and incur stupefying debt with impunity. For better or worse, many oil customers and producers such as Japan and the Saudis tacitly pay for US protection by buying US Treasury debt. The corporate military budget is sacrosanct, with a shifting list of global clients and potential enemies to enforce funding demands.

Since 2001, in the same vein, Washington has pumped up a weakening economy with a vast Homeland Security industry, and bulked up private security companies in Iraq such as scandal-plagued Custer Battle and Blackwater. "The scale of the revenues at stake," says Naomi Klein, "is certainly enough to fuel an economic boom. Lockheed Martin, whose former vice-president chaired the Committee for the Liberation of Iraq, which loudly agitated for the invasion, received $25 billion in U.S. government contracts in 2005 alone. Democratic Congressman Henry Waxman noted that the sum 'exceeded the gross domestic product of 103 countries [and] was larger than the combined budgets of the Department of Commerce, the Department of the Interior, the Small Business Administration, and the entire legislative branch of government.' Lockheed itself deserved to be characterized as an emerging market"[30]

From the days of the Pinkertons private "security" agencies have operated to enforce discipline and to suppress labor activism as well as crime, with some famous rampages punctuating the historical record. After hurricane Katrina private security forces intervened in New Orleans as in a third world country. "'This vigilantism demonstrates the utter breakdown of the government,' says Michael Ratner, president of the Center for Constitutional Rights. 'These private security forces have behaved brutally, with impunity, in Iraq. To have them now on the streets of New Orleans is frightening and possibly illegal.'"[31] The alarm is akin to anxieties about mafia muscle.

Americans take the protection economy for granted. At the heart of the derivatives implosion in 2008 were financial instruments and agencies that advertised a fantastic new scale of "securitization" and guarantees. From the Brinks armored car to the Pentagon and the insurance and pharmaceutical industries, protection is a symbolically charged business, sublimating the ancient fantasy roles of warrior, priest, patriarch, and mother. Yet the demand for government protection at all costs is matched by fear of "big government" intrusiveness in personal lives.

The Sopranos raises this ambivalence to a radical pitch. Beneficiaries of government's guarantees and yet living under a constant threat of surveillance and usurping governance whenever possible, the Soprano families are at once patriots, rebels, and outlaws. They resent government intrusions, yet their protection racket is ruthlessly intrusive. Like a tax collector, Tony Soprano squeezes rewards from vulnerable "civilians": sex from women, dinners from his restauranteur friend Artie, and Rolex watches and other tribute from assorted clients. Like Fitzgerald's Gatsby stopped for speeding—"I was able to do the commissioner a favor once, and he sends me a Christmas card every year"—mafia and officialdom may cooperate.

As in mainstream American culture, the Soprano mob complements the anxiety and boredom of the protection economy with investments in a thrilling shadow market that includes prostitution, money lending, gambling, and drugs. The Bada Bing club and Tony's exclusive high-stakes card games are the local mafia incarnation of the national craze for casinos, lotteries, easy credit, and the pleasure palaces of Las Vegas. Tony's frantic gambling parallels the inflation of the stock market bubble of the 1990s, which led intoxicated investors to pitch money at stocks like chips on a roulette table.

In this context *The Sopranos* dramatizes the end of an era in which immigrants were establishing families and local mafia could seem heroically purposeful. Now that ethos is myth. Worse, as younger generations discover its dark side, they try to deny or reinvent that haunted myth of origins. This is what Tony does in therapy and his daughter Meadow does in coming to resent law enforcement's "persecution." What finally count as heroism in the saga are the tragic efforts of particular individuals to face up to demystification, the loss of nostalgic consolations, the reality of their predatory greed and cruelty.

Tony's families are forced to grapple with creaturely motives in themselves and others, and that can make them seem more significant than humdrum, sheltered "civilians." To the extent that Tony's world dies trying to turn its death-anxiety to account, the scripts are modeling heroic purpose for modern audiences the way gladiatorial combat gripped spectators in the Roman amphitheater—but with the camera now able to take spectators down into the subterranean dressing areas where the abject and admired protagonists of death strap on their armor struggling to master their terror.

With "casino" economics and failing wars in the background, Tony's families mirror an America dangerously overconfident and frightened of decline. The point is not that the United States is equivalent to a New Jersey mob, but that in stressful historical moments group fantasies operate across unlikely boundaries. This is why Tony's inner turmoil and need for psychotherapy are such a useful vehicle for insight into the cultural moment.

Tony's sessions with Dr. Melfi (Lorraine Bracco) "may be the most realistic depiction of therapy ever depicted in a mainstream movie or television show."[32] His inner life comes to light in his unruly feelings toward her. He's attracted to her, grateful, humbled, resentful, and frightened. He wants to be noble and protective but helplessly bullies and lies to her. The sessions resolve nothing yet they humanize Tony and provide a lens on the culture that has shaped him.

Tony's distress crystallizes with his glimpse of a family of ducks abandoning his swimming pool at the end of summer. He's been feeding—parenting—them, and their flight panics him as an omen of old age, rejection, and death. He panics when showing his mother a nursing home. In fact death-anxiety has shadowed him since childhood. He remembers his father, the original family godfather, hacking off the finger of a butcher who failed to repay a gambling debt. Only when his father brought home "the bacon," Tony recalls, did his wife Livia (Nancy Marchand) ever reward him with sex.

In this psychic economy men pay for love—trust, nurture, conviction—with "bacon," by making a killing. The young strive for heroic patriarchal authority that turns out to be grounded in predation. Young Tony fainted in a panic attack at the sight of his father carving a roast at the dinner table. Livia's love of meat is a marker for cannibalistic appetite, borne out in her old age when in revenge for imagined offenses she plots with her brother-in-law Uncle Junior (Dominic Chianese) to have her son Tony killed.

The threat of cannibal frenzy is the toxic heart of the mafia mentality. In Ernest Becker's innocent-sounding premise: nobody ever gets enough life. In different ways Tony's parents dramatize the sinister greed for life that springs from survival-anxiety. Their appetites are the more frightening for being so fully naturalized in local mafia culture. The child fears that his own inadequacies, his inescapable failings, condemn him to punishment and death. In reaction he may lash out at scapegoats trying to identify with godfatherly invincibility. But he may also be overtaken by insoluble childhood dread, the terror that makes Tony's panic attacks also a berserk loss of control, but directed inward as well as at scapegoats around him. Mafia proves to be a theater of heroic cruelty and risk, and also of intensely rationalized punishment. In this way mafia epitomizes the hopes and terror of intimate life, since a god-"father" can turn a child into a "made man" or—like the ancient Roman patriarch empowered to kill disobedient children—destroy him.

Tony grew up in the force field of predatory appetites, feeling inadequate and ungrounded, with reason to fear real as well as social death. Having steeled himself to be tough, he complains of feeling "like a clown" inside. But that appreciation of life's absurdity never fully translates into letting go. In therapy he begins to recognize his mother's malice, but though he tries, he never really comes to terms with the survival rage aroused in childhood, and his capacity for empathy remains tragically impaired.

Dr. Melfi can probe the subject of death-anxiety, but for her it remains philosophically distanced, whereas for Tony it is close but numbed. When Tony is upset by Jackie Aprile's death from cancer, Dr. Melfi says, "That's the mystery, isn't it? God or whatever you want to call it? That we're given the questionable gift of knowing we're going to die?" But nothing comes of the question. They are never able to examine the terror and compensatory rage in Tony and a dog-eat-dog world. They come closest to the reality after Dr. Melfi has been raped. To Tony she pretends it was an auto accident, fearing he will go after her attacker. You can't control everything that happens to you, she argues. Tony objects: "But you can get pissed off."

Dr. Melfi: "And then what? Lose control?" (That is, run amok?)

Tony: "Who said anything about that? You can direct your anger where it belongs."

Dr. Melfi replies that a panic attack "occurs when feelings of anger, revenge, or whatever overwhelm you. . . . Behavioral therapy can teach you to control these triggers." She speaks as if they agree that they are discussing berserk panic.

Tony: "Then how do you get people to do what you want?" That is, how can you use berserk style's threat-displays to control others?

The exchange articulates two conflicting modes of coping with violence. While the psychiatrist recommends understanding and forbearance, Tony argues for strategic anger. One mode emphasizes self-control, negotiation, life as politics; the other dreams of masterful warrior force. It is the difference between diplomatic and military strategies. Both modes have limits. In the extreme, forbearance may lead to futile resignation, while in Tony's formula the equation of anger with desire, not to mention the tragic proximity of mastery and madness, opens the way to rage. Dr. Melfi fears running amok where Tony sees it as a tool for "getting what you want." The problem appears to be morale: the need for courage to overcome depressive fatalism in one direction, and self-control to forestall violence in the other.

But there is a cultural problem as well: both the therapist and the gangster see violence as purely personal. Neither has any faith in law as the will and guarantees of the community. After Dr. Melfi's boyfriend Randall is beaten up by a corrupt cop who is unbeknownst to her on Tony's payroll, she says to Tony, ruefully skipping over the failure of the law: "I guess I lead a sheltered life. I'm out of touch with the climate of rage in American society."

In a moment dizzy with ironies she proposes that American culture is governed by berserk style. And Tony, the suburban godfather, affirms mafia mentality as the sensible way to be American and get results. She speaks out of therapeutic culture, whereas the godfather defends a culture of macho confrontation. She underestimates the need for will—without which Tony would feel like an impotent child again. And in spite of therapy Tony cannot see the roots of the anger within him.

YOUR MONEY OR YOUR LIFE

Since the mob believes in a dog-eat-dog economy, survival greed is always eating away at inhibitions, threatening a war of all against all. As a result the group tries to police its motives though a paramilitary structure of "capos" and "soldiers" and a relentless threat of quasi-judicial killing for disobedience. Yet for all the macho cockiness, calculation, and paramilitary severity, gangs are susceptible to contagious panic, and much of Tony Soprano's torment originates in the conflict between dangerous appetite and a rage for order and security. To chop off a debtor's finger in front of your son is to demonstrate the berserker's godlike power but also the victim's terrified—castrated—insecurity. The moment is the more terrifying for flaunting the treacherous rationality of the gambler's contract.

Order becomes rage when carried beyond measure. His mother's whining passive aggression masks a potentially murderous demand for order. Less violent but nevertheless part of the underlying psychic economy is the demand for security made by mafia women. Like many Americans in the bubble years, Carmela frets about retirement. Insecurity disposes her to mistrust Tony as well as government Social Security, and brings her to gamble on a crooked "spec house" so she can participate in the nationwide real estate mania that ran amok in 2008. In effect, women express fear that would unmake "made" men. Insofar as it allows the men to deny their own fears, the system is a form of dissociation.

The system comes apart as the Sopranos's marriage does. The burden of stress is plain enough today. Early immigrant families also labored under daunting stress, but they could find support in a heroic story of discovery and survival in addition to the patriarchal and clan bonds from the old world. In the myth-tinted heyday of La Cosa Nostra, Mario Puzo's *Godfather* epic (1969, 1972) portrayed the inheriting son Michael as soulless but triumphant. As the new godfather he is despicable yet queasily admirable: a figure as compelling as one of the great murderous dictators of the twentieth century.

By contrast, Tony Soprano lurches toward disorder and death. In anxious, sentimental moments his circle mourns for bygone days. Trying to reconnect with the Old World mafia of legend, he finds the Neapolitans he visits eerily cosmopolitan, with a woman godfather. His family is adrift in a tidal wash of exhausted narratives. The older generation decays in nursing homes. In the new world of brand names and industrial glitz, religious rituals and mawkish ethnic songs are empty gestures. Funerals and weddings are vacantly stereotypical. When Carmela breaks with Tony, she and her girlfriends gather to watch old movie "classics" on television in a wishful gesture at self-improvement, seeking consoling cultural authority in Hollywood's fading lowbrow heroism. Carmela knows women's roles are changing, and she can imagine rebellion but no story beyond that.

Alienated souls try to substitute loot for story. The behavior is poignantly childlike, as when Tony's face helplessly lights up at an underling's gift of a glitzy watch. More often it has the frightening force of addiction and triggers manic aggression. In this light mafia is a metaphor for what Dr. Peter Whybrow calls a "mania" for status and possessions: an "outbreak of greed" that drives Americans to live turbocharged lives at the expense of relationships with others.[33] Whybrow sees greed as biologically wired, implicated in the same brain chemistry as drugs such as cocaine and caffeine. But greed is also more difficult to manage in a depersonalized global economy no longer regulated by the neighborly market restraints envisioned in classical economics. In the credit crack-up of 2008 it was epitomized in the infantile self-indulgence of Wall Street executives buying fabulous corporate jets and Ali Baba office furnishings while begging for a government bailout.[34]

Fetishistic frenzy is stressful and exhausting. Like addiction, it escalates, since berserk style tries to dispel or explode stress by concentrating the self in the furious moment, or by focusing on the beyond. Either way it moots reflection, depression, and self-doubt. As identities fray in *The Sopranos*, the families become more recklessly excessive. Tony increasingly abandons himself to gambling, intoxication, desperate sex, and paroxysms of aggression.

The younger, insecure mobsters try to emulate legendary mob exploits and end up amok and usually dead, the fate of Jackie Aprile Jr. (Jason Cerbone). As Tony's nephew Christopher (Michael Imperioli) tries to write screenplays, he becomes aware of his inner chaos. He complains to Big Pussy Bompensiero (Vincent Pastore) about unnerving murders he has committed: "I have no identity. I have bad dreams every night." The older man sympathizes: "The more you do [kill], the better you sleep." He recommends habituation and desensitization. But habituation kills stories. What's more, this is a recipe for addiction and berserk style: escalating violence ("the more you do") in search of stability that is perversely destroyed by the search and usually ends in a convulsion. Before long the "family" will destroy Big Pussy himself, along with Christopher and his fiancée Adriana (Drea DeMatteo).

The grisly film Christopher scripts reveals the death-anxiety that underlies so much aggression. Christopher grasps at the delusion that killing makes the self more secure. As a film within a film (*The Sopranos*), the metadramatic quality of his story becomes a way of showing the power of berserk style to control behavior. The gory torture in his film is at once real—a disguised "confession" of actual sadism Christopher has been involved in—and also a horror genre cliché that controls its audience by cueing applause. In effect, a subculture such as Hollywood or the Mafia projects genres that govern responses. The mobsters at the movie preview attend in order to see berserk style objectified on screen for thrills and thrilling profit. For Christopher, by contrast, the film is a means for the "made man" who is terrified of his own emptiness to inflate his life on screen, and use audience applause to substantiate himself. Given the outcome—Christopher's return to drugs—his Hollywood triumph demonstrates the way berserk lifestyle destroys character.

Christopher unwittingly arouses fatal suspicion in Tony by incorporating facets of Tony's story into his movie script. The irony is brutal: mafia mentality can make any contact with personal lives lethal. Yet the process of writing and listening to others in workshops makes Christopher and also his fiancée more aware of imaginative sympathy. Yet that opening weakens their capacity for denial and makes them fatally conflicted. This is a version of the dilemma Tony faces in seeing a therapist. Like fundamentalists, other mobsters refuse to see that the self is ultimately ungrounded and therefore depends on social bonds and self-examination for substantiation and coherence.

The pressure of death is electrifying in the series' violence, but it is most disturbing in the subtle markers that the scripts use to evoke the imprisoning and doomed human body. Tony always breathes noisily, as if running out of breath, struggling for air. After an auto accident leaves Christopher unconscious Tony, fearing his betrayal, pinches off his breathing to suffocate him. Tough guy godfathers Jackie Aprile (Michael Rispoli) and Johnny Sacks die of cancer, their machismo wasting away. Uncle Junior's senility leaves him finally marooned alone in the cavernous gloom of a state mental hospital. Outraged nerves call for alcohol and drug binges. More gruesomely, the corpses of murder victims are a chronic reminder of the body's persistence as macabre, guilty waste. From time to time they have to be dug up to avoid detection, and then moved or further destroyed.

The attempt to replenish vitality plays out in the trope of predation and specifically cannibalism, which in turn links the motives to popular culture's preoccupation with vampires and other monsters of survival greed. As in *Dracula,* the mafia predators are organized around an alpha leader who can transform himself and has enviable access to life. As boss, Tony Soprano takes in roles as he does food and blood money. The roles expand him. They give him access to sexual conquests, dominance displays, booze, bling, and other markers for fertility and vitality. He can be tender, amused, or sadistic: father, warlord, bandit, killer, gambler, judge, entrepreneur, and needy child, without end. Each change promises liberation, new life. The scripts shrewdly capture these efforts at self-creation. The gangsters try to emulate impressive fashions and vocabulary. Christopher would aggrandize himself in his screenplays.

What makes Tony poignant is his fitful ability to be wise enough to recognize the futility of his survival greed. It brings him to the verge of tragic insight. Living out multiple selves with criminal abandon, Tony half-perceives that his self-expansion subverts and vitiates identity even as it feeds his appetite, yet he keeps reaching for more.

At the point of abandon, the development of multiple incompatible selves is the Jekyll and Hyde paradigm. Tony is a regular guy but also a monster. The neighbors suspect—they "know"—that he is a criminal, but they're tantalized by the forbidden beyond: taboo power and appetite. Tony's compartmentalized identity—the orgiastic gambler in Las Vegas, the moralizing middle-class dad—evokes the larger cultural fantasy celebrated in the 1980s and 1990s as "multiple personality syndrome." Although debunked by research, the syndrome remains popular, presumably because it offers an explanatory tool for the conflicted motives people wrestle with, just as Victorian novels used Jekyll and Hyde to dramatize urgent questions about identity in the nineteenth century.

Tony's risk-taking and especially his binge gambling make sense as an attempt to break out of the chronic unfulfillment of affluenza and the strain of inner conflict. He invests in a racehorse to enjoy the "break neck" abandon of the race. His trips to Las Vegas are headlong lunges at fortune. He is an acute expression of the risk-taking that infected the national mood in the go-go1990s. Many churches and state governments relaxed traditional strictures on gambling. Indian tribes erected gaming palaces. Investors called the stock market a casino. Tony's Las Vegas is more intoxicated than imaginative, an infantile Disneyland goosed up by winking sin. In Mike Figgis's *Leaving Las Vegas* (1995) the casino's glitter stands for exhausted sexual greed and suicidal compulsion. The mob's formative role in the gambling "industry" links making a killing to the tabloid "Murder Incorporated" associated with Vegas through Meyer Lansky and Bugsy Siegel. Martin Scorcese chronicled these mob exploits in *Casino* (1995), and now the city has a museum to enshrine its shopworn gangster mythology.

The corporate counterpart of the Vegas casino was the glitzy Enron tower in Houston, in which one trading floor was a stage set designed to fool visitors while executives gambled on future valuations and manipulated markets to favor the house. The trading floor was a "boiler room" operation of the sort mobsters use to peddle crooked securities. CEO Ken Lay infiltrated regulatory agencies, plying politicians up to the White House the way mafia pays off public officials. In the end speculation crowded out any semblance of productivity, and Ponzi dynamics took over. What *Fortune* magazine called "America's Most Innovative Company" turned out to be relying on frantic momentum and mafia deceit.

Enron's godfather and his inner circle projected godlike confidence. They could be suavely brutal as their millions of victims found out. Alex Gibney's documentary *The Smartest Guys in the Room* (2005) shows them verbally flogging their underlings to do-or-die exertions, while on private weekend retreats, like macho adolescents, they show off their daredevil bravado on dirt bikes. The biker play-acting suggests the unreal atmosphere surrounding their world-conquering ruthlessness. Abetted by unscrupulous accounting, the inner circle acted out a more elevated version of Tony Soprano's greed not just for loot, but for meaning. What we can glimpse of their inner lives is scripted by phony gentility and macho posturing, refining into banality the animal fury and anguish the scriptwriters attribute to Tony Soprano.

The firm's violence damaged millions of lives. Indicted on 98 counts of fraud, conspiracy, insider trading, money laundering, and more, Andrew Fastow received a "discounted" prison sentence from a judge who said that he had been "the subject of great persecution," including threats and religious slurs." The former executive could "shave" another year off his sentence by participating in a drug program "to help wean him from the undisclosed substances he used to mask his anxiety." He was sentenced on the same day that Bernie Ebbers, founder of World Com, reported to prison. One former Enron employee working three jobs to stay afloat commented, "I'm not guilty of anything, but my sentence will be longer than Fastow's."[35] Even behind bars the executive still had leverage and unspoken connections working for him.

The Enron chiefs' adolescent derring-do on dirt bikes illustrates the quality of play-acting that Robert Reich called "A Culture of Paper Tigers."[36] The fantasies resonate with the "bad boy" self-image of bejeweled, paunchy rap stars or a president being landed aboard an aircraft carrier dressed up as a fighter pilot. This is the romance of abandon, the executive magic so crisply summed up in *The Leadership Secrets of Attila the Hun* (1985), where recycled aphorisms come dressed up in barbarian warrior garb, prescribing loyalty, courage, decisiveness, and other virtues, but also fiery ambition and a sharp sword. The would-be leader could profit from Attila's example without fretting that the Hun's business plan was literally cut-throat, and that all empires eventually dissolve.

The Sopranos dramatizes the tragic absurdity of survival greed. The more the mobsters grasp at illicit immortality fantasies, the more terrifying the abyss that opens beneath their feet. It should not surprise us that as the neocon United States overreached in its quest for an American century, the doom of the Roman Empire began to haunt op-ed writers. In financial culture Wall Street bankers with nicknames like mafia chieftains chased magical profits and ended up in a vertiginous global credit collapse.

That queasy sense of the abyss creates the survival rage that drives even the striped-tie psychopaths in the executive suite. In the film *Wall Street,* Gordon Gecko is given to outbursts that turn mafia-style enforcement into berserk rage, "When I get a hold of the son of a bitch who leaked this," he screams, "I'm gonna tear his eyeballs out and I'm gonna suck his fucking skull." This is cannibalistic, vampire rage. The tantrum telegraphs creaturely motives ordinarily masked by the opaque windows of a limousine.

The social scientist Robert Hare concludes that many top executives "are callous, cold-blooded individuals. . . . They have no sense of guilt or remorse . . . if I wasn't studying psychopaths in prison, I'd do it at the stock exchange."[37] In a *New Yorker* cartoon (August 10 and 17, 2009) a personnel manager tells a Viking applying for a job: "Your resume is remarkably similar to our C.E.O.'s." In other *New Yorker* cartoons the boss's office usually commands the skyline with a window so huge that it evokes the "primary narcissism" of the young child who wants, as Ernest Becker says, to "swallow the world" (37). It may have a trapdoor that drops fired underlings into the abyss of social death.

Enron's magic factory was not just a flashy glass showplace. Like the rules and rites of "mafia" that turn a gang of appetites into the enabling fiction of Tony's "family," the Enron tower was above all manufacturing an illusion of heroic purpose desperately needed in a culture whose convictions and consolations cry out for renewal.

CHAPTER 5

RAGE FOR ORDER

Government . . . derives its moral authority from God. It is the minister of God with powers to 'avenge' to 'execute wrath' including even wrath by the sword. . . . Indeed, it seems to me that the more Christian a country is, the less likely it is to regard the death penalty as immoral

Supreme Court Justice Antonin Scalia

Conventional wisdom thinks of "what is right" as an abstract principle or a cosmic code such as "the word of God." But the need to feel right is built into us. It is part of the operating system that enables an ephemeral creature to feel at home in an overwhelming world. It supports the conviction that our lives have lasting meaning: that we matter. When that conviction falters, self-esteem suffers, and we face the fear "not so much of extinction, but extinction with insignificance."[1] No wonder people will kill to feel right.

This chapter explores the way berserk style conditions moral outrage. Research shows hatred of unfairness to be linked in the brain's "conflict detection" circuitry (the dorsal anterior cingulated cortex). Some people are especially primed to feel personal indignation, and outrage can seethe beneath outward calm.[2] Moral aggression is routinely and transparently engrained in childhood. In Disney's hugely popular *Beauty and the Beast* (1991) the jealous lout Gaston fires up Belle's neighbors to attack the Beast-Prince. After a treacherous clash with the Beast-Prince on the parapet of his palace, the defeated Gaston "falls" into an abyss and the rampaging neighbors gratuitously vanish. Happiness comes about not through negotiation or law but through annihilation. The neighbors have run amok, but berserk style enables

Belle and the Prince to exterminate them in a wink and live happily ever after, to the satisfaction of young audiences.

An adult version of the exterminating wink is a vigilante film such as *Death Wish* (1974). In James Wan's *Death Sentence* (2007) a father (Kevin Bacon) loses nearly his entire family to evil gang members and righteously slaughters them all. The fight to the death takes place with the connivance of the police and ends in catatonic exhaustion, with the hero gazing at his chirpy ideal family singing onscreen in a home video. Berserk exertion, that is, equivocally idealizes—and derealizes—the family. But it is also the film's only reason for being. One critic complained that the director was "too busy jamming the accelerator to realize that his movie's spinning out of control."[3]

Magical annihilation can be an instrument of public policy. After the September 11 attacks, for example, President Bush proclaimed "this crusade, this war on terrorism." As CNN reported on September 16, he "vows to rid the world of 'evil-doers.'" The president later disavowed the word "crusade," but there was no mistaking the use of moral abandon to justify his heroic stature and the wars to come. His rhetoric blocked any curiosity about motives and shades of guilt. As governor of Texas, Bush cultivated a reputation for denying mercy in death penalty cases, a symptom of his "willingness to make punishment his preferred response to social problems."[4]

Like torture, punishment uses pain to engrain what is right, and the ultimate punishment is of course death, as Adam and Eve found out. But punishment is a protean tool with as many guises as it has applications. To be forced to write a rule a hundred times on a black-board counts as education. When Bart Simpson does it, satire scolds hypocrisy. Punishment calls for attention in this book when, as moral aggression, it goes amok.

In the Vietnam era the global policeman sought to punish Ho Chi Minh's upstart regime and teach a lesson to Communists every-where. At home, on behalf of President Nixon's "silent majority" (1969), police faced off against marchers for social justice and a "counter-culture" bent on sex, drugs, and rock 'n' roll. At the extremes, each position in this agon was conflicted and inconsistent. The exasperated Weather Underground tried to enforce social justice with homemade bombs. The "Revolution" that would "tune in and drop out" was also morally strident about the rightness of "doing it in the road" and "letting it all hang out." Grotesquely, in mid-skirmish, some of the silent majority's rectitude went to jail with the moralizing Vice President Agnew, and into forced retirement with President Nixon.

The cultural stress convulsed in the Detroit and Watts riots, in police brawls with antiwar demonstrators, and in political assassinations. Nixon and the dissenters were both right that the nation was reinforcing its image as universal policeman. As futility and humiliation loomed in the war, demands for "law and order" at home began trying to restore self-esteem by "getting tough" on scapegoats in John G. Avildsen's vigilante movie *Joe* (1970), which imagined a wealthy New Yorker and a factory worker joining forces to massacre a commune of drug-indulgent "peacenik" hippies. In this domestic echo of My Lai bloodlust one of the vigilantes tragically kills his own daughter, driving home the film's moral ambivalence.

But outrage was armed and punitive outside the movie theater as well. To choke off dissent at Berkeley, then Governor Reagan sent in military helicopters to teargas students. Resurrecting the war against Hitler, he vowed: "If it takes a bloodbath, let's get it over with. No more appeasement!"[5] Challenged about this incitement to a "bloodbath," he dismissed critics as "neurotic." He managed to project righteous wrath while falling back on style—the put-down—to sugar coat it. A few days later, in May 1970, the Ohio National Guard shot four Kent State University students to death, and later that month at Jackson State College police killed two more students. The underlying trope of the "shootout" echoed the plot logic of cop and cowboy melodramas and the psychological plunge into action associated with hair-trigger high noon confrontation. Reagan's "shoot from the hip" language was using melodramatic materials from his movie career, even as forces within the culture were using him to legitimize a rage for order.

In the 1970s the lost war in Vietnam and the abandoned war on poverty transformed into a war on drugs. The Nixon and Reagan drug wars went beyond public health concerns, cracking down on the oppositional spirit that had "lost" the war. In the depressed post-Vietnam economy the drug war worked to police the inner city as suburban flight left a stranded cohort of young black males in need of jobs. By 2007, when Marc Mauer and Ryan S. King of the prison advocacy group published "A Twenty-Five Year Quagmire: The War on Drugs and Its Impact on American Society," the demand for punishment had mushroomed. The number of drug offenders incarcerated since 1980 had increased 1,100 percent, the majority—60 percent—with "no history of violence or high-level drug-selling activity."[6]

Still, drugs were only part of the prosecutorial boom. "Around 1975 . . . the United States became radically more punitive. In thirty-five years, the incarceration rate ballooned [from 100] to over 700 per

100,000, far outstripping all other countries."[7] The data point to a slow-motion criminal justice rampage. In part it was a response to economic distress following the guns-and-butter binge and the dashed hopes of the war on poverty. By the 1980s middle-class families faced growing insecurity and journalists were discovering homelessness and "latchkey kids."

Anxiety about family contributed to the moral panic that kept the prison system expanding. Almost as soon as the last helicopter fled Saigon, *Time* magazine was targeting youth crime as the new enemy: "How can such sadistic acts—expressions of what moral philosophers would call sheer evil—be explained satisfactorily by poverty and deprivation? What is it in our society that produces mindless rage?"[8]

By the 1990s economic blight had magnified the alarm. In the decade of the Los Angeles riots (1992) the riot zone lost 50,000 jobs. "In the vacuum, youthful rage exploded again in gang warfare." In this atmosphere all parties resorted to berserk style to account for carnage and the failure of public policy. Tom Hayden warned: "We need to find alternatives to the 'embedded sense of self-hate' that propels so many inner-city youth to lash out in killing sprees." By contrast, "conservatives such as William Bennett and James Q. Wilson began attaching the label of 'super-predator' to all the [potential killers]. Their notion seemed to be that a fixed percentage of kids were natural-born killers who just couldn't be helped by better schools or jobs—a neo-Darwinian philosophy that fit neatly with the de-industrialization and budget cuts that swept across inner cities like chain saws through old-growth forests." In turn, "The super-predator thesis justified the most massive prison expansion in American history, with its epicenter in California, where there were about 150,000 inmates in any given year, two-thirds of them reputed gang members."[9]

As more urban black men went to prison, "bad boy" or "gangsta" role-playing became a calculated product of industrial entertainment, celebrating themes of kamikaze defiance, starry glitz, and sexual dominance. Like Prohibition-era gangster epics, the rap phenomenon was richly ambivalent: socially aware yet also regressive and reactionary. The performer Biggie Smalls (Christopher Wallace) sold "ready to Die" (1994) to become a celebrity, and was murdered two weeks before his release of "Life After Death" (1997) at age 24.

The youth scare had its ambivalent counterpart in the remarkable upsurge in "child abuse hysteria" that lasted into the 1990s.[10] Just as long-simmering frustration overreacted to the Great Society "war on poverty" with urban riots, so efforts to redress inequality and domestic violence unexpectedly contributed to an acute sensitivity to abuse.

A sense of emergency eventually generated a cluster of group fantasies centered on "multiple personality disorder" (MPD) and "recovered memory"—phenomena reminiscent of the spectral evidence seized upon in witchcraft panics.[11] Fantasies about satanic cults, abduction by aliens, and mind-control inflated abuse to supernatural proportions— a story for the following chapter.

Pressured by alarmed parents and police, some children began reporting sensational sexual predation that entangled innocent day care providers and fathers in the criminal justice system. "The recovered memory movement readily embraced the idea of male violence, particularly that of repressed C.S.A. [child sexual abuse] at the hands of fathers, step-fathers, and other male authority figures. Women (overwhelmingly white and middle class) who sought counseling for alcohol and drug problems, depression, eating disorders, and a variety of other conditions were told by their therapists that they were abuse victims because they showed the "symptoms" of C.S.A., despite the fact that most had no conscious memories of such childhood violence. Many were encouraged to "abreact," or recover and relive the repressed memories, and to join ongoing incest survivor self-help groups to aid in their "recovery."[12] In a classic case former police officer Clyde Ray Spencer spent 20 years in prison after a conviction for sexually molesting his son and daughter. He was released in 2009 when his children testified that the abuse never happened.[13] Belatedly the children recognized that their divorced mother apparently used berserk style as a weapon against her ex-husband. Only when psychological research and the courts reasserted evidentiary standards, barring recovered memory as testimony, did the hysteria abate.

The policeman's imprisonment is a telling parable of berserk style in a complex historical moment. The real suffering of women and children was badly served by popular self-help books such as *The Courage to Heal*. The authors advise readers that "[i]f you think you were sexually abused and your life shows the symptoms, then you were." In their view nonspecific and subjective complaints of anxiety, depression, and their somatized effects qualify as symptoms. The authors go on to incite self-intoxicating rage: it is "[a] little like priming the pump, you can do things that will get your anger started. Then, once you get the hang of it, it'll begin to flow on its own. . . . Many survivors have strong feelings of wanting to get back at the people who hurt them so terribly. You may dream of murder or castration. It can be pleasurable to fantasize such scenes in vivid detail. Wanting revenge is a natural impulse, a sane response. Let yourself imagine it to your heart's content."[14] The payoff for this berserk abandon, predictably, is the release of superhuman resources: "Imagine all women healed—and all that energy no longer used for mere survival but made available for . . . freeing political prisoners, ending the arms race" (129).

This advice ignores the self-intoxicating, self-destructive dangers of rage, which is after all the reason Christianity advocates mercy and forgiveness. But the advice also ignored the actual experience of victims, which as psychologist Susan A. Clancy has reported, usually does not involve violent injury, however reprehensible the violation.[15] As in so many other incarnations of the berserk trope, convictions of victimization have perverse consequences: "a newer 'third wave' of feminism has produced scathing critiques about feminist theory and practice that is rooted in the concept of victimization. . . . Requiring women to assume the role of the 'victim,' a person who is perpetually in recovery, has been criticized for being disempowering as well as being a suppression of women's rights to sexual, psychological, and economic freedom. Nonetheless, "victim feminism," as it has been dubbed, was an integral part of the recovery culture that emerged in the 1980s" (Robbins).

DYING TO BE RIGHT

The core themes of victimization and outraged justice are nowhere more tragically visible than in the debate over capital punishment. Advocates of the death penalty resist international calls for a ban and deny the evidence that led Governor George Ryan to impose a moratorium in Illinois after 13 people on death row were exonerated (January 31, 2000). The debate foregrounds conflicting data about capital punishment's effectiveness as a deterrent, as if those percentages, one way or another, could be sufficient grounds for policy. The emotions aroused—fury, guilt, and terror—understandably conjure up berserk style. Although more than 130 prisoners on death row have been exonerated since 1976, some prosecutors continue to fight to discredit DNA and other evidence. Supreme Court Justice Scalia has openly maintained that "this court has *never* held that the Constitution forbids the execution of a convicted defendant who had a full and fair trial but is later able to convince a habeas court that he is 'actually' innocent."[16] The peculiar tone of this chilling statement, with its scare quotes around "actually," raises troubling concerns that go beyond courtroom debate.

In an unsettled historical moment prosecutors and public opinion are outraged on behalf of real victims whose suffering cries out for justice. Opposed to executions in the days of the liberal Warren Supreme Court, majority public opinion became more aggressive as the criminal justice system did. In recent decades politics and popular Christianity have relentlessly foregrounded hot-button issues such as abortion and homosexuality, and racial prejudice undoubtedly bears upon the disproportionate number of minority males put to death. At the same time television dramas have distorted forensic science and occult detection to allay doubts about justice.

Even at the highest level Supreme Court Justice Scalia uses morally charged and unaccountable beliefs to justify capital punishment. Though ostensibly a "strict constructionist" in constitutional law, the Catholic Scalia maintains that

> for the believing Christian, death is no big deal. Intentionally killing an innocent person is a big deal: it is a grave sin, which causes one to lose his soul. But losing this life, in exchange for the next? The Christian attitude is reflected in the words Robert Bolt's play has Thomas More saying to the headsman: 'Friend, be not afraid of your office. You send me to God.' . . . For the nonbeliever, on the other hand, to deprive a man of his life is to end his existence. What a horrible act! Besides being *less* likely to regard death as an utterly cataclysmic punishment, the Christian is also *more* likely to regard punishment in general as deserved. The doctrine of free will—the ability of man to resist temptations to evil, which God will not permit beyond man's capacity to resist—is central to the Christian doctrine of salvation and damnation, heaven and hell. The post-Freudian secularist, on the other hand, is more inclined to think that people are what their history and circumstances have made them, and there is little sense in assigning blame.[17]

"Death is no big deal" unless of course you happen to be wrongly put to death. The justice reduces the bewildering variety of religious experience to "the Christian" and attacks a straw man, the "post-Freudian secularist." In this rhetoric Christian theology shrinks to a historically shadowy anecdote used by a dramatist in a popular hagiography. Murder is terrifying—"a horrible act!"—yet in theory Christian murder victims achieve bliss with God, so the rhetoric boxes in deep ambivalence. Scalia's Gospel sees no incoherence here and has no room for Christian mercy. The justice is weighing the power to kill accused individuals, but his argument refuses to contemplate actual behavior. Its stereotypes foster psychic impunity by polarizing categories and ignoring the quality of evidence. At no point does Scalia acknowledge that he is talking about faith in immortality that by definition is beyond any rational standard: and that such faith could be used to legitimize judicial murder or a genocidal crusade. At the same time he imagines that all murders are deliberate acts, ignoring the roles of panic and accident, not to mention organic dysfunction.

Rage for order is both a behavior and an idea about behavior. Justice Scalia, for instance, is attracted to the idea of punishment: "the Christian is also *more* likely to regard punishment in general as deserved." He imagines a world cleanly divided between the righteous and the damned—believers and nonbelievers, Christians and "Post-Freudian secularists," and so on. In this mindset the deep structure is melodrama. Differing imaginations don't overlap, wonder at the infinite varieties of creation, agonize over how to get at the truth, or rue our tragic inadequacy ("God will not permit [temptation] beyond man's capacity to resist"). Social life is not a matter of trade, negotiation, mutation, and adaptation, but rather an adrenalized struggle to identify and punish, empowered by a conviction of godlike invulnerability.

The issue is not whether judgment will exist, but what form will it take? How much is enough? Who gets to judge? On what evidence? And who will police the system? History groans with mass movements and cults that have thrived on predatory righteousness. The self-intoxicating effects of moral aggression stand out in Philip G. Zimbardo's famous Stanford Prison Experiment, which had to be halted early when student volunteers in the roles of prison guards began slipping into sadism and the inmates' depression became self-confirming. But this was only an experiment, not the living horror of a false conviction and judicial murder—the likely fate of people such as Cameron Todd Willingham, whom Texas officials put to death in 2004 despite demonstrably faulty evidence and a feckless appeals process.[18]

In his retirement, with moving humility, Justice John Paul Stevens abjured his support for the death penalty decades earlier. Reviewing reasons that capital punishment is "unwise and unjustified," Stevens called attention to the creaturely motives underlying American cultural practices that make the law perverse, quoting the argument of David Garland's *Peculiar Institution: America's Death Penalty in an Age of Abolition* (2010). Not only is the death penalty not a deterrent to crime, it actually promotes "gratifications," of "professional and political users, of the mass media, and of its public audience." With its demonstrable racial biases and its role in the Republican Party's "southern strategy" as well as in the post-Vietnam "culture wars," capital punishment has served political ends. But beyond these motives, even beyond revenge, Stevens and Garland see at work "the American fascination with death"—specifically, the "emotional power of imagining killing and death. [Garland] concludes that 'the American death penalty has been transformed from a penal instrument that puts persons to death to a peculiar institution that puts death into discourse for political and cultural purposes.'"[19]

How much order is enough? During the 2008 financial crisis and political transition, partisan media began accusing the new mixed-race president of "Nazi" socialism. Journalists in turn favored stories about the threat of civil disorder and an apparent spike in gun sales. Though in January 2009 the FBI reported that crime had declined in 2008, "Nearly a third of Americans surveyed in the Rasmussen poll say crime has increased in their neighborhoods, and 72 percent say it's very likely that crime will grow in the near-term. . . . The fears are in some cases taking on a Y2K-like fervor, forecasting total social meltdown. In times such as these, Americans have always reached for their guns, says David Kopel, research director for the Independence Institute, a free-market-oriented think tank. . . . He digs up a clipping from a Massachusetts newspaper published three months before the 'Shot Heard Around the World' that started the Revolutionary War. . . . Modern fears are fueled by the prospect of an apocalyptic economic failure." Gun-toting rage for order predictably invokes the Revolutionary War and the Constitution. "'The logic is simple,' says Tom Lee, a member of the Virginia Citizen Militia, which traces its roots to the Revolutionary War. 'People are seeing a looming economic collapse that will lead to a prolonged and possibly worsening breakdown of law and order and, eventually, a We-the-People vs. armed-government-enforcers scenario.'"[20]

"We-the-people" here are rhetorical phantoms, a means for Tom Lee to pump up his morale and his cause. Rather than fighting off the US military and anarchic marauders, Tom Lee is fortifying self-esteem with firearms. In July 2009, Tennessee prepared to enact a law allowing loaded handguns in bars. The deep motives are thoroughly masked and denied by Kentucky pastor Ken Pagano, who "told his flock to bring handguns to church in what he said was an effort to promote safe gun ownership." Disguising survival dread as patriotism and placing more faith in guns than God, he boasts that "[i]f it were not for a deep-seated belief in the right to bear arms, this country would not be here today" (BBC News, July 13, 2009). His determination to "send a message" uses a phrase associated with combat berserking and mafia threat. It also exemplifies the "emotional power of imagining killing and death" to which Justice Stevens refers.

Potentially such thinking enables "God-fearing patriots" or "we the people" to take the law into their own hands. Such extralegal behavior mirrors mafias, which also operate as a primitive legal system, adjudicating disputes and interpreting local codes. To be sure, a godfather caricatures a judge and jury, particularly when mafias resort to the death penalty, as in the nickname of Albert Anastasia, "the Lord High Executioner" of Murder Incorporated. Mafia's "soldiers" impose a surreptitious form of martial law and "tithes" on behalf of an unelected elite. In *The Sopranos*, whether they are punishing an allegedly abusive girl's soccer coach, a closeted gay, or a traitor, the mobsters talk themselves into a fury. And since they live in chronic fear of rivals and law enforcement, punishment of scapegoats allows them to discharge their own worst terrors as rage against others.

STRIKING BACK

The most spectacular sign of rage for order is the nation's record-breaking prison population.[21] With less than 5 percent of the world's population, the United States has almost a quarter of the world's prisoners. "Indeed, the United States leads the world in producing prisoners, a reflection of a relatively recent and now entirely distinctive American approach to crime and punishment." Americans "are locked up for crimes—from writing bad checks to using drugs—that would rarely produce prison sentences in other countries. And in particular they are kept incarcerated far longer than prisoners in other nations." What is more, the criminal justice system has corralled a disproportionate number of black men, women, and immigrants. Statistics show no upsurge in crime to explain the phenomenon. "Criminologists and legal scholars in other industrialized nations say they are mystified and appalled by the number and length of American prison sentences."[22]

Michael J. Moore's film *The Legacy* (1999) records some of the ways in which berserk style affected the abandonment of reform and rehabilitation—hope—as the goal of the criminal justice system. Moore documents the process that forced California's draconian Three Strikes law through a skeptical legislature. By the Turn of the 21st Century, California had a larger proportion of its population in prison than any country on earth. The film centers on two parents who lost daughters in brutal murders and took leading roles in the frenzied process that led to passage of the law. In 1992, during what began as a minor mugging, two recently released ex-convicts murdered college student Kimberly Reynolds in a flash of cold rage—the berserker's "flaming ice." The heavily armed killer later died in a firefight with police that was tantamount to a combat rampage.

In reaction to his daughter's death at the hands of repeat offenders, Mike Reynolds, a Fresno wedding photographer, began organizing a push for the "Three Strikes and You're Out" initiative (Proposition 184). The witty allusion to baseball trivializes the law's overkill, which mandates prison terms of 25 years to life for a third felony conviction, even though the third strike could be petty theft, shoplifting, a forged check, or another nonviolent offense.

At first legislators found Three Strikes simplistic and counter-productive, and Reynolds's campaign stalled. A year later, however, an ex-con abducted and killed 12-year-old Polly Klaas. The public anguish and outrage reached around the globe, amplified by inflammatory media coverage. In time police arrested the feral-looking repeat offender Richard Allen Davis, and the public outcry attracted politicians and new financial support, and turned Reynolds's flagging campaign into a crusade.

Early on in the referendum process critics foresaw the danger of overkill: "Data clearly shows that counties that vigorously and strictly enforce the 'Three Strikes' law did not experience a decline in any crime category relative to more lenient counties."[23] And in fact a majority of "Three Strikes" sentences have been for nonviolent offenses. California has imprisoned a disproportionate number of young black men, many for drug-possession.[24] The bill's coauthor, California politician Bill Jones, vowed that the goal is "zero" crime, a goal as unrealistic as it is perverse. For as in distressed Flint Michigan during General Motors' epic triage of its workforce, the demand for control and punishment diverted to the prison industry resources for productive investment in education, job training, and therapy.[25]

Despite criticism of the bill's excesses, Reynolds was able to step up his campaign when the appalling murder of Polly Klaas roused a paroxysm of public anguish and fury. As the Proposition 184 initiative became a hot-button issue, Michael Huffington and other political figures appropriated some of its energy. The National Rifle Association, the prison guards' union, and other parties contributed funds; a corporation loaned a plane; and talk radio shock jocks scapegoated skeptical lawmakers and inflamed "the court of public opinion." Under pressure the reluctant legislature began to respond.

Conceptually the Three Strikes movement took on some of the features found in large-scale group violence. Polly Klaas's murderer came to stand for an out group that public imagination expanded to include all repeat offenders menacing or not. "Our" survival—the posterity embodied in vulnerable young women—depended on overcoming this "monster." So intense was the fear and outrage that Governor Pete Wilson reversed his opposition and in the legislature attempts to tame the Three Strikes bill's excesses failed.

Before the camera Mike Reynolds does not dwell on his anguish at his daughter's death. Rather, he presents himself as a resolute citizen humbly triumphing over arrogant, indifferent politicians. Looking back from a position of considerable influence as the "father" of the law, now depicted on the Three Strikes website as a heroic rescuer of untold potential victims, he makes self-effacing gestures. But more complex posttraumatic motives show through. Criminals are "those animals": he has no curiosity about their motivation and makes no distinctions about levels of threat. He remains fearful that some day a criminal will murder him as the father of Three Strikes.

As the campaign intensified, Reynolds defied criticism of the initiative. He needed to appear humbly reasonable, but the role of crusader counters depressive feelings of helplessness and grief, and in the film he admires the radio shock jocks whose aggression helped to whip up public fury. "Those guys are a couple of chainsaws!" he gushes. His language imagines not reform but annihilation of any opposition, and evokes Tobe Hooper's sadistic thriller "The Texas Chain Saw Massacre" (1974). In his zeal to punish, Reynolds began to treat government itself as culpable in the murders, as if "the authorities" can eliminate all risk from life. At one point, like a terrorist, he exults that Three Strikes supporters phoning legislators in Sacramento "melted" the switchboard and brought government to a halt.

The media "chainsaws" inflamed—and prospered from—the public's concerns. The issue perfectly suited the theater of righteousness and retribution that talk media had been perfecting for a decade or more. Like supermarket gossip tabloids, the shock jocks operate in a zone of half-knowledge, screening out inconvenient inhibitions and complexities in order to intensify "the money shot"—the thrill of venting self-righteous wrath. Rupert Murdoch's Fox is famous for the stagey indignation of commentators such as Bill O'Reilly, who in 2005 "had one of his tantrums and told would-be terrorists to 'go ahead' and blow [gay San Francisco] off the map."[26] O'Reilly's widely broadcast threat-display is of course itself a form of terrorism, acting to cow some people and pump up others.

When Governor Wilson signed the Three Strikes bill and handed Mike Reynolds the ceremonial pen, Reynolds brandished it before the cameras and declared: "This pen, with this bill, is like the .357 magnum of pens. This is the toughest, hardest crime bill not only California has proposed but the entire country has ever seen." He was wielding a symbolic equivalent of the weapon that killed his daughter, and the pen reveals the pressure of rage. Although Reynolds's conviction of power arguably helped him cope with traumatic loss, his fantasy of merciless punishment mirrors the killers' cold rage—the berserk state's "flaming ice."

The injured father wanted total revenge, no matter how many people might lose their lives to unjust prison sentences. His fantasy aligns him with the vigilante fathers who run amok in movies such as Michael Winner's *Death Wish* (1974) after attacks on wives or daughters, or with soldiers who slaughtered "enemy" villagers in Iraq to avenge dead comrades. In addition to assuaging personal agony, the role of vigilante hero in American movies is tacitly messianic: a fantasy of rescuing society by exercising power over life and death. Yet Reynolds sees the pen—prison—not primarily as protection from harm, but as a vindictive weapon to kill all the "animals." Since a Three Strikes conviction mandates a de facto life sentence, the law does impose social death. In this sense Reynolds is reenacting the original murder of his daughter, but this time armed with a legislative pistol and personally taking the lives of a potentially endless mob of killers.

After wrestling with his own anger, Marc Klaas, Polly's father, came to see the overkill in Proposition 184, finally persuaded that the law would be indiscriminate and unjust. Although he joined others to oppose the referendum, it passed by an overwhelming margin. Even so, having suffered the same grief, Klaas recognizes the depth of Reynolds's rage when he excuses him for ignoring the family's request that Polly's name not be used to promote the Three Strikes agenda.

One sign of overkill in the legislation was the provisions that make modifying it exceptionally difficult, even though prison costs have soared, taking money from social services, and crime rates fail to confirm the law's effectiveness. A chart in Moore's film shows funding for higher education cut back by nearly the same amount as prison costs were rising. In March 2003 a divided Supreme Court upheld the convictions of two Three Strikes prisoners serving 25-year-to-life and 50-year sentences for stealing golf clubs from a country club and videotapes from two convenience stores. The justices reversed a federal appeals court that had declared the 50-year sentence "grossly disproportionate," violating the Eighth Amendment's ban against cruel and unusual punishment. Twenty-six other states adopted "three strikes" statues, although none were as severe as California's version.

After passage of the law Reynolds continued to be frightened about murder. On camera he fantasizes about retaliation against him for fathering "the toughest, hardest crime bill . . . the entire country has ever seen" At a traffic light, he says, a criminal "could recognize me as that Three Strikes guy, and I'm gone." Even with the "toughest, hardest" punishment at work, fears persist. Reynolds imagines himself as an important enforcer meeting a martyr's end.

ZERO TOLERANCE

The cry for "zero tolerance" played tout in an atmosphere of heightened insecurity. Magazines in the dentist's office warned of inner-city gangs and teen "superpredators." While ads for SUVs stressed size and comfort, the subtext was always survival in a hostile world. GM's tank-like Hummer featured the slogan "HOPE: Hummer Owners Prepared for Emergencies." Not by coincidence, news stories of "road rage" grew along with the cars, usually describing a vigilante driver bent on punishing someone else for aggressive driving.

The traffic jam is a vivid trope for the larger social problem of surplus people. As in Flint Michigan, law enforcement and new prisons triaged the troublesome unemployed along with society's unruly, unlucky, and incompetent losers. The criminal justice system aggressively prosecuted low-status black males. Where the "great society" of 1960s had imagined society as a system of shared concerns, moral alarm depicted a familiar neighborhood menaced by intruders—Mike Reynolds's "animals."

Television generally reinforces insecurity by exaggerating the incidence of violence in everyday life. But broadcasters try to frame threat in ways that excite thrills while keeping fear within bounds. In the late 1990s "real-life" cop shows showed triage at work as the camera followed police into the incoherent, squalid world at the bottom of society. Television shows such as COPS watch local police as they subdue a "group of people who are permanently down on their luck for a variety of reasons: momentarily or chronically dysfunctional, inveterate 'outsiders' and misfits . . . weak of character and prone to the worst kind of judgment. When encountered, most are under the influence of drugs or alcohol." They include incompetent petty criminals, immigrants, and mentally ill as well as homeless people, "But since the concept of homelessness has no place in the universe of COPS, these individuals are simply part of the population who are endlessly and violently out of control and in trouble with the law." They inhabit "a world of nothing but brawls, bars, hookers, mental breakdowns, and outbursts. It is difficult to comprehend any of it in any human or social terms."[27]

In each episode of COPS, that is, berserk style frames life at the bottom as alien, out of control, and beyond help—which absolves the viewer of any responsibility. The camera especially lingers on "a person going more and more out of control, in ways that are painful to watch. Often the person will be wildly, violently rebellious and hysterical. Unkempt, often barely clothed, and surrounded by filth and chaos, he or she is allowed to gyrate and gesticulate as the cops show saint-like restraint." They are "tabloid criminals . . . marked as subhuman and different than 'normal' Americans like the police" (264).

In this scheme the berserk quality of moral citizens is euphemized as zero tolerance law enforcement at any cost. To pay for expanded prisons, the cost went up tenfold—and far beyond cuts in social services, education, and in the quality of life for inmates. "Three Strikes" zealots such as California Secretary of State Bill Jones frankly prescribed subsistence conditions for inmates. "Free market" ideology imagined that privatization and technology could make punishment cheaper. In many states inmates became commodities managed for profit by companies such as the Corrections Corporation of America. Overcrowding, inadequate medical care, and the overuse of solitary confinement are dangerously stressful for prisoners while behind bars and after their release. Five states spend as much on corrections as on higher education, and in California's prisons job training and education were cut virtually to nothing. Says one analyst: "there are large numbers of people behind bars who could be supervised in the community safely and effectively at a much lower cost—while also paying taxes, paying restitution to their victims and paying child support."[28]

As berserk stress ratcheted up, in short, the cultural system disabled ever-larger numbers of citizens instead of fostering their productivity. In such explosive conditions inmates' demands for humane treatment and institutional reflexes periodically escalate into bloody insurrection. During the prison population explosion since the 1980s, says Jeanne Woodford, the warden of San Quentin, "[t]he violence went out of control. . . . And then the programs started going away. I was there during an 18-month lockdown. It was unbelievably horrific."[29] The nominal recidivism rate of the 1980s shot up to 70 percent.

The folly of the system crystallized opposition. In a "scathing" order, for example, federal judges ordered the state of California to reduce its overcrowded prison population because that was "the only way to change what they called an unconstitutional prison health care system that causes one unnecessary death a week."[30]

Moral Fanaticism

We are deeply ambivalent about police "force." In its most radical form "Zero tolerance" means tyrannical control and extermination—the police state. Hence the fascination of dystopian sagas such as Orwell's *1984* and its offspring, Ridley Scott's *Blade Runner* (1982), Paul Verhoeven's *Robocop* (1987), and Andy Wachowski's *The Matrix* (1999). In these stories the corporation is an ambiguously cybernetic, totalitarian police state, persecuting its human subjects with the berserker's icy fury. When their victims resist, they fight back as insurgents in the equivalent of a workplace rampage.

As pure berserk force, the policing is implacable. In the *Terminator* films, for example, a computer called Skynet has gone amok, fusing global corporation and government in a drive to exterminate humanity. It dispatches a humanoid Terminator robot (Arnold Schwarzenegger) to assassinate a boy who would become a rebel leader. Skynet's behavior is moral aggression amok. To accomplish its mission of murder—"what is right"—the terminator evinces all the symptoms of the berserk state on the psychiatrist's list. The cyborg is godlike and beastlike, indifferent to pain, fear, and inhibitions. Repeatedly "killed," he recomposes or resurrects himself with invincible purpose, fixed on killing.

Today's military analog to the cyber assassin is "smart weapons." They are selfless warriors but can turn on the innocent, as in US-occupied Afghanistan, where for insurgents, the remote-controlled Predator drone that mistakenly kills civilians became a symbol of an American empire amok. In Paul Verhoeven's *Robocop* a policing cyborg goes haywire and destroys everything in sight. As the robots become increasingly superhuman, controls become treacherously critical. The US military is developing "self-governing, armed robots that could find and destroy targets on their own," says Ronald Arkin in a study commissioned by the Army. "The pressure of an increasing battlefield tempo is forcing autonomy further and further toward the point of robots making that final, lethal decision," he predicted. "The time available to make the decision to shoot or not to shoot is becoming too short for remote humans to make intelligent informed decisions."[31]

Skynet is a caricature of the "big government" that the electorate loves to fear and despise. On the deepest level, however, the police state speaks to the infantile guilt that is built into us. The vast world-machine can crush such puny mortals at any time. On this ("Skynet") scale we die because Death (or God) is punishing us for our unworthiness like Adam and Eve. Craving security, therefore, humans pour tremendous resources into rituals to placate the gods. Religious narratives insist on God's love and our obedient devotion.

In the *Terminator* films Skynet, like Satan's regime, has displaced the loving God and sent a demonic terrorist to destroy humankind's hope of leadership. In this cosmic frame the *Terminator* scenario fits an imaginative pattern that was ready to be put into service in interpretations of the September 11 terrorism. After the attacks people commonly saw the suicide terrorists as inhumanly machine-like assassins from a globe-girdling Islam akin to Skynet. They took the terrorists to be moral fanatics fixated on immortality and a paradise of virgins. Just as the later films in the series dramatize the *Terminator's* conversion to the human cause, so ranters such as Ann Coulter played to injured American righteousness by calling for the carpet bombing and conversion (!) of Muslims. In a larger frame, absurdly, not a few Muslims shared a version of the same fantasy dynamics, conceiving the United States as Skynet sending its terminator troops to exterminate Muslims and assassinate the heroic Osama bin Laden.

Closer to home, moral fanaticism has inspired rampage killers such as Timothy McVeigh, who bombed a federal office building to punish "big government" for attacks on marginal groups such as David Koresh's Branch Davidians. Hatred of the corporate state spurred the Unabomber, Ted Kaczynski, to hole up in an isolated shack and fabricate mail bombs to kill victims that he associated with the juggernaut he detested. His behavior illustrates the mirroring symmetry of moral aggression, since he was at once a crusader and a terrorist. It makes sense to regard his rage against depersonalizing, destructive institutional force as a blind effort to fight off the cold fury consuming his inner world.

Cinematic robots and cyborgs regularly dramatize the trancelike, solipsistic quality of fanaticism. On a personal level audience fascination with the metallic, indestructible Terminator, say, is akin to the public fear of—and fascination with—autism and an alleged epidemic of autism that developed in the 1990s. The popular conception of the autistic personality as an uncanny, hyperfocused savant unable to relate to others easily overlaps with the idea of the godlike, insensate berserker.

The most literal use of the autistic trope is the HBO television series *Dexter*, in which the protagonist Dexter Morgan (Michael C. Hall) is a crime lab technician by day, and by night a righteous serial killer of criminals who have evaded the law. The premise is that Dexter is autistic. Adopted, he learned from his stepfather, a Miami cop, to mimic enough social skills to mask his alienation from ordinary human feelings. Though his emotional life is all studied play-acting, the sentimental kicker is that he is more sensitive than ordinary people.

As a vigilante, Dexter sneaks about like a conventional gumshoe. Like the unemotional Sherlock Holmes, he dramatizes the fantasy that release from empathic inhibitions makes possible masterful penetration of the masks and illusions of ordinary life. Like Holmes in his reckless cocaine addiction, Dexter is a creature of berserk style, compulsively risking his life to "execute" lawbreakers by pseudo-surgical vivisection in a clinically tidy version of the psychopath's secret torture chamber and the forensic lab's deconstruction of cadavers. In his words, "I'm a very neat monster." Like the Sopranos's mafia, Dexter's autism is meant to fascinate and allure as well as scare viewers.

Despite its novel rationale for sadistic aggression, the series has a recognizable lineage. As executions, Dexter's operations are a sanitized replay of the "death by a thousand cuts" recorded, for example, in the photograph of a vivisected Chinese assassin that haunted Georges Bataille.[32] To the extent that his laboratory life is believable, Dexter is a version of Mary Shelley's "mad doctor" Victor Frankenstein and his misunderstood, murderous creature. Dexter's vigilante dissections recall anatomists' experiments upon the cadavers of criminals moralized in Hogarth's ghastly *The Reward of Cruelty* and a history of illicit practices going back to the middle ages.[33] The dissection of immobilized victims also euphemizes Jeffrey Dahmer's attempts to turn his victims into living dead "zombies" with injections before satisfying his fetishism for body parts: a sequence Dexter follows when he injects his former lover Lila with a spinal epidural, lays her out on a sofa, and stabs her in the heart. From his victims Dexter draws and collects blood samples as clinical souvenirs. The fetish for blood evokes vampire lore in treatments such as John Landis's film *Innocent Blood* (1992), in which the beautiful Anne Parillaud plays a cosmopolitan vampire who preys only upon gangsters, making her an irresistible vigilante.

In keeping with the series' sordid ironical tone, Dexter disposes of body parts from his powerboat as Tony Soprano does. The boat's jokey name, "Slice of Life," locates one of the series' seductive features: like its marketing taglines ("He's Got a Way with Murder") and Dexter himself, it advertises forbidden fantasies with deadpan irony. Vicariously, voyeuristically, *Dexter* cannot help exercising the sadistic feelings that its hero supposedly transcends—or at least cannot imagine. In this way the show resembles the thrillingly equivocal *24*, in which torture is also assumed to be inexhaustibly righteous. Its cruelty vibrates to the fascination that has made Jack the Ripper's disemboweling of prostitutes in the 1890s a staple of entertainment.

Dexter's America is a nation of theatrical surfaces and crass procedures. The script's basic assumption is that everyone is tacitly autistic, faking authentic feeling, but only the "genuinely" autistic can see it. Catching a teenage killer, Dexter tells him: "I'm a lot like you . . . I'm empty. But I found a way to make it feel less bottomless. Pretend. You pretend the feelings are there for the world. For the people around you. Who knows. Maybe one day they will be." This is the core anxiety of modernity: the discovery that the self is finally ungrounded and therefore free—and also forced—to spin a sustaining web of fictions that can function as family and "family" do in mafia. In this light Dexter's emotionless vigilante rampage represents a desperate resort to judicial murder to ground the self in a world made uncompromisingly moral by vengeance. This is a euphemized form of authoritarianism or fundamentalism. Combined with the hope that pretending will one day "come true," it is also magical thinking: a belief that thinking can make things so.

In the first season, Dexter is taunted by an invisible serial killer who spies on him with the uncanny penetration of Satan. The idea that society abounds in serial killers is a cliché of pulp fiction, but it also echoes fundamentalist anxieties about a demon-infested world. At the same time the plot plays out the sadistic reactions to death-anxiety exploited in a new generation of crime shows and movies in which bodies are openly mutilated or "scientifically" cut apart in a forensic lab, as if to discover some physical source of evil. The programming resonates with the merger of fundamentalism and sadistic pseudoscience in the "war on terror," with its ideological absolutes, devilish religious enemies, chimerical "weapons of mass destruction," and the astonishing defense of extrajudicial—cf. vigilante—torture and surveillance.

PUNISHING LIFE

The fantasy of the autistic vigilante invites a reconsideration of the exhaustively reported Columbine High School killers, Eric Harris and Dylan Klebold (1999). The media initially moralized their motives, speculating that they had been victimized by a clique of bullying jocks. But the icy cruelty of their rage squared poorly with most of the conventional explanations proposed. Pulling the trigger on helpless classmates, the pair was gratuitously vicious, closer to the berserker's flaming ice than to any thematic rage.

The FBI's psychological assessment found Harris a psychopath: grandiose, cold, and homicidal. His journal opened explosively: "I hate the f—-ing world." On his website the rant was self-intoxicating:

YOU KNOW WHAT I HATE!!!? Cuuuuuuuuhntryyyyyyyyyy music!!! . . .

YOU KNOW WHAT I HATE!!!? People who say that wrestling is real!! . . .

YOU KNOW WHAT I HATE!!!? People who use the same word over and over again! . . . Read a f—-in book or two, increase your vo-cab-u-lary f*ck*ng idiots.

YOU KNOW WHAT I HATE!!!? STUPID PEOPLE!!! Why must so many people be so stupid!!? . . . YOU KNOW WHAT I HATE!!!? When people mispronounce words! and they dont even know it to, like acrosT, or eXspreso, pacific (specific), or 2 pAck. learn to speak correctly you morons.

YOU KNOW WHAT I HATE!!!? STAR WARS FANS!!! GET A FaaaaaaRIGIN LIFE YOU BORING GEEEEEKS!

The behavior is a tantrum, but as the FBI's consultant psychologist recognized, at its core is contempt. "He is disgusted with the morons around him. These are not the rantings of an angry young man, picked on by jocks until he's not going to take it anymore. These are the rantings of someone with a messianic-grade superiority complex, out to punish the entire human race for its appalling inferiority."[34] What clinches the rant as berserk style is Harris's use of self-conscious, show-off, shock-jock hyperbole.

Like survival, purity and morality are imperatives, and potentially tyrannical. Outwardly Harris was a nice kid—in military terms a model recruit. But he took pleasure in lying, and in his more private moments he projected infantile vainglory, feelings of persecution, and a rage to punish. In a typical passage under "Society" he rants: "I live in Denver and god damnit I would like to kill almost all of its residents. [Expletive] people with their rich snobby attitude thinkin they are all high and mighty and can just come up and tell me what to do and then people I see in the streets lying their [expletive] asses off about themselves." Under "Philosophy" he declaimed: "My belief is that if I say something, it goes. I am the law, and if you don't like it, you die. If I don't like you or I don't like what you want me to do, you die. . . . I'll just go to some downtown area in some big ass city and blow up and shoot everything I can. Feel no remorse, no sense of shame."[35] These threat-displays culminated in fantasies of extermination. In his America Online profile, Harris allegedly snarled, "'Kill 'em AALL!!!"

Behind the rant is an inner life that strikingly recalls the themes dramatized in *Dexter*. Like the autistic vigilante, Eric Harris consciously pretended to be a smart, likable guy. Yet like Dexter, Harris also culti-vated a hidden "real" identity as a cold-blooded vigilante preparing death for a world of offenders whose feelings and motives are totally alien to him. Like the suicidal 9/11 terrorists, Harris and Klebold demanded superhuman confirmation. Harris's "enemies" were people who think "they are all high and mighty"—like God. But in his fantasy he is God or more exactly the merciless cosmic wannabe, Satan: "I am the law, and if you don't like it, you die. If I don't like you or I don't like what you want me to do, you die."

The paranoia and delusion in the voice invites psychiatric perspectives. It may be significant that Eric Harris took the prescription drug Luvox, which is licensed for treatment of obsessive-compulsive disorder and in the same family as Prozac. Luvox is often prescribed to treat depression and obsessive thoughts. Did the drug fail to bring equilibrium to a disturbed mind? Many an adolescent male and Hollywood blockbuster has shared Harris's fantasies about warrior heroism, monstrous power, persecutory feelings, and invincible rightness, but not everyone acts on them. Harris was unaware of his contradictory desires to be a heroic Marine killing enemies (he was turned down because of his drug prescription) but also an infamous monster.

The contradiction is a familiar characteristic of berserk style. As Harris and Klebold were dreaming about crashing an airliner into a New York skyscraper, an entrepreneur was planning a chain of theme restaurants to be called Crash Cafe, each featuring a DC-3 passenger plane that has crashed into its façade. According to developer Patrick Turner, the restaurant would "aggressively" appeal to the public's "undeniable fascination with the destructive, erotic nature of crashing, colliding, and exploding objects."[36] The death-anxiety and aggressiveness underlying this self-parodic chic blazed into consciousness when the 9/11 hijackers acted on the "undeniable fascination."

Like cult members obsessively ritualizing their convictions, Harris and Klebold worked on their passions day after day in mutual fantasies of competitive self-intoxicating wildness. In the psychiatrist's office Harris's obsession is unhealthy; for the Marines his treatment with a prescription drug disqualified him from enlistment; but in the larger, unofficial atmosphere of militarized American culture his rage for glory was a form of basic training. Obsessing over guns and enemies, the young men were playing out a self-inflating survival scenario and yet losing touch with the social reality of the self.

As the son of a career Air Force officer, Harris "thought about war, fantasized about war and wrote about war. He was an angry teenage rebel planning disciplined military revenge with the most destructive weapons he could command. He was thrilled when he heard, one morning in philosophy class, that the United States was about to bomb Yugoslavia. Rebecca Heins, who sat next to him, remembers

Harris saying, 'I hope we do go to war, I'll be the first one there.' He wanted to be in the front lines, he said. He wanted, as he put it, to 'shoot everyone,' Heins recalls."[37] In fantasy the suburban student was under fire, cut off from his culture, running amok.

The combat soldier, again, is at once a slave to command yet also possessed of godlike power over life and death. Likewise Harris and Klebold were at once adolescent small-fry and haughty, cruel warlords in the mold of Idi Amin or SS big shots. Harris sounds like a nasty authoritarian parent, but pumped up to cosmic dimensions. "The killers, in fact, laughed at petty school shooters. They bragged about dwarfing the carnage of the Oklahoma City bombing and originally scheduled their bloody performance for its anniversary. Klebold boasted on video about inflicting "the most deaths in U.S. history." Columbine was intended not primarily as a shooting at all, but as a bombing on a massive scale. If they hadn't been so bad at wiring the timers, the propane bombs they set in the cafeteria would have wiped out 600 people. . . . The climax would be captured on live television. It wasn't just "fame" they were after—[FBI] Agent Fuselier bristles at that trivializing term—they were gunning for devastating infamy on the historical scale of an Attila the Hun. Their vision was to create a nightmare so devastating and apocalyptic that the entire world would shudder at their power" (Cullen).

The tragic cultural paradox is that roles meant to guarantee security and survival may instead spawn havoc. That goes not only for para-military and executive behavior but also for law and religion. In the Columbine massacre one of the killers reportedly asked a cornered student named Cassie Bernall if she believed in God. When she said she did, he shot her. This story became headline news. Her pastor vowed that "'Cassie died a martyr's death. She went to the martyr's hall of fame. She has graduated,"' he told mourners, "'while the rest of us still have tests ahead of us.'"

What is troubling about this reaction is its association of a tragic death with sports (the "hall of fame") and school bureaucracy ("tests ahead of us"). This is the language of boosterism, echoed by *Time* (May 31, 1999) when it did a follow-up article about the murders as an inspiration to teen evangelicals, titling it "A Surge of Teen Spirit" in a play on team spirit. This sort of cheerleading threatens to turn religion and a grave community injury into a special achievement. Indirectly it contributes to the berserk style in its glib celebration of death as a heroic and ultimately useful blaze of glory, made possible by notorious killers.

These voices too are naively caught up in fantasies of righteous competition and a "hall of fame" like the Valhalla of ancient pagan heroes. Their narcissism uncannily echoes that of the murderers, who also dreamed of performing an "immortal" story for vast audiences. "Directors will be fighting over this story," Dylan Klebold bragged in his video diary. He was avid for the approval of parent-like directors who would substantiate his identity through fame. Not incidentally he imagines glory itself to be substantiated by the directors' "fight" or competition. Klebold's boast echoes a soldier named Kreutzer. As he "set out to mow down a company of soldiers at Fort Bragg with an assault rifle and a semiautomatic pistol" in 1995, Kreutzer "told a friend he knew what the record number of multiple killings was."[38]

While males are far more likely to kill than females, reactions to the Columbine rampage show a complex gender system at work. On the playing field and off, young men compete for status with aggression that society manages with a suite of rewards. In wild-west jargon low-status males—or males looking for heroic exaltation—are especially apt to look upon weapons as tools of triumph and apotheosis. A real or sublimated military context substantiates the fantasy of elite warrior prowess. Young women, too, get caught up in competition for status, but some reactions to the Columbine mayhem show culture reinforcing traditional fantasies of sacrificial victimization for women. This is the pattern that surfaces so often in domestic violence: fear of social death and greed for self-esteem turns men's aggression outward, and encourages aggression to turn inward in women.

Time approvingly quotes "sixth grader Susan Teran" in Wichita, Kansas, who "has reached a personal decision . . . based on the example of her new hero," the "Christian victim" Cassie Bernall. 'If there was a shooter in my school,' declares the 12-year-old gravely, 'I'd volunteer to sacrifice my life. I'd say, 'Don't shoot my friends, shoot me,' because I know where I'll go when I die.'" The unrecognized, nightmarish irony is that in his video ramblings just before the rampage, Dylan Klebold allegedly voiced a similar fantasy: "It's a half hour before Judgment Day. I didn't like life very much. Just now I'm going to a better place than here." Yet more ironical is that both Susan Teran's and Klebold's convictions about death echo Justice Scalia's boast that "for the believing Christian, death is no big deal."

Aliens Amok

In a globalized world, outsiders threaten to suck away jobs, wealth, and vitality as vampires do. When they cross the border as immigrants, they can be seen as invaders. In an economic slump, when American invasions of other countries such as Iraq and Afghanistan have backfired, we should not be surprised that renewed hostility toward outsiders relies heavily on berserk style, calling for soldiers to defend the border with Mexico and ringing in alarms about immigrant infiltration, crime, and parasitism.

These themes have long been seething. As Mike Davis noted, "The overtly fascist apocalyptics of survivalist fictions were complemented throughout the 1980s by a growing obsession with a clandestine and eroticized extraterrestrial presence. Hollywood likewise was experimenting with the concept of shipwrecked aliens as Los Angeles's next ethnic minority. In the shadowlands of white anxiety, the distinction between the images of space alien and illegal alien was subjected to repeated elision. Immigration and invasion, in a paranoid register, became synonyms."[39]

A case in point is Barry Sonnenfeld's popular satire *Men in Black* (1997).[40] The film imagines space aliens living in human guise on earth, mostly in New York City, policed by clandestine government agents euphemistically called Men in Black. The agency resembles a corporate version of the CIA, FBI, Immigration and Naturalization Service (INS), and the National Security Agency (NSA). According to the veteran agent Kay (Tommy Lee Jones), the aliens are "intergalactic refugees" from persecution and violence, "most of them decent enough, just trying to make a living." The agency is in transition, with two white male agents recruiting replacements so they can retire. They choose a young black New York City policeman (Will Smith) who combines street smarts with the physical superiority stereotypically associated with black athletic celebrities. A plucky, attractive pathologist named Laurel (Linda Fiorentino) earns the second agent's position.

The movie's villain is an alien called "The Bug" (Vincent D'Onofrio) with the qualities of a berserker: "a giant cockroach with unlimited strength, a massive inferiority complex, and a real short temper." The Bug has come to earth to assassinate a refugee prince of the Arquillian Empire, who lives in New York City disguised as a jeweler named Rosenberg (Mike Nussbaum). After a crash landing in upstate New York, The Bug devours a local redneck named Edgar and puts on his skin. The alien-redneck murders the elderly jeweler in order to steal a galaxy belonging to the Arquillians that he has hidden inside one of his jewels. The Bug is greedy for space and victims because "that means more food for my family, all seventy-eight million of them. That's a lot of mouths to feed." In reaction, a formidable Arquillian battle cruiser threatens to annihilate the earth if the Men in Black fail to retrieve the stolen galaxy.

The film parodies Cold War melodramas such as *The Hunt for Red October* (1990) and *Crimson Tide* (1995) in which heroic agents thwart an apocalyptic nuclear holocaust. While the primary threat is immigration and globalization, the Bug's rage also anticipates post-9/11 terrorism that triggers the threat (and in Iraq and Afghanistan, the reality) of war. In the process the film spoofs and validates an evolving corporate police state and rage for order.

The film's extraterrestrials satirize conflicted attitudes toward immigration, as evident in Arizona's contested immigration enforcement law (2010) and California's Proposition 187 (1994). In 2008, the organization of vigilante groups to police the border with Mexico drew on berserk style, evident in an article deploring "Operation Return to Sender: The government's immigration enforcers run amok."[41]

In the film's opening scene, Border Patrol agents intercept a van smuggling Mexicans into Texas, unaware that one of the illegals is actually a criminal space alien. When two Men in Black detect the impostor and he runs amok, they destroy him. In post-9/11 America they could be intercepting a terrorist at the border. The Men in Black calm the astounded, naive Border Patrol agents by "shooting" them with a gun-like "neuralizer" whose blinding flash obliterates recent memory. The gun induces amnesia or dissociation, keeping the aliens' existence secret and sanitizing a reality supposedly too disturbing to be public knowledge. In movies the border interception usually inspires ambivalent sympathy for the homeless migrants and relief that "our" boundaries are policed, so the neuralizer also distracts the audience from its ambivalence. The neuralizer gun also suggests the manipulative secrecy surrounding Washington's antiterrorism, surveillance, and disinformation apparatus so prominent in the propaganda surrounding the Iraq War.

Men in Black jokes about official and everyday use of dissociation to protect ignorant earthlings from terrifying awareness that behind the faces of humdrum reality lurks alien monstrosity and berserk chaos. The repression operates on two levels: to manage hostility between newcomers and native humans, and to control the basic existential terror of cosmic alienation and death that the immigrants from space represent to earthlings. With its special guns, including the memory neuralizer, the mysterious police agency keeps the groups and spheres of awareness dissociated. When the agents do come in contact with the underlying berserk state, however, behavior goes amok.

From time immemorial migration has meant competition for resources and sometimes genocidal displacement. Ideally, immigrants to America are fellow refugees from oppression. But in practice, newcomers have always been a source of cheap labor and therefore vulnerable to exploitation even as they implicitly threaten the nation's working poor. When competition intensifies and assimilation falters, newcomers may be, or seem to be, parasites or predators.

Psychologically the newcomers represent dangerous infantile orality: too many mouths to feed and in turn a threat of cannibalistic hunger and survival rage.

Men in Black winks at this pulp imagery. The cockroach-like assassin called The Bug reveals a horrific shark-like maw. The Bug caricatures oral rapacity on behalf of "my family, all seventy-eight million . . . mouths to feed." The aliens can usurp someone's skin the way immigrants or outsourced "alien" workers may take over someone's job and social position. Ultimately, according to this symbolic logic, immigrants compete for nothing less than autonomy and identity itself. The Bug devours the redneck Edgar and appropriates his skin, acting out the immigrants' threat to bring social death to marginal members of society.

This nightmare has antecedents in the conflicts over the surge of immigration from 1890 to 1910 and American imperialism, which worried that the project of civilizing the world might weaken American manliness. Teddy Roosevelt warned against degeneration and effeminacy and the specter of "race suicide." Coined by Edward A. Ross in 1901, "race suicide" was associated with "immigration and women's advancement, as well as the falling birthrate." Anxiety focused on "civilized but inferior" immigrants, especially Asians.[42] With the closing of the frontiers, distances shrank, competition over colonies increased, and surplus populations now had no room to expand—in Hitler's charged language, no *Lebensraum*.

These conditions contributed to the genocidal warfare of the twentieth century, a history evoked by the ultimatum that drives the plot of *Men in Black* when the Arquillians demand that "their" stolen galaxy be returned or the earth will be annihilated. H. G. Wells anticipated this pressurized atmosphere in *The War of the Worlds* (1898), in which Martians invade Britain. And global "others" threaten psychic as well as bodily usurpation, as in western worries about being overrun by the "yellow peril" of faceless Asian hordes, or as Jerry Falwell warned in the Reagan years, by "foot people" from Central America. "Our" rampage must preempt "their" rampage.

Men in Black's aliens neatly condense these ambivalent historical attitudes. Their insect-like and squid-like body parts make them both derisively primitive and frighteningly powerful. The aliens arouse human distrust, yet their behavior is virtually indistinguishable from human behavior, and the film satirizes the humans' visceral xenophobia.

Much of the aliens' menace lies in their ambiguity. On earth the agency monitors them in a parody of late twentieth century industrial surveillance technology. But how many aliens finally exist out in the cosmos? If they can adapt so readily to earth and mutate at will, can they be trusted to keep to any reliable form, or are they beyond any sort of psychic or bodily integrity? In this respect they suggest the relativism that has shocked people since modernity began to discover evolution and the range of cultures across the globe.

In this century's fantasies, then, immigration may presage the fall of empires and personal annihilation.[43] Although most of the aliens in *Men in Black* seem benign, the seasoned agent Kay explains that the agency maintains strict secrecy because people would panic if they realized that aliens lived among them, already invisibly—if harmlessly—displacing them. The film maintains a deftly ambivalent attitude toward the newcomers. For one thing, the aliens seem to represent an elite that travels like intergalactic business executives and cooperates with the immigration agency on earth. They resemble the moneyed elites of post–Cold War capitalism, the new breed of global entrepreneurs and financiers who buy citizenship in countries like the United States or Canada when economic home bases become untenable. At the same time they can be despotic, as in the Arquillians' threat to destroy the earth when the Bug steals their galaxy. Panicked by the Arquillians' ultimatum, most of the aliens on earth manage to flee back into space without consulting their official minders, as if they are actually more autonomous than officialdom has admitted. In their superhuman adaptability, these elite beings more nearly fulfill immortality wishes than their human counterparts.

The men in black operate on the margin of conventional awareness. Unlike ordinary people, they confront the cosmic insignificance of humankind, but they also share some of the superhuman capacities of the aliens, thanks to their surveillance technology and high-tech guns. To become an agent, the black policeman James has to sacrifice his identity, and a computer expunges all records of him. "You will sever human contact," Jay is told. But in compensation "You're no longer part of the system. You're above the system. Over it. Beyond it."

This fantasy institutionalizes the berserk state. In effect, the neuralizer amnesia gun enables the agents to enjoy the exalted morale of the berserker, living on the threshold of the beyond, free to plunge into all-out violence and then to return to stable reality. The core threat to the fantasy is of course inescapable mortality. The pressure of underlying death-anxiety only reveals itself when age and fatigue begin to overcome the agents who wish to retire.

The relatively youthful Kay is still absorbed in the warrior-police role, and the film draws much of its ironic energy from his style as an agent. His coolness—the sunglasses, business suit, and nonchalance—seems to signify absolute composure. Yet in the larger symbolic context, these qualities are a comic mask for hypervigilance, numbness, and diminished subjectivity akin to combat trauma. Confronted by overwhelming terror, agents are ready to plunge recklessly into battle, with superhuman force.

Like other tools, guns magnify the force of the human body. When the body itself becomes a vehicle and potential weapon for an "alien," then it can actually be a kind of gun. With its robot-like limp and grotesque strength, the redneck's body is charged with explosive force and serves The Bug as a cybernetic weapon. In a paranoid universe, radical existential motives such as survival-anxiety and striving for heroic power tend to bind self and gun so closely that they fuse. In the hero's hand the gun symbolizes godlike control, yet like Faustian magic, it also threatens to dissolve inhibitions and "possess" the soul, as in so-called impulse killings.

Men in Black dramatizes these magical associations. Using the memory-zapping gun, an agent transcends ordinary "repressed" life, comprehending it but also initiated into cosmic mysteries beyond it. As in fantasies of "blowing away" a target, the agents' high-tech weapons dissolve alien bodies into harmless, lurid goo. In the final showdown at the World's Fair site in Flushing Meadow, Kay acts out the stages of berserking. When The Bug disarms him by swallowing his assault rifle, Kay taunts the monster into attacking him, then plunges headlong into its fearsome maw to retrieve and fire his weapon, exploding the creature from within. As if reborn, Kay emerges like a newborn infant, smeared with the gooey essence of the creature. In the imagery of berserking, conventional categories magically dissolve: killing and sacrifice produce life; the macho enemy becomes perversely maternal; and reincorporation into this devouring parent-figure generates uncanny autonomy. Smeared in goo, the agent acts out the berserker's urge to tear apart the enemy's body. What's more, the rebirth also marks Kay's decision to retire, surrender his memory, and finally accept mortality.

Like the aliens, the idea of berserking assumes many disguises in the film. Despite the agents' professional cool, the agency epitomizes the berserk state, transcending conventional legal and institutional restraints. The agents' cryptic letter names neatly evoke their dissociation, as their high-tech car does in rocketing about New York City at speeds too great for personal control, freed from traffic laws and even natural laws. Racing upside down on the roof of the Lincoln Tunnel, "over the heads" of everyone else, the agents' car demonstrates the magical potency of ultimate heedless daring. When the novice Jay accidentally touches a supercharged ball in the agency's terminal, the sphere goes amok. When it ricochets wildly throughout the building, its furious trajectory magically defies the usual laws of physics.

The film also implicates women in berserk magic. Although the rookie Jay covets the hefty assault rifle his mentor Kay requisitions in the final crisis, he is issued a little "ladies'" pistol called a "cricket." However, the derringer-like pistol packs a tremendous punch whose recoil invariably knocks Jay over backward. The pistol mocks gender stereotypes and flatters women in the audience by implying that "ladies" pack a concentrated wallop that a man cannot control. An analogous inversion appears when Jay is dispatched to help an alien mother give birth in the backseat of a car. In the throes of labor the mother reverts to her underlying alien form, and her tentacles pick up and violently whirl the helpless agent about. Childbirth is akin to going amok. In a flattering gesture toward blacks, the screenplay insists that despite this shock, Jay has soul. Although his partner Kay is impassive, Jay can still feel, cooing over the newborn alien.

Magical berserking is of course ideologically charged. The Bug's violence is atrocious; the agency's rescues humanity. This ideological disguise keeps us from recognizing that at bottom the agency is a corporate police state with a lawless program of surveillance and enforcement. The film's ideological implications are evident in the bodies of the aliens. The disguised alien Rosenberg is a gentle, avuncular shopkeeper who is rescuing part of his "homeland"—the disputed galaxy—from the rapacious Bug. He is "Daddy" to his pet cat Orion. During the autopsy after his assassination, his face swings open on hinges to reveal an infantile ET-like creature inside the head that is operating the body like a machine. Innocents, the film argues, use cybernetics and illusion to compensate for their inherent vulnerability.

By contrast, the alien assassin assumes the form of a hostile if bumbling redneck, a type regularly vilified in Hollywood films. He is uncouth and abusive to his wife (Siobhan Fallon). But as the climax of the film argues, inside this skin or form of a man is a more primitive evil, the cockroach-like Bug. The monster is intrinsically evil as Rosenberg is "really" a childlike, elderly incarnation of ET. The film's symbolic logic makes the jeweler the admirable old man that retiring agents like Dee and Kay would become, while projecting onto the redneck monster all their darker motives as agents. After all, in his survival rage and lust for the Arquillians' galaxy, the Bug acts out a lawless greed for life that is only too human. By destroying the monster, the agents tame death-anxiety and greed for life in themselves. In emerging from the grave-like crater, animating a grotesque male body, the rampaging assassin resembles the Frankenstein monster. As in Mary Shelley's novel, the ungainly body parts evoke proletarian incoherence, in this instance not the revolutionary mob of nineteenth century Europe,[44] but the marginalized white men associated today with neo-Nazis, white supremacists, and militia terrorism. One such figure is Buford O'Neal Furrow, who assaulted a Jewish day care center in Los Angeles on August 10, 1999. In effect, the Bug is a caricatured redneck gone amok, with a prosperous Jewish victim (the urbane jeweler Rosenberg), and the intergalactic war threatened by the theft of the stolen galaxy actually euphemizes a more disturbing prospect of class violence.

Men in Black envisions a radical gap between an invisible elite and ordinary people. It imagines a corporate state whose unseen executives manage the affairs of an even more dissociated alien elite, editing reality for everyone else. Select, gun-toting recruits from the lower ranks serve the corporate state and preserve the "galaxies" of an alien elite from brutish enemies.

Those at the bottom of society are epitomized by the redneck monster and associated with immigrant stereotypes of a century ago. As scapegoats, greedy and malicious, they draw off guilt that corporate insiders might otherwise feel. The redneck Edgar abuses "his" wife, behaving like the immigrant in Alice Guy Blache's didactic, pseudo-documentary film *The Making of an American Citizen* (1912).[45] In the film an immigrant husband named Ivan mistreats his wife as he did in the old world, until his new American neighbors reeducate him through chivalrous exhortation and, as a last resort, a prison term.

In *Men in Black,* that despised, uncouth barbarian once again invades America's genteel shores. After debriefing Edgar's wife, preparing to zap her memory, the young black agent Jay wants to give the woman a new feisty identity to remember when she awakens. He tells her that she "kicked out" her boorish husband and should now "hire a decorator" and get a new wardrobe. But this is Hollywood feminism, deflecting attention to personal style, when the deeper problem is the woman's poverty and the ownership of "galaxies" by a coercive and inaccessible global elite.

But there is also another way that immigration lore serves the film's fantasies about the present. If the Bug represents white trash subculture, his opposite is his victim, the jeweler "Gentle Rosenberg." The grandfatherly Rosenberg euphemizes a privileged business class that feels older and vulnerable to ruthless foreign rivals, afraid of losing its wealth and real estate—the prized galaxy. The jeweler belongs to an "alien" Arquillian royal family, but he can also be seen as a representation of the new corporate elite, disguising its acquisitiveness and arriviste insecurity. He possesses a "galaxy" that suggests the immense wealth—the business "empire"—controlled by this financial elite, just as the redneck monster embodies the rage of the underclass. This is an "alien" elite insofar as it has cut itself off from the poor.

The galaxy-in-a-bauble is supposed to be an invaluable "sub-atomic energy source," even as the mild jeweler puts a harmless face on the military-industrial aggression projected in the Arquillian battle-star. But in the new century, the jeweler better represents the deindustrialization and reliance on showy finance and hoarded consumer wealth that has been draining postwar America. The malice of the Bug in turn projects an elite fear that eventually the new economy will reduce the working poor to desperate antagonism.

In an era of identity politics, the manipulation of ethnicity and class markers is good box office. Like the film's black and woman superheroes and its demonized redneck, Rosenberg is part of an ideological formula. His Jewishness is an honorific, sentimental marker that celebrates ethnic pride yet also leaves out the real struggles of past immigrants chronicled by Henry Roth and others.[46]

The transforming magic of berserk style supports the film's equivocations. The selected agents can be happy serving their human and alien overlords because the agency allows them an illusion of professional autonomy signified by their high-tech guns and surveillance devices. Guns make the men in black not servants but free agents, not only morally superior to the elite they rescue, but also capable of policing and if necessary even killing them. Just this rebellious potential makes it necessary to have demonized enemies like the Bug to deflect anger away from the social world. Berserk style insulates the agents from awkward questions about status and social justice, while the memory-zapping neuralizer can switch them into amnesiac bliss.

In their doomsday ultimatum, the Arquillians dramatize the old American wish for both exterminatory supremacy (as in the genocidal "taming" of the American frontier or the wish to bomb Vietnam "back to the stone age") and innocence worthy of "the new Jerusalem." In the Bug's rampage, the film dramatizes fears that the prosperous postwar era is passing, its baby boomers aging, and that sinister, prolific new rivals will run amok.

These fantasies call into question the nature of subjectivity. The idea of aliens dramatizes anxiety that the core of self is foreign and manipulative. It personifies the Freudian unconscious, making it to some extent controllable through surveillance and guns. As in some fashionable psychological therapies, the film wishes for a purgative berserk abreaction. In plunging down the Bug's throat in the climactic confrontation, Kay dispels the threats of the primitive unconscious. He magically undoes the terror of cannibalism associated with the man-eating insect, hungry immigrants, and aliens who can devour humans' innards and wear their skins. In plunging into the belly of the beast, shedding all inhibitions, going out of his conventional self, the berserker puts himself in the grip of a deeper will analogous to the alien inside a human. The berserker, that is, implicitly participates in the aliens' cosmic reality.

And yet this pseudo-religious transcendence is eerily equivocal. An autopsy discovers inside Rosenberg's head a diminutive alien being something like the philosopher's "ghost in the machine." What agency moves the ghost? The question has long haunted modernity. Industrial technology produces tremendous power by anatomizing things, reducing them to manipulable components. It can overcome death by replacing body parts in organ transplants and even clone living beings. Yet these same processes also arouse fears that we are nothing more than biomechanical gizmos, even in mental life—that reality is always virtual and intelligence ultimately artificial. They invite us to look for a ground of being that can never be seen, if it's there at all. Though democracies deny it by appeals to patriotism and community, societies are also assemblages of competing individuals, subgroups, and classes, each swayed by powerful external forces, from the time clock to headline news, themselves manipulated by even more remote agencies. *Men in Black* closes with a vision of galaxies being knocked about like croquet balls in an absurd game played by agents as capricious as the ancient gods.

Like the growing disproportion in wealth and freedom in post-Vietnam America, the disproportions of scale in this absurd cosmology resist practical thinking. With an executive elite ever more removed and invisible, ordinary people understandably appreciate fantasies about aliens stealthily taking control of their minds. To some extent this is in fact what media monopoly does by determining the vocabulary and arguments available to people. But there is another problem of scale no less disturbing. At least some of the aliens are refugees from life-or-death territorial disputes, perhaps a small elite escaping from overpopulated home planets.

This scenario resonates with Richard L. Rubenstein's thesis that the "demographic explosion that began in Europe during the eighteenth century" initiated "the modern, worldwide phenomenon of mass surplus population" and an "age of triage."[47] Rubenstein contends that technological, economic, and demographic pressures have been making whole groups of people expendable, resulting in mass migrations and genocidal horrors. His examples range from the enclosures that eliminated entire villages in seventeenth-century England, to the Holocaust. In the new century anxiety about triage has intensified—or resurfaced—with increasing globalization, and the economic quakes and new waves of immigration. As the frontiers have closed off outlets for emigration and the great powers have lost their former empires, imperialistic rhetoric has claimed space as the last frontier. Intergalactic fantasies such as *Star Trek* routinely envision the future in terms of expanding empires and dangerous competition over colonies. Closer to home, and symptomatic of American dein-dustrialization, Michael Moore's *Roger and Me* (1989) documents the automotive industry triage that desolated Flint Michigan and scattered "surplus" population to the winds in rental trucks. As in the Social Darwinist nightmare of the Gilded Age, the haunting ques-tion remains: Is there nothing but insane competition at the core of experience?

Men in Black worries this question. The film imagines urbane wit, technology, and daring precariously keeping order on an imperiled planet. But behind this cool demeanor, like an alien inside a humdrum human body, is a darker fantasy that the stress of globalization, immi-gration, and the emergence of a corporate police state are pressuring human populations toward the berserk state, psychically disembedded, open to hair-trigger rage over life-threatening shortages: of vital energy, autonomy, and even subjectivity itself.

CHAPTER 6

THE LIVING END

Apocalypse has become banal.

Anthony Giddens, Modernity and Self-Identity

Rampage killing is figuratively an apocalypse. Eric Harris wanted in caps to "Kill 'em AALL!!!" Narcissism tells us that "the world is me. After my death nothing matters." The doomed self can see no future and can scarcely help resenting the lucky ones who will live on. Annihilation resolves all conflict. Given the right story, total death can be totally significant.

Still, total oblivion is a big order. We are cognitively disposed to see endings as change. In Christianity the end of the world is really a conversion experience: translation from earthly to heavenly or infernal existence. Victory in warfare annihilates an enemy and inaugurates a new age or confirms a new compact with the gods. In the Bible, God sends the Israelites to exterminate the Canaanites. In nations nearby "which the Lord your God is giving you as a heritage, you shall not let a soul remain alive. No, you must proscribe them . . . as the Lord your God has commanded you" (Deut. 20:18).[1] In rationalizing ethnic cleansing and appetite for land, the rhetoric of the beyond substitutes "us" for "them." Life goes on, but under new auspices.

Ideas of the beyond frame consciousness. Within the boundaries of Eden, there was no death, anxiety, and alienation. Following our eviction, we have depended on symbolic materials to create a prosthetic beyond that can frame life and make it seem enduring and significant.[2] Medieval crusaders stormed out of Europe in manic sallies that amassed treasure in heaven as well as in pack trains. Conquest was theology. The spectacular rampage killings at the World Trade

Center and at the Pentagon in 2001 were also framed by fantasies of the theological beyond.

For the purposes of this book, apocalypse is best understood as a tool. For all the insistence on the terrorists' alien fanaticism, for example, their behavior mixed religious and worldly motives in the cauldron of berserk style. Likewise, public responses summoned berserk style to manage morale and integrate the terrorist rupture into the familiar stories we live by. Globalization has shaken traditional verities around the world. China goes home with Walmart shoppers; Coca-Cola and the US Army are familiar in countries around the planet. Subatomic science and radical advances in cosmology have dispelled traditional certainties and controls. Modernity disenchants even the possibility of ultimate frames.

Viewed as a form of rampage killing, the September 11 terrorism has some intriguing features. For one thing it could have elicited an international police response rather than the opportunistic, berserk-style "war on terror." As an analog to workplace and school rampage, the attacks were a perverse solution to serious conflicts in the lives of relatively affluent young men under pressure to find heroic purpose in countries such as Saudi Arabia in which modernity and reactionary repression are maddeningly in conflict. Career plans, sex, and family were problematical for almost all of the hijackers. While none lacked for opportunities, they grew ever more obsessed with "what is right." The plot of cosmic jihad against the American Satan's front office, as it were, allowed them to feel right—and while the spell lasted, supremely important. As in most such attacks, suicide allowed them to escape any modern ironies and tragic postmortem analysis.

The jihadis' pious exaltation can be understood as the berserker's seething sense of injustice, godlike transport, and cold fury. They plotted to go postal in the aisles of everyday life, yet they were also self-consciously amok as soldiers under the banner of God. Remind-ers of medieval crusaders infuriated them, though they were crusaders themselves. They were also self-anointed priests righteously carrying out holy duties. In "the most blood-curdling sentence" of his final instructions to the hijackers, [the ringleader Mohammed] Atta com-manded: "You must not discomfort your animal during the slaughter." This phrase "is well beyond anger or hatred. It is the utmost in dispar-agement. . . . By having mercy on one's animals, one is imitating God, who rules over death."[3]

Carrying out this human sacrifice, Atta emulated ancient priests, but he identified with God. For all his piety, he is also a judge like the Columbine killers sentencing everybody to death. Recall Eric Harris's

"Philosophy" on his website: "My belief is that if I say something, it goes. I am the law, and if you don't like it, you die. If I don't like you or I don't like what you want me to do, you die. . . . I'll just go to some downtown area in some big ass city and blow up and shoot everything I can. Feel no remorse, no sense of shame."[4]

As at Columbine, the execution is also a suicide, so the priest-judge is sacrificing all the "animal" bodies in the plane and in the twin towers. This is in keeping with the asceticism that progressively overtook Atta from his student days. Like Dylan Klebold, he told himself he was "going to a better place." As Ruth Stein concludes in her analysis of Atta's final letter, evidence points to a breakdown of reality-testing familiar in cult behavior and psychosis. "Being immersed in a state of intense focus on God in word and thought, not detaching from attending His presence for one minute, in a kind of numbed, awed adhesion, yet at the same time functioning with extraordinary vigilance and competence, may be likened to cold psychotic paranoia at its height. The subject adheres to the idealized persecutory inner object, while the world, become insignificant and contemptible, vanishes into derealization" (Stein, 106).

The "contemptible world" we are trapped in is first of all the human body. And if it won't agreeably "vanish," then it can be starved or done away with. The purification of the self promises an escape from repulsive mortality. As in anorexia, the cruelty of this syndrome lies in its distortion of rewards and defenses, so that the individual's self-protective systems short-circuit, and instead of triggering alarm and disgust, physical self-destruction generates mental exaltation. Although research has yet to make clear the interplay of neurological and cultural influences, the self-intoxicating quality of anorexic behavior is psychocultural. The nervous system responds to repeated bouts of stress, and as Atta's history shows, the mind seeks out or imagines sympathizers who will support the belief system. The more you starve yourself toward perfection, the louder the applause and the fiercer your resolve.

Rage and self-aggrandizement can be just as self-intoxicating. Hatred of unworthiness and injustice fuels an urgent search for release, in this instance a world-shattering rampage meant to open the gates of paradise. The hijacker's obsessive prayers are the equivalent of the rampage killer's seething fixation. The climax is an addictive, terminal binge. As it gathers momentum, anorexic self-denial resembles suicidal berserking insofar as growing disgust at the real body heightens the panic of being trapped: trapped not only in the ugly body and the "fat," ugly world, but also trapped in feelings of disgust. Rage at the grotesque, affluent enemy can feed righteous self-regard.

For all his supposed foreignness and religiosity, Atta's fantasies are pitifully familiar. Strange to say, pulp-and-science fiction resonate with his narratives. In describing *The Matrix* (1999), Mervyn Bendle uncannily echoes Ruth Stein's clinical observation of disgust and messianism: "The idea that everyday life is a vacuous illusion is central" in the film. The critic's account of the plot catches echoes of the terrorists' inner life. The hero, Neo, is a nobody working in a corporate cubicle until he meets the rebel leader Morpheus, who reveals that everyday reality is in fact the Matrix: a computer-generated virtual reality engrossing the entire globe and powered by energy drained from infantilized humans immobilized in artificial wombs. This is industrial-scale vampirism.

> At the end of the movie Neo, in a voice-over, contacts the sinister and hegemonic AI system, declares his status as the Messiah and his intention to reveal to the denizens of the Matrix an alternative world without rules and controls, borders or boundaries, and where anything is possible. The Matrix registers "system failure" and Neo steps forth into the hustle and bustle of a busy city, watching the masses hurry by in their mindless everyday toil, before he ascends into the heavens to await the outcome of his intervention. . . . Contemporary cinema offers extremely misanthropic representations of the apocalyptic near future and communicates a fear and hatred of everyday people. The masses are depicted as mindless, barely functional vermin, ready to tear each other apart in a desperate rage for survival. Accompanying this is a depiction of the heroes and survivors being readily transformed into effective killers, capable of butchering large numbers of people who, perhaps only hours before, may have been their friends, allies, or even family members.[5]

From the "butchered" animal masses to the hero's ascent to the beyond, it is all there: the persecution, the derealization, and the messianic rebellion. Even Atta's conviction that the industrial world is robbing Muslims of their vitality echoes in the fantasy of battery-farms and infantilization. The remedy is the cosmic heroism of the terrorist mastermind.

Media and officials depicted Atta and Bin Laden as criminal geniuses. But rampage killers can be strategic even in the throes of an inner storm. Consider Mark O. Barton, who kept a mask on his inner turmoil until the summer of 1999, when he murdered his second wife and two children, nine people in two Atlanta brokerage houses, and finally himself. Barton had quit his job as a chemist and suffered financial ruin as a day trader. "I have been dying," he wrote just before the end. Like a soldier trapped and overwhelmed by death-anxiety, "I wake up at night so afraid, so terrified that I couldn't be that afraid while awake. It has taken its toll. I have come to hate this life and this system of things. I have come to have no hope." In his "hate [for] this system of things," he could be speaking out of a terrorist manifesto. Even as his character was disintegrating, he was systematic in his assault on the brokerage houses. Failing as a trader, he attacked fellow brokerage customers who "greedily sought my destruction."[6] Like the Islamists who reviled US prosperity, Barton hated the "greed" that meant happiness for others and marked his failure.

Barton, too, matched acute persecutory feelings with a special sacrificial relationship to God. Generally journalists examine religious pathology with euphemistic discretion because the taboos are so explosive. But like Atta, Barton used the beyond to rationalize his murders. In the note he left behind, waking and dream life blurred for him. He repeated a ritualistic formula naming the wife and children he had just slaughtered, then offering them to God as in an ancient ceremonial sacrifice. "I give you my wife, Leigh Ann Vandiver Barton. My honey, my precious love. Please take care of her. I will love her forever." The children follow, one by one, as he repeats the formula. Through this sacrificial murder, talking to "Jehovah," Barton shed his failures and hatred by playing the benevolent priest-judge as Atta did, but in a script meant to be read by sympathetic posterity.

Killing your family, you destroy your intimate life space in a personal apocalypse. In his role-playing Barton is lover, priest, judge, and executioner, and about to be a terrorist wreaking vengeance on his enemies. Meanwhile he lovingly summons divine protection for the family he has slaughtered as they accompany him into death like the sacrificed dependents of an ancient warrior-king.

What the doomed warrior-king does not say is that the police had good reason to suspect him of murdering his first wife and her mother on a camping trip half a dozen years earlier. Nor does he connect those crimes to the shattering turmoil inside him.

After slaying his family, Barton visited his lawyer to change his will, appearing composed. In the berserk state of exalted, vicious calm—the psychiatrist's "flaming ice"—he then resumed his rampage. A witness reported that "[h]is eyes had this enormous sadness; he was flat-out hopeless."[7] His emptiness recalls Anne Greaves' description of Mohamed Atta at the flight school in Florida training for death: "he had a terribly sad expression on his face. Totally emotionless cold eyes . . . such a fixed purposeful expression on his face. Almost as though he was hypnotised in a way . . . just this sort of almost dead expression. Just no life in him whatsoever. Robotic. Not a flicker of emotion or excitement or anything. Nothing at all."

These observations show both men withdrawing from life, "hypnotized" by the beyond: filling up the "vacuous illusion" of life with God and death. Ruth Stein's description of Atta's "cold psychotic paranoia" suggests an organic etiology. But that would by no means eliminate psychocultural influences. The seeds of the deadness resonate eerily in the phenomenon the Romans called "the demon of noontide"—the experience of peering out a doorway at noon and suddenly finding the world utterly meaningless. What we know for sure is that both killers fought this depressive void by coming "to hate this life and this system of things." Barton coped with the feeling that "I have been dying" by forcing his death, just as Atta undertook a slow-motion suicide that reached apotheosis in the twin towers funeral pyre.

Apocalyptic Rescue

Hatred of "this life and this system of things" could scarcely be more telling than in the career of the Rev. Jim Jones. In a cruel parody of the original Puritan settlement of New England, he herded his Peoples Temple faithful out of California, where the law was beginning to investigate the cult, to build a new city on a hill in the bush of Guyana, where he murdered almost every one of them with cyanide, in a drug-addled, absurd apocalypse.

Childhood friends say that as a schoolboy Jim Jones (1931–1978), like Jeffrey Dahmer, was fixated on death and funerals.[8] As an abused child of an alcoholic family in rural Indiana, he found shelter in a Pentecostal church group. As a young preacher of a social gospel, he cultivated marginalized minority followers. In time berserk style enabled him to act out a fantasy solution to his own tormented childhood by taking the role of "Father" rescuing "his" children. He used utopian sympathies and criminal guile to build a shaky cult empire that collapsed in a spasm of rage and self-pity. As he directed the murder-suicide of over 903 followers, many still thought of him as father and God.

From the start Jones embraced berserk themes in the cultural materials around him, especially Cold War ideology. Jeanne Mills, who defected in 1975, wrote one of the earliest first-hand accounts of the Peoples Temple (1979).[9] She first fell under Jones's spell in November 1969, when the nation was shuddering through antiwar and civil rights clashes, nearly three dozen urban riots in three years, and the Bobby Kennedy and Martin Luther King assassinations

(1968). The Black Panthers were loudly arming in self-defense, and President Johnson had been pressured out of office.

In this queasy atmosphere Mills and her husband Al attended a service at Jones's church in Redwood Valley, California. At this early stage Jones brought together a few middle class and many marginal members, white and black, young and elderly. His sermon that day was "about political problems, the war in Vietnam, which he claimed to have prophesied, the government-supported drug racketeering in our country, the social injustices committed against the minorities," and religious hypocrisy. At the climax he announced: "I have seen by divine revelation the total annihilation of this country and many other parts of the world. . . . The only survivors will be those people who are hidden in the cave that I have been shown in a vision. Those who go into this cave with me will be saved from the poisonous radioactive fallout that will follow the nuclear bomb attack. . . . It will be up to our group to begin life anew on this continent" (122). In the ideation of race war, "poisonous" fallout, and mass death the end was already present.

Like Jones's healings, this doomsday sermon made fear of death a shared group experience, even as the cave and the dream of repopulating the earth countered terror with fantasies of invulnerability, fertility, and special destiny. Jones played on Cold War themes of nuclear holocaust and backyard bomb shelters. In Stanley Kubrick's *Dr. Strangelove* (1964), the sinister Strangelove advises the government elite that they can survive an imminent nuclear strike underground and with a harem, godlike, repopulate the earth—a fantasy personally appealing to Jones. Jeannie Mills had been raised in a "deeply religious" Seventh Day Adventist family (111), so she was used to millenialist theology. But the story spoke to her fear of nuclear war, and she responded to the racial harmony in the congregation.

Jones preached makeshift messianic doctrines increasingly centered on his superhuman powers to rescue followers from death. Services came to focus on miraculous testimonials contrived with a suite of confidence tricks and cunning confederates. Impersonating a cripple, responding to a command from Jones, a church secretary stood up from her wheelchair and walked. An elderly black woman praised Jones for helping her "spit up" a stomach cancer. After his sermon his psychic powers identified another woman in the congregation with a stomach cancer, and he dispatched her with a nurse to the toilet to disgorge it. The deadly flesh produced for all to see and smell was in fact rotting chicken guts and a prop. The congregation exulted at this exorcism.

In time Jones's fantasies of apotheosis became less sublimated. All along he mocked conventional belief in a fraudulent "Skygod," projecting onto this religious deception his own sinister motives. By 1972 he was asking to be called "Father" and hinting that "he was none other than 'God Almighty'" (180), as in this Peoples Temple song:

> Father is God,
> And we are blessed,
> I know you're God, I know you're God,
> I know you're God, God, God, God, God. (203)

His followers learned that he had been incarnated before as Buddha, the Bab, Jesus, and Vladimir Lenin (181).

As a seminarian Jones had been obsessed with inequality and exploitation. But like that other seminarian Josef Stalin, Jones's communistic benevolence gradually transformed into predatory survival greed. He seduced prospective followers by making them feel loved, bombarding them with testimonials from his followers—in cult jargon, "love bombing"—and promising rescue. But the craving for love became obsessive for him as well. He jealously attacked any follower who held back from hero-worship or showed desire for others.

As in classic domestic abuse, "Father" professed love for his family even as he viciously "disciplined" them. Surrendering autonomy and worldly goods to the cause, working themselves into a state of befuddled sleep-deprivation, his followers became increasingly dependent. That made them less threatening to "Father," but also less profitable and more burdensome. Since his business dealings were often irresponsible or inept, with no real goal beyond endless self-expansion, the organization was bound to be self-disabling in the long run.

As the man's criminal ambitions ratcheted up his stress, his demands for veneration and dominance followed suit. With mainstream American culture as the enemy, he was implicitly in combat, a guerrilla leader or mafia godfather. In his accelerating rampage during the 1970s he extorted property, defrauded the state welfare department, used children as hostages, and instigated assaults on "traitors." As his fear of exposure and punishment mounted, so did his compulsion to punish others, especially "disobedient" children, with public beatings and humiliation. As his excesses threatened everyone's sense of stability, his demands for loyalty became fanatical. Defections left behind an increasingly infantilized core of believers. Week after week his punishment of children modeled the helplessness of his adult followers, even as it allowed him to feel mastery over his own terrors. As his tyrannical violence became increasingly self-intoxicating, it required ever more sadistic excess to maintain his godlike exaltation.

As Jones experimented with abandon, testing limits, promising supernatural protection while making outrageous demands on the faithful, he became more openly paranoid. In 1971–1972, evoking the assassinations of the Kennedys and Martin Luther King, he began to stage fake attempts on his life in which he would feign gunshot injuries and miraculously "dissolve" the bullets. He built a watchtower in his backyard and armed the bodyguards who would be his enforcers during temple services and abet the murders in Jonestown.

By 1974, Jones was pushing berserk style toward abandon. He openly took the role of alpha male. "It was nauseating to listen to him tell a congregation of a thousand or more adults and children that he had the biggest penis of any man" (258). He humiliated rival males: "If you think you can fuck women, prove it here, in front of everyone. If you think you know how to make love, then show us. You fuck your wife and I'll fuck mine, and we'll see who is able to do it longer and better" (258). The emphasis on stamina, his terror that anyone should see his penis, his dyed graying hair, and his embarrassing potbelly enabled the once-transfixed Jeannie Mills to recognize the turmoil in the man. In 1975, several years before the mass murder in Guyana, he began to test his inner circle by pretending to poison them and watching to see who would die willingly for "the Cause"— for him. The messiah would not go alone into failure and death.

In the year or so before the move—or flight—to Jonestown, the Peoples Temple took on an air of saturnalia. Financially the empire was coming apart. Despite blackmail and death-threats, defectors were pressing for legal sanctions to recover family members held hostage. Jones openly cultivated the berserker's godlike and beastlike abandon. He fulminated against imaginary enemies and looked for excuses to punish. During services he bragged about sexually servicing his followers as if they were his harem, forbidding sexuality among themselves. Defying legal advice to mask his emergent homosexuality, he reveled in it and taught that everyone was basically homosexual, incoherently boasting of superhuman powers of procreation. At times he would mock his sexual partners in his sermons, ridiculing them for infecting him with venereal warts or failing to use an enema before he sodomized them, his self-hatred deflected onto the sexual acolytes.

Poignantly, Jones half-acknowledged his mental illness: "He explained that he had a sugar imbalance which caused people to go crazy. 'People who have this problem usually become murderers,' he said, 'but I am able to stay in control.' He explained to his bodyguards that there might be times when he would be unable to control his 'righteous indignation' because of this sugar imbalance. His instructions to them were, 'Watch me if I should begin to lunge toward someone. Pull me away from them so I don't harm an innocent person in my anger'" (272). And in fact there were occasions when he began to run amok and had to be restrained.

Jones's insanity played out the ambiguity in berserk style: at critical moments it was difficult to determine how in or out of control he was. For all his vehement iconoclasm, his "Apostolic socialism" shared many of the ideals of Vietnam-era counterculture, its communes, and its frequently toxic gurus. His hodgepodge of doctrines borrowed from Communism but also from Cold War militarism, which like the Temple demanded a huge share of its citizens' wealth every year to protect them from demonized enemies who would eventually crumble with the Berlin Wall. According to Mills, in 1974 Jones confided to his inner circle that he was "negotiating the purchase of an atomic bomb for us" (277). Surrounded by armed guards, seeing traitors on all sides, he echoed the berserk rhetoric of groups as different as the Black Panthers, the John Birch Society, and the Manson family.

As a utopian project, the Peoples Temple espoused communitarian ideals. In its public image the group identified with the ethos of Lyndon Johnson's Great Society programs—the first national effort since the New Deal to bring all Americans into mainstream economic life—and with therapeutic culture. Economically, however, Jones pursued a boom-bust business model. While advertising self-sufficiency—planting crops in Guyana, for example—the group depended on Ponzi-style growth. The organization absorbed its members' personal resources, taking houses and salaries in exchange for paternalistic guarantees, in some cases stealing social security and welfare payments. Jones ruthlessly exploited the labor of his followers in maintaining high-visibility public relations.

Working through an elite inner circle, "Father" was godfather in a tacit mafia that bled the largely black membership in a protection racket. With a plant in the state social services department he could divert benefit payments. The gang had its code of silence and a repertory of intimidation tactics. As a de facto aristocracy, Jones, his natural family, and his inner circle lived on the labors and resources of the ordinary members. As in mafia, with ritualized Orwellian doublethink, the leadership stressed love and loyalty even as it established a tacit prison system, with armed guards, work details, supervised social relationships, spies, and punishment for rebels.

As a spokesman for the poor, Jones was able to woo politicians by providing them with campaign workers and flattering endorsements. To parry criticism, he emulated corporate public relations blitzes, mounting letter-writing campaigns and stage-managed protests. Playing on public opinion, he was able to intimidate editors and silence reporters, quashing Lester Kinsolving's early expose in 1972.

By the time that disaffected followers, alarmed relatives, and investigators finally began closing in, Jones had good reasons for his persecution mania. Congressman Leo Ryan's fatal visit to Guyana eerily evoked the trips up river in search of a berserk renegade in Conrad's *Heart of Darkness* (1902) and Francis Ford Coppola's contemporaneous *Apocalypse Now* (1979). Jones's mental instability and drug use were by then well advanced. Having stockpiled cyanide, he was entertaining a homemade apocalypse of cosmic victimization and vindication.

Jeannie Mills was convinced that Jones planned to survive the mass poisoning of his followers, and it remains unclear how he came to be shot to death. In exhorting the followers to accept death because "we" were tired of life, he was confessing his own exhaustion and the futility of the Peoples Temple scheme. For a long time he had taken no pleasure in alpha male sex and triumphal fraud; investigations were cutting off his financial resources and any hope of expansion; and the group that remained with him, now wholly dependent, would be an insoluble burden to him. Expecting to be "terminated" like Coppola's renegade warlord and former Col. Kurtz (Marlon Brando), who has become a self-appointed god presiding over native warriors in the jungle, Jones was overcome by a form of combat stress. Using his guards and cyanide as his weapons, he launched the rampage that killed reporters, a US congressman, and nearly a thousand followers.

Jones's paranoia was palpable, yet the clinical term flattens out the ambiguity of his actions. Given his predatory behavior, his fear of retaliation was realistic. Yet like the desire to be a god, the fear was also limitless. This is the miserable truth evident in the tape of Jones's final harangue as the faithful were swallowing the cyanide-laced fruit juice he called "the medication." In the murder of Congressman Ryan and the journalists at the airstrip, Jones behaved like a rampage killer slaying a boss and severing connections to the world. Now he faced certain punishment, taking out his guilt and numbed anger on his flock. Like Mark Barton killing his family, the warrior-king wanted company in death. "His" group death magnified his martyrdom even if he was holding out hope for his own magical last-minute rescue.

The tape begins with Jones at the microphone declaring his love for the group, defusing resistance from the group and his own fury and guilt from the murder of the congressman's party. As usual he mixes grandiosity, flattery, and self-pity. He—"we"—had been "born too soon" into a despicable world. We are revolutionary heroes but engulfed by enemies. Logically, some of his victims propose carrying on the fight or escaping. The con man instantly counters that their deaths are not a spectacular suicide at all, but the routine practice by which every revolutionary group in history has "passed over" when finally cornered.

Pitching his plan for suicide, Jones is unctuous, emotionally dissociated. He rambles a little, lisping or slurring words as if under sedation. As resistance and turmoil circulate in the group, urgency begins to strain his crooning pleas for relaxation and peace: "Let's get gone. Let's get gone. Let's get gone. (Children crying.) We had nothing we could do. We can't—we can't separate ourselves from our own people. For twenty years laying in some old rotten nursing home. (Music.) Taking us through all these anguish years. They took us and put us in chains and that's nothing. This business—that business—there's no comparison to that, to this."[10]

The "rotten" nursing home and chains are the fears of the exhausted, aging criminal who in fact faces life in prison. Warning that "they" are coming to kill "our babies," he projects onto enemies the murders he is actually directing now, attested by the shrieks of poisoned children in the background. Babies stand for rebirth and immortality, but also for the hope of reintegrating personality splintered by lies and internal conflict, the hope of finding a coherent self: "They've robbed us of our land, and they've taken us and driven us and we tried to find ourselves. We tried to find a new beginning. But it's too late."

As he pretends that the decision is voluntary and democratic, Christine Miller, an articulate sixty-year-old black woman, brings up his past promise that the Russians have "given them a code" and in a crisis a plane would take them to Russia. The magician pulls more excuses from his hat. Maybe "next time," after reincarnation, she may go to Russia. And when she persists that she has a right to her own opinion and the babies have a right to their lives, Jones tops the lie without missing a beat: "Right now I'm making a call to Russia. What more can I give you?"

Grasping for arguments, he observes that the defectors who left with Ryan's party were white, playing on racial fears and animosity. When an elderly woman picks up on the theme, he interprets her feelings to her, crystallizing her vague sense of racial betrayal. "Broke my heart completely," she agrees. Her reasoning reveals the tremendous need for self-esteem and acceptance in so many of the followers: "All of this year the white people had been with us, and they're not a part of us. So we might as well end it now because I don't see . . ."

Jones replies by insisting on his own concerns: "It's all over. The congressman has been murdered. (Music and singing.) Well, it's all over, all over. What a legacy, what a legacy." In response to an inaudible comment soon after he reinforces the mixed confession-denial: "I didn't, but my people did. My people did. They're my people, and they've been provoked too much. They've been provoked too much." Presumably he means the guards who carried out his murders at the airstrip instead of restraining him as he'd once commanded in less desperate days.

When protests flicker, he cries to the nurses, "Can we hasten with that medication?" And to the victims, "You don't know what you've done"—as if the group, not he, killed the visitors. Later on he refers to defector Tim Stoen as if Stoen is murdering the group. The exhausted rage to punish scapegoats comes out in his vow that enemies "brought this upon us. And they'll pay for that." He becomes urgent as the group's mood wavers. "Please. For God's sake, let's get on with it. We've lived—we've lived as no other people lived and loved. We've had as much of this world as you're gonna get. Let's just be done with it. Let's be done with the agony of it." (Applause.) His own fear of death surfaces again: "It's far, far harder to have to walk through every day, die slowly—and from the time you're a child 'til the time you get gray, you're dying."

The supreme leader wants to merge with—to hide in—the group. So the group can share his burden of guilt he half-confesses that he has had the visitors murdered. "You can't separate yourself from your brother and your sister. No way I'm going to do it. I refuse. I don't know who fired the shot. I don't know who killed the congressman. But as far as I am concerned, I killed him. You understand what I'm saying? I killed him. He had no business coming. I told him not to come."

Unless the group "passes over," they will be tortured and killed. In reality of course Jones is killing them. And he cannot quite believe he too will die: "I want to see you go. They can take me and I don't care what they do with me." It is possible, as Jeannie Mills believed, that he was scheming to escape. The feint at martyrdom plays to the persistent hero-worship in the air. A handful of true believers come to the microphone and give testimonials as if this is just another temple service or an infomercial.

He tries to talk down the anguish before him. "Lay down your life with dignity," he coaxes. "Don't lay down with tears and agony. There's nothing to death. It's . . . it's just stepping over to another plane. Don't be this way. Stop this hysterics. This is not the way for people who are Socialists or Communists to die. No way for us to die. We must die with some dignity. We must die with some dignity. We will have no choice. Now we have some choice. Do you think they're gonna allow this to be done—allow us to get by with this? You must be insane." Not he is insane, but they. "Look children, it's just something to put you to rest. Oh, God." Children are crying. Jones begins to plead, and it is hard not to hear appeals to a fantasy mother akin to his sentimentality about his "seniors" even as he apparently scolds a woman trying to resist: "Mother, Mother, Mother, Mother, Mother, please. Mother, please, please, please. Don't—don't do this. Don't do this. Lay down your life with your child. But don't do this."

Like a dutiful child, a woman tells him, "We're doing all of this for you."

"Free at last," he replies evoking emancipation and Martin Luther King's civil rights rhetoric. "Keep—keep your emotions down. Keep your emotions down. Children, it will not hurt. If you'd be—if you'll be quiet. If you'll be quiet." With babies screaming in death throes and eddies of distress in the group he implores them all to "Stop this hysteria." At the evidence of their death agonies he is responding to the pressure of guilt and panic in himself as well. "So be patient. Be patient. Death is—I tell you, I don't care how many screams you hear. I don't care how many anguished cries. Death is a million times preferable to ten more days of this life. If you knew what was ahead of you—if you knew what was ahead of you, you'd be glad to be stepping over tonight." He can't resist some fatherly scolding: "Adults, I call on you to stop this nonsense. Stop exciting your children. Hurry, my children. Hurry . . . hurry." Quickly quickly quickly quickly."

In his effort to make rhetorical theater preempt fatal reality the rational mind snatches at fragments and formulas: "Death, death, death is common to people. And the Eskimos, they take death in their stride. Let's be digni—let's be dignified. If you quit tell them they're dying—if you adults would stop some of this nonsense. Adults, adults, adults. I call on you to stop this nonsense. I call on you to quit exciting your children when all they're doing is going to a quiet rest. I call on you to stop this now if you have any respect at all. Are we black, proud, and Socialist, or what are we? Now stop this nonsense. Don't carry this on anymore. You're exciting your children."

The children can't rationalize. They sense panic.

In the closing turmoil incoherence spreads. "No, no sorrow—that it's all over," he says. "I'm glad it's over. Hurry, hurry my children. Hurry. All I think (inaudible) from the hands of the enemy. Hurry, my children. Hurry. There are seniors out here that I'm concerned about. Hurry. I don't want to leave my seniors to this mess. Only quickly, quickly, quickly, quickly, quickly." There is a pause in which one of the victims apparently professes some sort of devotion, and with stupefying dissociation Jones replies in the scripted formula of everyday business, "Good knowing you."

Several true believers praise the Cause and Father's love. One woman brings out the infantile subtext: "Right. Yes, eh. Dad's love and nursing, goodness and kindness and bring us to this land of freedom. His love—his mother was the advance—the advance guard to socialism. And his love (inaudible) will go on forever unto the fields of—"

She runs out of clichés. But Jones is anxious to get on with his business plan, the final act of their play: "Where's the vat, the vat, the vat? Where's the vat with the Green C on it? The vat with the Green C in. Bring it so the adults can begin."[11]

That is, die.

As in Mohammed Atta's final instructions to his gang, Jones the God-priest was concerned that they "must not discomfort [their] animal during the slaughter." But like Atta, he had come too far to turn back to a world of self-doubt and guilt. There was nothing left now but sweaty bodies, needy dependents, and squalling babies. The glorious possibilities lay in the beyond, an illusion—what did it matter as long as no one was left to be happily rescued by others and to testify to his failure and criminal rage?

The final Jonestown tape shows not a cadre of suicidal fanatics or, despite the menace of Jones's armed guards, crushing force. On the contrary, the collapse gathered momentum among disoriented, conflicted followers marooned in a jungle, alienated from home and familiar landmarks. They had literally abandoned familiar cognitive boundaries. Now they depended on group solidarity, Jones, and a flattering ideology for coherence and willpower. The tape reveals only wavering resistance to abandon and death. The few true believers who take the microphone tell us that confused imaginations clung to Jones's grand themes—including martyrdom—to ground themselves. A few voices objected to death, but nobody proposed a realistic alternative or condemned the murder of Congressman Ryan and his party. The followers had surrendered much of their autonomy to Jones and to the nebulous community. Like Jones's euphemism of "passing over," the poisonous fruit juice made an apt metaphor for the pressure of conformity in the group. Under stress, berserk style disposed them to reach for purpose in the hallucinatory beyond.

STAR WARS

In the following decade evangelical ministries took to the airwaves as a route to expansion. They banished the sinister Jonestown themes with variety show entertainment and an upbeat message. Rev. Jim Bakker drummed up a media ministry and in North Carolina opened a popular theme park, Heritage USA. As in politics (Reagan) and industrial entertainment (Disney), the emphasis on heritage combined religion and patriotism to reaffirm a feel-good ground of identity for post-Vietnam America. Nevertheless, in a 1986 sex scandal Bakker lost his empire and was convicted of swindling his followers in a 158 million dollar real estate fraud, among other counts. He went to prison decrying a plot that mixed themes of mafia and martyrdom. "My enemies are trying to kill me," he told the largest audience in *Nightline's* seven-year history. "They plot my ruin and spend all their waking hours planning treachery."[12] The traitor was another televangelist, the Rev. Jerry Falwell, who inveigled the tainted "Heritage USA" for his own empire.

After this sunny interlude berserk themes darkened again. Infuriated by the Federal government's incineration of David Koresh's band of Branch Davidians at their compound in Waco Texas, Timothy McVeigh blew up the McMurrah Federal Building in Oklahoma City (1995) in the deadliest terrorist attack in the United States before the World Trade Center inferno. Based on his interest in the white-supremacist novel *The Turner Diaries* (1978), McVeigh's racial convictions were the opposite of Jones's. Still, the novel fantasizes a doomsday nuclear race war of the sort that terrified Jones's followers. Where Jones fantasized about buying an atomic bomb, McVeigh actually built a 5,000- pound ammonium nitrate bomb that killed nearly 200 people and damaged more than 300 buildings in Oklahoma City.

The Christian right achieved new visibility in the post-Vietnam decades with its rousing attacks on social issues such as abortion, evolution, and homosexuality. While some of this militancy has been strategic—acquiring political influence and donors, for example—the core themes exercise a soft version of survival rage. On its website a "pro-life" organization called "Survivors," for example, directly inflames personal death-anxiety with ominous music, photographs of concentration camp corpses, and the warning that "[i]f you were born after 1972, we challenge you to consider yourself a Survivor of the Abortion Holocaust. 1/3 of your generation has been killed by abortion in America! The Survivors are taking an active stand on behalf of those who have already been lost, and for those who are scheduled to die through abortion. We are empowered by the truth, enabled by extensive training, and unafraid of condemning the death of innocents." Although carefully inexplicit, this rhetoric is paramilitary and judicial. "You" are part of a special group, "your generation," and in a genocidal war. You need "training" to "rise up . . . willing to be used by God to 'defend those unjustly sentenced to death.'" This is the language of jihad, directed at a nation that "schedules" annihilation through "death sentences." It calls for a heroic battle for survival, with "you" enacting a version of "the greatest generation's" triumph over Nazism—the nation's last righteous war.

Circulating on the web is a video titled "Battle Cry." Prefaced by Christ's threat-display, "I come not to bring peace, but a sword," the video uses crusader swords and portentous melodrama—Carmina Burana chant, cascading echo effects—to beef up this mantra for Christian "soldiers":

I'm not an innocent bystander,
I am a threat to my enemies
I am powerful
I am strategic and bold
I will not sit idly by
I will take ground
I will advance
I will tear through my enemy
I will not avoid the difficult fight
I will fight
I will be wounded
I will be targeted & I will bleed
I will not tire
I will see tragedy I will feel pain
But I will be restored
My feet will not stumble
My hands will hold fast
I will not be intimidated
I cannot be stopped
I will stand by my brothers in arms
I will fight until my last breath
I will push the limits
I scale the mountains
My enemy will cower
For I serve a great king!"

This is not the Christianity of the Sermon on the Mount. The chant directs teenagers to role-play at berserk abandon: "I will bleed, I cannot be stopped, I will fight until my last breath." The mantra mixes adolescent narcissism, idealism, and a need to belong with suicidal self-sacrifice and the demonization of enemies.

The crusader chant honors the Christian story of the crucifixion less than the mystical group-bonding rituals of the Nazi SS and other paramilitary cults. The predominance of style and play-acting makes possible the nation's polite obliviousness to the literal meaning of the fantasies. The media paid little notice when vice presidential candidate Sarah Palin's church, the Wasilla Assembly of God, handed out Samurai swords—the emblem of Japanese fascism—to young adults in the congregation, with the incitement to use "a double edged sword in their hands to inflict vengeance on the nations, and punishment on the peoples, and to bind their kings with fetters, their nobles with shackles of iron, and to carry out the sentence written against them" (Psalms 149 verses 6–9).[13]

Projection of berserk tropes onto the "enemy" has supported attacks on abortion clinics and the assassination of doctors. Scott Roeder, who allegedly murdered Dr. George Tiller in a Kansas church on May 31, 2009, fits a familiar profile: a man divorced, preoccupied with death-anxiety (abortion), and according to his brother David, mentally ill at various times of his life. But Roeder acted in an atmosphere that legitimized the murder. The son of clergyman Frank Schaeffer posted an apology online explaining that his father had written the best-selling *A Christian Manifesto* (1981). "In certain passages he advocated force if all other methods for rolling back the abortion ruling of Roe v. Wade failed. He compared America and its legalized abortion to Hitler's Germany and said that whatever tactics would have been morally justified in removing Hitler would be justified in trying to stop abortion. I said the same thing in a book I wrote (*A Time for Anger*) that right wing evangelicals made into a best seller."[14]

Schaeffer apologizes for unintentionally contributing to a "climate" that could encourage murder. As a style, however, incendiary language paradoxically seems "natural" or normal, even as its furious zeal makes it hard to see that style takes on a life of its own in which motives may be unaccountable. At the time of Dr. Tiller's murder, for example, antiabortion rage was formulaic in rant media. Bill O'Reilly was vilifying Dr. Tiller for "Nazi stuff" and "operating a death mill." Columnist Kathleen Parker referred to media-savvy activists such as Randall Terry as "fire-breathers.[15] As the genre desensitizes audiences and yesterday's fire-breathing becomes today's stale breath, rhetoric escalates toward abandon. During the health care debates of 2009–10, for example, survival anxiety glibly switched to the specter of "death panels" that would triage the elderly.

The teenagers' crusader vision has a counterpart in the fundamentalist subculture within the US military, in which the "global war on terror" is commonly construed as "a spiritual battle." "The Source of Combat Readiness," an Officers' Christian Fellowship (OCF) Bible study text, proclaims that spiritual battle means "continually confronting an implacable, powerful foe who hates us and eagerly seeks to destroy us." Another study, unfortunately named "Mission Accomplished," draws on the logic of witch panic: "If Satan cannot succeed with threats from the outside, he will seek to destroy from within." The defense is to subsume secular America into a militant theocracy. "God was to be Lord of all or not Lord at all."[16]

This crude Manichaean language makes inner life a combat zone. It converts fear to wrath and invites group solidarity. People are always looking for ways to legitimize scapegoat psychology and make its arguments credible. Since it ultimately involves survival fears and killing, it always opens toward the beyond, as religion and politics repeatedly demonstrate. Senator John Ensign, for example, belongs to a Pentecostal denomination, the International Church of the Foursquare Gospel, that "promotes a new health care paradigm in which both physical and psychological maladies can be cured through the casting out of demons. In the new approach, individuals can even heal themselves by exorcising their own demons."[17]

The "new approach" is of course an ancient fantasy system given topical authority as a "movement." The "demon-deliverance movement" or "Theophostic Ministry" ignores its historical affinity with early modern witch-hunt hysteria. Its style of thinking risks inflaming paranoid symptoms by attributing supernatural powers to troubling thoughts and, given the plasticity of imagination, seeing infiltrating enemies everywhere. By reducing experience to a melodrama, favoring hyper-vigilance, it intensifies preoccupation with the self even as it closes off other explanations, inviting self-intoxication. In a word, this is berserk style opening into magical thinking. "One very distinctive characteristic of Third Wave Christianity is its emphasis that average Christians can perform the same magnitude of healing miracles described in the New Testament to have been performed by Jesus Christ—including raising the dead."[18]

The totalizing character of the ideation is classic berserk style, echoing the psychodynamics of Islam's radical jihadis who would dominate society by imposing their own versions of history and sharia law. The preacher-proprietors of aggressive new religions like to claim millions of adherents, but in the absence of reliable data, zeroes tend to be promiscuous. The "neo-Apostolic" empire builder C. Peter Wagner speaks in terms of "megablocks" and boasts that "postdenominational" and more radical movements number hundreds of millions and are growing faster than the earth's population and faster than Islam. His claim revisits the ancient appetite for life more plentiful than the stars in heaven, and in the process outdoing a sinister rival. Such is the power of survival greed.

SUPERNATURAL ABUSE

In the post-Vietnam decades witch-hunt ideation assumed many guises. The previous chapter described the wide net spread by the idea of abuse in the post-Vietnam years. In the foreground the term referred primarily to domestic violence and sexual aggression against children. Religious militancy gave the term florid cosmic coloration. Sexual abuse offered a logical hypothesis for a range of disturbances in American culture. Economic stress heightened awareness of gender inequities, women's personal safety, and the welfare of children. With more families needing both parents to work, "latchkey kid" became a familiar term. Antiabortion protests declaimed against a "slaughter of the innocents." Media and even milk carton advertisements inflamed anxieties about an epidemic of child kidnapping that turned out to be an urban legend. In this climate the actual kidnapping and murder of Polly Klaas, which radically changed the California criminal justice system, became a catalyst in the panic around abuse.

The most unlikely exponents of berserk style proved to be a subculture of psychotherapists who used sexual abuse to explain a wide host of symptoms. They were especially excited about dissociative disorders such as multiple personality (MPD, now called dissociative identity disorder) and recovered memories (suddenly recalled but unsubstantiated abuse). Before long a subset of clinicians and patients were entangled in a classic iatrogenic feedback loop. Encouraged by popular self-help books and media hype, credulous sufferers reinforced each other's beliefs and gave social reality to some wildly implausible theories. By insisting they be called abuse "survivors," as if sexual abuse was lethal, the groups participated in a process akin to a conversion experience, assuming roles based on heroic rescue, with the prestige of overcoming death. Real or imagined experiences of sexual abuse became enemy attacks. The possibility of "recovered memory" gave the interpretation of distress an uncanny quality.

Feelings of persecution by evil parent figures have venerable precedents, from fairy tales to witchcraft lore, in which crones and the "father" of lies Satan supposedly cannibalized babies, sickened children, practiced loathsome sterile sex, and worse. The fascination with multiple personality owed much to Flora Rheta Schrieber's *Sybil*, (book 1973, film 1976) and Dr. Lawrence Pazder and Michelle Smith's *Michelle Remembers* (1980), each presenting a case study with sensational symptoms, and each reliably debunked.[19] Michelle's story explicitly borrowed heavily from witchcraft lore. By the 1990s child sex abuse and MPD featured in novels for adolescents and critics could shake their heads at "The Vogue of Childhood Misery."[20]

The clinicians' ignorance of history included the history of their profession, in particular the belated recognition of iatrogenic and transference phenomena in the days of Charcot and Freud.[21] If nothing else, the elasticity of the theories should have raised warning flags. One of the most unsavory variants of the abuse theme proved to be "Satanic ritual abuse syndrome," which held that patients were suffering the effects of programming by a shadowy global cult whose satanic rituals called for the abduction, sacrifice, and prostitution of children. Like medieval panic about Jews feeding on Christian children, the theory imagined the cult to be a wealthy, clannish elite bent on consuming the vitality of innocents.[22]

The cult supposedly exercised mind control through brainwashing techniques that could induce amnesia, giving the perpetrators a totalitarian cast dramatized in John Frankenheimer's Cold War thriller *The Manchurian Candidate* (1962). Mind control is a deeply engrained human preoccupation, evident in ancient beliefs about possession, in the fascination with Satan, in the allure of "animal magnetism," and in the cult delusions generated around Hitler's personality.[23] In *The Shock Doctrine*, Naomi Klein traces the origins of that corporate-military ideology to the CIA and Cold Warriors' obsession—and experiments—with brainwashing techniques. The web of analogy is dense, and colors a wide political spectrum.

These improbable materials haunt—no other word will do—the two cases reported in Ofra Bikel and Rachel Dretzin's lucid PBS *Frontline* investigation "The Search for Satan" (October 24, 1995). While the patients, Patricia Burgus and Mary Shanley, eventually won lawsuits against their psychiatrist Bennett Braun and other therapists, they both suffered dangerously destabilizing treatment driven by berserk dynamics.

"Mary S" (Shanley), a young teacher, sought treatment for persistent anxiety symptoms after some painful setbacks in an otherwise healthy middle-class life. In a brief intake interview psychiatrist Roberta Sachs at Rush-Presbyterian-St. Luke's Medical Center in Chicago diagnosed multiple personality disorder caused by membership in a satanic cult that Mary had been "programmed" to forget. The diagnosis led to two years of heavily drugged hospitalization and a regimen of interrogation meant to force the patient to "abreact" the spectral horrors of the childhood that the therapists projected on her. By the time she won her release in a lawsuit, she had been transferred to clinic in Texas, was in seriously impaired health, and destined for a nursing home—and her insurance policy had topped out at a sum in the millions.

To be sure, the absurdities of the diagnosis were in plain view. Mary S's family, the doctors told her, had been "cult royalty." The cult encoded its brainwashing programs using letters of the Greek alphabet. Her young son was dragged into the net, also hospitalized, and held to be in mortal danger. Nevertheless, as the woman tells the filmmakers, the doctors "were the authorities, the experts." And crucially, berserk style in the culture around her seemed to corroborate their diagnosis. She had heard her local pastor warning about Satan's infiltration of their neighborhoods. The media thrilled to stories about teen satanists.

The diagnosis had coercive features reminiscent of Soviet psychiatry. The healers isolated the patient in their hospitals, blocking ordinary reality-testing and dosing her with inappropriate psychotropic drugs. Tape of one of the therapy sessions records a pitiably distraught and helpless Mary S shrieking in anguish while a circle of therapists browbeat her to remember cult atrocities and confirm their narrative. The therapists form an accusing circle as a pack would. More than a sufferer to be healed, the patient is a presumed perpetrator. This is not a figure of speech, since the doctors accused Mary S of being an agent of cult malice, endangering the lives of her husband and son and by implication her doctors. As in witch hysteria, the accusers imagine an evil mother in the service of a satanic regime with what amount to superhuman powers.

Like brainwashing, the treatment devised by Dr. Braun and others perversely undermined the patient's identity. Accused of harboring murderous motives beyond her control while simultaneously being a target of cult assassination, the patient was consumed by panic. Drugged, sometimes held in restraints, stripped of her own life story, bullied to substitute a nonexistent cult childhood, she was suffering on the edge of an abyss. If abuse is so damaging because it is traumatic, and trauma is an effect of overwhelming terror, then patients such as Mary S, who presented acute anxiety and depression, needed serenity, trust, and a renewed sense of life purpose, not an emergency crusade against a hallucinatory past injury with features that resembled post- 9/11 "harsh interrogation tactics." Relief from terror depends on restoring trust and social bonds, not on imaginary triumphs over "perpetrators" and the Ultimate Perpetrator, Satan.

At the same time the ritual abuse narrative made the patient death-tainted and a threat not just to her family and self, but also to the doctors. They were caught in a cognitive trap of their own devising. If they believed in their own story and therapy, they faced a menacing woman beyond their control. If they admitted the failure of their story, they faced guilt as well as helplessness: in effect, an attack on their own ground of experience. In short, the situation readily generated berserk panic, and the cruel absurdity of the therapies followed.

The therapists' anxieties were fuel for their heroic roles. In the film Patty Burgus describes how Dr. Braun coached her hospitalized sons to "remember" cult atrocities, rewarding them with stickers for a good performance. Braun in turn used the fabulations to prove his theories. At one point, as an expert witness in court, he testifies about the child's report of a cult rite in which he had witnessed a man's abdomen cut open and entrails spilling out with a putrid smell. Braun knows the story is true, he vows, because he's done surgery where such an eruption is a concern. How, he demands, would a five-year-old boy come by such information if not through the cult?[24]

The answer, says Patty Burgus, is that as she tried to tell Dr. Braun, her son was recounting an episode from *Star Wars* in which Luke Skywalker cuts open the gut of a space creature and gags at the smell of the erupting entrails. The doctor evinces anxiety about death-tainted bodies while blindly seizing on the tale as proof of his heroic narrative as physician. Similar turmoil underlies the hostility of practitioners when challenged by skeptical nurses.

The satanic abuse fad developed out of banal cultural materials provided by psychologist D. C. "Corey" Hammond, among others. Hammond was a clinician and consultant with degrees in counseling psychology, marital and sex therapy, and clinical hypnosis. His background in suggestive techniques is evident in his own dreamlike suppositions. Behind the Satanic cult, he argued, was a Jewish doctor who had survived the death camps by collaborating with the Nazis and surfaced in the United States as "Dr. Green"—a clone of criminal masterminds from pulp fiction. Exposure to traumatic death-anxiety (the death camps) arouses berserk survival greed that gorges on children and forbidden sex. "Dr. Green" is the evil twin of the good therapist who happens to be profiting from engaging with the suffering and terror of mental illness.

Just this potent elixir of dread and heroic aggrandizement links berserk therapy to forms of making a killing discussed in earlier chapters. The abuse phenomenon coincided with increased Federal funding for child abuse research. Dr. Braun ran a multimillion dollar dissociative disorders clinic at Rush-Presbyterian that was, after all, a business depending on insurance plans. "Bennett Braun seems to be a promotional genius," said John Hochman, a California psychiatrist who likens Braun's own professional following to a cult. "He started [The International Society for the Study of Dissociation] and a journal. There were the conferences. . . . They were just very excited about what they had and nobody challenged them in a very big way" (AP, March 7, 1999).

What finally broke the self-confirming paradigm was the data analysis of clinical outcomes by independent auditors who noticed that patients' conditions worsened rather than improved, and a combination of patients' lawsuits and the formation of critical groups such as the False Memory Syndrome Foundation. In the meantime the billing for care resembled the unchecked extravagance unfolding in Wall Street finance.

For a time recovered memory and mind-control themes pervaded many areas of American culture. Futuristic thrillers such as Kathryn Bigelow's *Strange Days* (1995) and Paul Verhoeven's *Total Recall* (1990) used fears of brainwashing technology. Like the Terminator saga, *Total Recall* is a digest of berserk themes. It envisions a criminal mastermind reminiscent of Antichrist using a cultlike regime to rule over a servile class (on Mars!) through mind-control and false memories. Like the Satanic abuse delusion, the film associates cognitive mischief with episodes of berserk rage.

During the 90s the courts finally barred recovered memory testimony as research exposed its unreliability and the damage it caused. Mary Shanley suffered terribly, but her induced "memories" could have put her, her supposedly satanic parents, or others in prison. Or worse. The State of Texas put Cameron Todd Willingham to death in 2004 after a conviction based on "junk science" and influenced by community fantasies about Satanism. The prosecution concluded that the unemployed father had deliberately set the fire that killed his three small children one morning while his wife was at work. Once gripped by the popular idea that they had discovered what the prosecutor called a sociopathic "demon," neighborhood witnesses reinterpreted their recollections of Willingham's behavior while the house burned. A psychologist testified that Willingham's rock group posters revealed pathological motives: "There's a hooded skull with wings and a hatchet. And all of these are in fire—it reminds me of something like Hell. And there's a picture—a Led Zeppelin picture of a fallen angel . . . I see there's an association many time with cultive-type of activities. A focus on death, dying. Many times individuals that have a lot of this type of art have an interest in satanic-type activities." Political culture in Texas militates against clemency, and the Board of Pardons and Paroles apparently ignored an appeal based on new scientific evidence. "A Texas appellate judge has called the clemency system 'a legal fiction.' "[25]

The "demonic" rock band imagery and the tattoo of a skull used to help convict Willingham are an ironic reminder of how explosively ambiguous death-anxiety can be. For adolescents, the "satanic" posters presumably objectify, and create some mastery of, fears of death and social death. The posters mark teenage solidarity. At the same time the imagery is a marketing tool to sell industrial entertainment. Unluckily for Willingham, the terrifying deaths of small children, in a culture limited by ignorance and latent anger, turned the fantasy images into grounds for judicial killing of a "demon" parent.

The cluster of fantasies around dissociative disorders and Satanic abuse defied reality-testing as long as it did in part because it drew strength from a confluence of unlikely voices, from fundamentalist preachers and law enforcement to MS magazine. In a keynote address at a 1991 conference on MPD in Chicago, Gloria Steinem praised Dr. Braun for his life-saving work. The demoralizing slump after the defeat in Vietnam saw antiscientific fundamentalism expand its appeal, amplified by aggressive new religious broadcasting, demographic transformation in the Bible belt, and the official sanction of figures such as President Reagan, who pumped up crusading spirit by calling the Soviet Union "the evil empire," and alluded in public to Armageddon and his Millenialist beliefs.[26]

THE LIVING END

As Otto Rank understood, nothing is more exhilarating than survival, and there is no survival more ultimate than doomsday. In Judgment Day theologies the divine parent defines the meaning of everything once and for all, and the blessed join Him in heaven. We can only think about such finality as we do death, in tropes. The process can take astonishing forms. In *The Pursuit of the Millennium*, Norman Cohn showed that Nazi and Soviet ideologies drew on millenialist mythologies. The "thousand year" Reich used an eschatological climax in the distant, unreal future to rationalize a berserk drive for expansion. The suicidal, blow-off climax of Nazi millennialism was effectively built in.

American Protestants have intermittently cultivated apocalyptic themes from colonial times. By the close of the twentieth century some American fundamentalists were lobbying for policies toward the Middle East that they hoped would fulfill biblical prophecies loosely associated with Armageddon in the book of *Revelations*. While there have been some political benefits for the believers, "Many of them have an ecstatic belief in the cleansing power of apocalyptic violence."[27]

An item in *L'Express* (February 26, 2009) reported that in a telephone call meant to persuade France's Chirac to join in the invasion of Iraq, President Bush asserted that "Gog and Magog are at work in the Middle East" and that "the Biblical prophecies are about to be fulfilled." Chirac listened with puzzlement and apprehension ("effroi"). After some research he was not amused. The absurd apocalyptic prophecy that Bush was invoking to justify his war plans—or the war meant to fulfill a prophecy—alarmed him. ("Chirac, lui, ne rit pas. Cette parabole d'une apocalypse annoncée pour réaliser une prophétie l'inquiète et le tourmente").

For decades fundamentalist Christians have been developing a feedback loop in which middle eastern turbulence substantiates the book of *Revelations* and, reciprocally, *Revelations* accounts for the tumult in the middle east. If we can trust the account in *L'Express*, Bush imagined that such millenarian ideas could persuade his French counterpart to join in a war. In theory, apocalypse frames the uncertain future, resolving anxieties and boosting morale. In the real world, as Bush's misreading of Chirac indicates, prophetic inspiration is prescriptive and not always attuned to the feelings of others.

Modernity is a history of traumatic disenchantments. The Renaissance thrilled and quaked at the rediscovery of magnificent civilizations that had perished. With science came evidence that humans may go the way of dinosaurs, and that life on earth will die out with the exhausted sun in a few billion years. Cable television documentaries especially favor doomsday topics from asteroids and dinosaur extinctions to nuclear weapons and global climate change. Like religious apocalypse, the documentaries frame overwhelming, disturbing information so that imagination can develop defenses and get used to it.

Since "end times" scenarios are pure speculation, criticism can only assess the work they do in the present. Like right-wing media rant, doomsday can be a vehicle for self-medication. Self-congratulating "end times" soap operas such as Tim LaHaye's entertaining multivolume "rapture" epic *Left Behind* can impart an adrenalizing morale boost, no matter how backward they may be as theology. The reported multimillion sales of the 12-volume *Left Behind* series appears to confirm the estimate that as many as a third of Americans believe the world is coming to an end soon. But the actual market share of such fantasies remains hazy. The quality of belief is always hard to measure, and there is a palpable quality of play about pop apocalypses akin to the pleasure in popular supermarket tabloids ("Woman Gives Birth to Martian Baby"). Belief in the imminent end of the world focuses many cults and can be a tormenting symptom of schizophrenia, but for many believers it is a tonic or a token safely tucked away, and nothing more.

The *Left Behind* story's Rapture domesticates the terrors of the end, translating the righteous to a heaven of abstract nouns with no more inconvenience than a change of wardrobe. Thanks to the Rapture, believers can participate vicariously in berserk rage against unbelievers. Here is an efficient summary of the fantasy:

> In the 19th century, two immigrant preachers [Edward Irving and John Nelson Darby] cobbled together a series of unrelated passages from the Bible to create what appears to be a consistent narrative: Jesus will return to earth when certain preconditions have been met. The first of these was the establishment of a state of Israel. The next involves Israel's occupation of the rest of its "Biblical lands" (most of the Middle East), and the rebuilding of the Third Temple on the site now occupied by the Dome of the Rock and Al-Aqsa mosques. The legions of the Antichrist will then be deployed against Israel, and their war will lead to a final showdown in the valley of Armageddon. The Jews will either burn or convert to Christianity, and the Messiah will return to earth.[28]

The cosmic battlefield ranges from the biblical Armageddon to the guidebook Israel of Tim LaHaye's propagandistic soap opera *Armageddon*, in which generic Christians and Jews slaughter minions of Antichrist with Uzis and comic book dialogue. Again Monbiot: "before the big battle begins, all 'true believers' (ie those who believe what THEY believe) will be lifted out of their clothes and wafted up to heaven during an event called the Rapture. Not only do the worthy get to sit at the right hand of God, but they will be able to watch, from the best seats, their political and religious opponents being devoured by boils, sores, locusts and frogs, during the seven years of Tribulation which follow." In this theology berserk style converts the sadistic horror of the "final showdown" to righteous joy, while sanitizing the killing frenzy with the bizarre amalgam of biblical torments (boils, locusts, and the like) and typical pulp fiction toys (Uzis, rockets).

"Most journalists find it difficult to take seriously that tens of millions of Americans, filled with fantasies of revenge and empowerment, long to leave a world they despise. These Armageddonites believe that they alone will get a quick, free pass when they are 'raptured' to paradise, no good deeds necessary, not even a day of judgment." John Basil Utley compares them to Islamic fundamentalist jihadis, then adds: "These end-timers have great influence over the U.S. government's foreign policy. They are thick with the Republican leadership. At a recent conference in Washington, congressional leader Roy Blunt, for example, has said that their work is 'part of God's plan.' At the same meeting, where speakers promoted attacking Iran, former House Majority Leader Tom DeLay glorified 'end times.'"[29]

In the run-up to the millennium Year 2000 the fear of apocalyptic extremism generated the FBI's Megiddo Report (1999), an inventory of groups such as the Christian Identity movement that blend racist and cosmic chauvinism with millenarian melodrama and a propensity for violence. "Megiddo" is another name for the biblical battleground of Armageddon. Although law enforcement did report the disruption of Y2K bomb plots aimed at targets as far-flung as Jerusalem and the Los Angeles airport, the anticlimactic outcome of the fateful day exposed the degree of berserk style at work.

In fact the "rapture racket," as Barbara R. Rossing calls it in *The Rapture Exposed* (2004), allows people to consider topical fears while keeping them safely unreal. The "rapture" website "leftbehind.com" hypes prophetic signs that read like a news index: "Political crisis, Economic crisis, Worldwide epidemics. Environmental catastrophe, Mass disappearances, [and] Military apocalypse." The September 11 terrorism popularized allusions to past and present religious crusades, satanic schemes, and mystified conspiracy. Equally salient is anxiety about the boundless growth upon which modern capitalism depends, environmental degradation, global pandemic such as bird flu, and new fears of global climate change. Doomsday ideation appears in television documentaries and movies that depict iconic cities sinking beneath the waves as in the myth of Noah.

In *Ecology of Fear,* (1998), urban critic Mike Davis calculates that Los Angeles has been destroyed in fiction and film 138 times.[30] Davis's "central claim is that the citizens of Los Angeles have imagined disasters through a lens of fear and misunderstanding and that the result is a profoundly unequal society that is apocalyptically out of balance with its environment."[31] Just such a cosmic imbalance or incommensurability is crudely dramatized in thrillers that play out variations on catastrophism.[32] In films such as Steven Spielberg's *A. I.* (2001) and Roland Emmerich's *The Day after Tomorrow* (2004) the pulp repertory of berserk convulsion and exhaustion is blockbuster box office. In films of the 1990s such as *Independence Day* (1996) and *Deep Impact* (1998), aliens and a rogue comet menace the earth with extinction.

In these films the catastrophe is actually a collision of everyday reality with cosmic ultimates. An imponderable universe crashes into the human world of flimsy, inadequate meanings. Humankind's deeply rooted guilt at inadequacy struggles against narcissistic survival greed. The imagery plays out harmlessly for most audiences, allowing people to entertain safely the wonder of life's absurdity. But for some, including the 39 members of Marshall Applewhite's Heaven's Gate cult, the crash can be unbearable. The aging, unwell guru taught that universal doom was imminent. Since the guilty earth was about to be wiped clean and renewed, he urged group suicide. His followers accordingly converted the threat of cosmic collision into a sci-fi narrative of escape through death into the paradise afforded by a passing comet. As in the conditioning evident in the Peoples Temple, the group had long been slowly building up to berserk abandon. And as with Jim Jones, the group death provided comfort and company for the ailing guru as he faced his own death.

Some versions of end times stress the idea of abreaction or purgation. The supreme battle is supposed to open the way to a spell of utopian peace something like the return to life after a harrowing illness and the expulsion of "germs"—a cognitive bias evident in the central role of exorcism and emetics in the history of medicine. In such scenarios the expulsion of demons, poisons, or germs corresponds to the divine judgment's banishment of the wicked to Hell.

Even in the realm of industrial entertainment we can only estimate the effect of paranoid fantasies on public attitudes, including the post-9/11 passions. This ambiguity is painfully evident in the military's quixotic, staggeringly expensive "Star Wars" visions of militarized space. Such a "theater" is boundless. Robert Jay Lifton identifies what is at stake: "The war on terrorism is apocalyptic, then, exactly because it is militarized and yet amorphous, without limits of time or place, and has no clear end. It therefore enters the realm of the infinite."[33]

This is the territory of abandon in which potentially bottomless terror fuels fantastic—superhuman—appetite for life.

CONCLUSION

THE ROMANCE OF ABANDON

To return to the beginning: "the concept of berserk abandon is far more pervasive than conventional wisdom recognizes." This proposition spurred a friend of mine to ask, "If the concept is so pervasive, how come it isn't immediately recognized?" An answer came to her in a flash: the berserk is hidden in plain view, like Poe's purloined letter. Since it shades into everyday behavior and ritual, and takes protean guises in berserk style, it is latent everywhere.

Every individual and every culture devises strategies for managing abandon. One such strategy is the idea of "the American dream,"[1] which packages the nation's aspirations and furies for retail consumption. Schools across the country teach the term through Fitzgerald's *The Great Gatsby* (1925), which associates the dream with erotic fertility: "the fresh green breast of the New World," "the milk of wonder," and a beloved voice "full of money." From personal experience Fitzgerald was wise to infantile appetites. He knew that the romance of abandon draws on radical ambivalence to keep the green light glowing on Daisy's dock, "the orgastic future that year by year recedes before us."

Fitzgerald's account remains astonishingly prescient. Gatsby has created himself through berserk style, at home among Madoffs and Enron smart-alecks: a celebrity impresario of thrilling bacchanals, exploiting what has become a perpetual war against substance abuse. His pal Wolfsheim's fix of the World Series bespeaks epic gambling, while his cufflinks, "the finest specimens of human molars," evoke cannibalism and mafia. Diddled by the wealthy Tom Buchanan and abandoned by his wife, the garage mechanic Wilson faces social death. "He's so dumb," sneers Tom, "he doesn't know he's alive." The valley of ashes foretells today's malign gap between rich and the working poor.

In Gatsby's fatal obsession with Daisy and Myrtle Wilson's blind rush into speeding traffic, appetite for life is amok. But in the emasculated husband's God-obsessed, suicidal rampage the novel recognizes the compulsion to enforce "what's right." Aware of Tom Buchanan's role in Myrtle's death and Gatsby's murder, Nick Carraway recognizes the crazed moral aggression: "I saw that what [Tom] had done was, to him, entirely justified." Nick points to the rhythm of rampage and retreat: "They were careless people, Tom and Daisy—they smashed up things and creatures and then retreated back into their money or their vast carelessness, or whatever it was that kept them together, and let other people clean up the mess they had made."

Or whatever it was that kept them together.

For better and worse, one of the things that has kept Americans together is berserk style. In the brawl and sprawl of postwar American life various groups have bonded around shared hopes and fears that are projections of the beyond. In countless ways berserk style has become a major tool for personal and institutional management of morale. But Americans have suffered—and enjoyed—the romance of abandon because abandon has stood for personal authenticity and creativity as well as rampage. The scale of the ironies defies summary when a globe-straddling empire that has tested the brink of prosperity and ruin still has its valleys of ashes, profligate punch bowls, and murderous ghosts—at a time when "the colored empires" in Asia have risen in an economic whirlwind and Gatsby's dubious medal from "little Montenegro" winks toward US military intervention in the Balkans in the 1990s. Post-Vietnam America still advertises the goal of making the world safe for democracy, but in an unruly world the global policeman can sound like the self-serving Tom Buchanan, that harbinger of conniving media rant: "Flushed with his impassioned gibberish, he saw himself standing alone on the last barrier of civilization."

In such a volatile, entangled culture everything is in motion and scale overruns boundaries. As the corporate state flatters and moots the lone citizen's will, submissiveness and rebellion mix in incalculable ways. Spooked by alienation and fear of social death, rage for order can handcuff creative ambition as well as criminal aggression. It can exhaust itself whipping scapegoats. Frenzy can be uplifting and energizing, but it can also override problem-solving faculties and the imaginative sympathy that enables us to respond effectively to others.

Like criticism, the emerging paradigm of sustainability offers a constructive means of managing abandon. As an ecological and philosophical outlook, sustainability stresses equilibrium and interrelatedness. Globalization could develop that way, but currently it is grounded in fantasies of unlimited expansion. Sustainability, by contrast, favors contexts and metrics that can put in perspective the spikes and anomalies in berserk style. It represents a different way of thinking about death-anxiety, appetite, and renewal.

If berserk style in the new century feels more electric, it is also because the "American dream" is more supercharged than ever: more globally ambitious, morally ambiguous, and more complexly in trouble. Anxiety about decline is in the air. Certainly the scale of things has changed. Only a decade or two before Gatsby the American president could still answer his own mail. The great Ponzi and traction scams of the day are proportional but still smaller than the corporate riots of the Enron era. Today the earth itself is a casualty in the headlines, and finite resources challenge scientific wherewithal to cope in time.

And these days the dream is also more evanescent, too: less like the magisterial iconic Miss Liberty chaperoning Ellis Island immigrants than like plasma held in a wink of space-time by fantastic invisible forces in a science experiment that may or may not illuminate the beyond. Altogether, that seething energy challenges our compulsive chauvinism and moral aggression, our mania and despair. Which is as it should be. With our limited understanding of the physiology of the berserk state and the difficulties of surveying a developing history at once vast and in motion, criticism has its hands full sorting out particular examples: a crucial project that is always only just getting underway, since berserk style itself is always in motion, changing shape, just beyond us.

NOTES

INTRODUCTION

1. Howard D. Fabing, "On Going Berserk: A Neurochemical Inquiry," *The Scientific Monthly*, November 1956, 232–37.
2. Jonathan Shay, *Achilles in Vietnam* (New York, 1997), 77, 217–18. "Bare sark" could also be taken to mean "without shirt = armor."
3. Jonathan Paye-Layleh, "I Ate Children's Hearts, Ex-Rebel Says," BBC News, January 22, 2008, http://news.bbc.co.uk/2/hi/africa/7200101.stm.
4. Ford Fessenden, "Rampage Killers / A Statistical Report," *New York Times* (April 8, 2000). The study counts 425 people killed and 510 injured in attacks since 1949. One-third of the attackers committed suicide; unlike ordinary murderers, virtually none made a serious attempt to escape.
5. According to E. L. Maguigad, *amok* derives from *amoq*, the Malay word for furious warfare. See "Psychiatry in the Philippines," *American Journal of Psychiatry* (121), 21–25.
6. Charles E. Silberman, *Criminal Violence, Criminal Justice* (New York, 1978).
7. Geoffrey R. McKee, *Why Mothers Kill: A Forensic Psychologist's Casebook* (Oxford, 2006).
8. Gary Rosen, e.g., criticizes developments "allowing George W. Bush and Dick Cheney to run amok," in "Constitutional Detour," *New York Times Book Review*, November 25, 2007, 31. Andrew Pollack reports "concerns that synthetic biology could be used to make pathogens, or that errors by well intended scientists could produce organisms that run amok." In "Researchers Take Step Toward Synthetic Life," *New York Times*, January 25, 2008.
9. John Seabrook describes the scientific background in "Crush Point," *New Yorker*, February 7, 2011, 34.
10. James Surowiecki, *New Yorker*, May 11, 2009, 38.
11. Nancy C. Andreasen, "Post-Traumatic Stress Disorder," in *The Comprehensive Textbook of Psychiatry*, ed. H. I. Kaplan and B. J. Sadock, (Baltimore, 1985), 919.
12. Shay, *Achilles in Vietnam*, 91.
13. July 6, 2000. William Pollack, an assistant clinical professor of psychiatry at the Harvard Medical School said, "reports of assaults by

parents at youth sports events 'have gotten much worse' in the last 5 to 10 years, and statistics show that the number of injuries in youth sports is also sharply up during the same period, a result at least in part, he said, of parents' encouraging their children to play more aggressively." Fox Butterfield, "A Fatality, Parental Violence and Youth Sports," *New York Times,* July 11, 2000.

14. David Aldridge, "Gambling Violence, Beer," *Washington Post,* September 18, 2008.

CHAPTER 1

1. Kimberly Flemke and Katherine R. Allen, "Women's Experience of Rage: A Critical Feminist Analysis," *Journal of Marital and Family Therapy,* January 2008.
2. Dolf Zillmann, "Mental Control of Angry Aggression," in *Handbook of Mental Control,* ed. Wegner and Pennebaker. Cited by Daniel Goleman, Emotional Intelligence (New York, 1995), 60–62.
3. Craig MacAndrew and Robert B. Edgerton, *Drunken Comportment: A Social Explanation* (Chicago, 1969).
4. As I noted in *Post-Traumatic Culture,* Kay H. Blacker and Joe P. Tupin, "Hysteria and Hysterical Structures: Developmental and Social Theories," in *The Hysterical Personality,* ed. Mardi J. Horowitz (New York, 1977), 113. See also H. B. M. Murphy, "History and the Evolution of Syndromes: The Striking Case of Lateh and Amok," in *Psychopathology: Contributions from the Social, Behavioral, and Biological Sciences,* ed. M. Hammer et al. (New York, 1973); and Lydia Temoshok and C. Clifford Attkisson, "Epidemiology of Hysterical Phenomena: Evidence for a Psychosocial Theory," in *Hysterical Personality,* ed. Horowitz (1977).
5. Malcolm Gladwell, "Drinking Games," *New Yorker* (February 15 and 22, 2010), 74.
6. For a revealing analysis of the interpretive processes affecting drivers' management of frustration and anger, see "Pissed Off in L. A.," in Jack Katz, *How Emotions Work* (Chicago, 1999), 18–86.
7. See Diane Binson and William J. Woods, *Gay Bathhouses and Public Health Policy* (New York, 2003).
8. Sam Delaney, "TV Preview: True Blood," *Guardian,* July 11, 2009.
9. *World History of Warfare,* ed. Christian J. Archer et al. (Lincoln, NE, 2002), 169–71.
10. See, e.g., Millon, T., and R. D. Davis (1998). "Ten Subtypes of Psychopathy," in *Psychopathy: Antisocial, Criminal, and Violent Behavior,* ed. T. Millon et al. (New York, 2003). 161–70.
11. Ernest Becker, *Denial of Death* (New York, 1973), 27.
12. Ernest Becker, *Escape from Evil* (New York, 1975), 2.
13. "Tankless Toilet Makes a Fashion Statement," Associated Press, March 29, 2005.

14. This is a premise of Terror Management Theory. See Tom Pyszczynski et al., *In the Wake of 911* (Washington, D.C., 2003).

15. To appreciate how thoroughly the need for "rightness" organizes human life, see Norman Cohn's *Cosmos, Chaos, and the World to Come* (New Haven, 1993): e.g., his account of ancient Egyptian culture and the comprehensively embodied concept of "ma'at," which meant "base," as in the base of a throne, but came to mean "a principle of order so all-embracing that it governed every aspect of existence. . . . [Nature] and society were imagined as two sides of one and the same reality: whatever was harmonious and regular in either was an expression of *ma'at*" (9). That meant all that is lawful, life-giving, and right, and it demanded repudiation, punishment, and death of all that was not.

16. Erich Fromm, *The Anatomy of Human Destructiveness* (New York, 1973), 222.

17. I have taken the term from Orlando Patterson's *Slavery and Social Death: A Comparative Study* (Cambridge, MA, 1982).

18. Jennifer Steinhauer, "Gunman Shoots 6 and Kills 1 in Fla.," *New York Times,* November 6, 2009.

19. Donald Dutton, *The Psychology of Genocide, Massacre, and Extreme Violence* (Westport and London, 2007), 142. Dutton is referring to the theory put forward by V. Nell, in "Cruelty's Rewards: The Gratification of Perpetrators and Spectators," *Behavioral and Brain Sciences* Vol. 29 (2006), 211–57.

20. Richard Slotkin, *Regeneration through Violence* (Hanover, NH, 1973), 156.

21. Nick Turse, "UnFair Game: Targeting Iraqis as Big Game," Tom-Dispatch.com, October 25, 2007.

22. Evan Wright, *Generation Kill: Devil Dogs, Iceman, Captain America, and the New Face of American War* (New York, 2007).

23. The definitive study of human pack behavior remains Elias Canetti's *Crowds and Power* (New York, 1978).

24. The extravagant, intoxicating sadism of the witch-hunts is palpable in Michael Kunze, *Highroad to the Stake* (Chicago, 1987) and Lyndal Roper, *Witch Craze* (New Haven, 2005).

25. Otto Rank, *Will Therapy* (New York, 1978), 130.

26. Dutton, *Psychology of Genocide*, 102–03.

27. Wendell Berry, "Faustian Economics: Hell Hath No Limits," *Harper's Magazine* (May 2008), 15.

28. Shaila Dewan et al., "For Professor, Fury Just Beneath the Surface, *New York Times*, February 21, 2010.

29. Dennis Ford, *The Search for Meaning* (Berkeley, 2007), 14–15.

30. E. J. Leed, *No Man's Land: Combat and Identity in World War One* (Cambridge, UK, 1979), cited by John Modell and Timothy Haggerty in "The Social Impact of War," *Annual Review of Sociology*, Vol. 17 (1991), 205–24.

31. Laurie Goodstein and William Glaberson, "The Well-Marked Road to Homicidal Rage," *New York Times* (April 10, 2000).

32. Robert D. McFadden, "A Long Slide from Privilege Ends in Slaughter," *The New York Times* (December 12, 1993), 1. See my *Post-Traumatic Culture*, 349–56.

33. Jane Mayer, "Covert Operations: The Billionaire Brothers Who Are Waging a War against Obama," *New Yorker*, September 2, 2010.

34. Becker, *Denial of Death*, 63.

35. Stephanie Armour, "Managers Not Prepared for Workplace Violence," *USA Today* (July 15, 2004), http://www.usatoday.com/money/workplace/2004-07-15-workplace-violence2_x.htm.

36. Goodstein and Glaberson, "Well-Marked Road to Homicidal Rage."

37. Stephanie Armour, "Inside the Minds of Workplace Killers," *USA Today* (July 14, 2004), http://www.usatoday.com/money/workplace/2004-07-14-workplace-killings_x.htm.

38. Goodstein and Glaberson, "Well-Marked Road to Homicidal Rage."

39. See, e.g., John Monahan, *Predicting Violent Behavior: An Assessment of Clinical Techniques* (Beverly Hills, CA, 1981).

40. Jarkko Jalava demonstrates that although the theory of degeneration stood discredited after World War II, the basic tenets of Lombroso's theory of the born-criminal type "have survived into mainstream scientific work regarding what is known as the psychopath." See "The Modern Degenerate: Nineteenth-century Degeneration Theory and Modern Psychopathy Research," *Theory & Psychology*, Vol. 16, No. 3, (2006), 416–32.

41. See the overview in *Criminology: Theory, Research, and Policy*, ed. Gennaro F. Vito et al. (Sudbury, MA, 2006), 86–87.

42. Ronald C. Albucher and Israel Liberzon, "Psychopharmacological Treatment in PTSD: A Critical Review," *Journal of Psychiatric Research*, Vol. 36, No. 6, November-December 2002, 355–67. Medications effective in treating PTSD include tricyclic antidepressants, monoamine oxidase inhibitors, and serotonin reuptake inhibitors.

43. Oliver Sacks, "A Summer of Madness," *New York Review of Books*, September 25, 2008, 57. Sacks is reviewing Michael Greenberg's *Hurry Down Sunshine*, an account of his daughter's manic-depressive psychosis.

44. Mike Nizza, "The Heroes Among Us," *New York Times*, July 9, 2007.

45. Karen Horney, *Neurosis and Human Growth* (New York, 1950, 1991), 39.

46. Becker, *Denial of Death*, 138.

47. Tim Shipman, "Sarah Palin Blamed by the US Secret Service over Death Threats against Barack Obama," *The Telegraph, UK*, November 08, 2008.

48. Michael Joseph Gross's profile of Palin in *Vanity Fair* (October 2010) described an offstage personality given to episodes of rage in private life: She can quickly "turn from kind to hateful, rational to unhinged."

49. Alex Ross, "Imaginary Concerts," *New Yorker* (August 24, 2009), 72.

50. As Pastor Steven Anderson did in a sermon screen on major television networks. See James Gilbert, "Tempe Pastor Prays for Obama's Death," *Yuma Sun,* September 1, 2009.

51. It seems to me significant that the concept of "temporary insanity" only evolved in the eighteenth century. Lennard J. Davis, *Obsession* (Chicago, 2008).

52. George Gerbner, "Who Is Shooting Whom: The Content and Context of Media Violence," *Popping Culture,* ed. Murray Pomerance and John Sakeris (New York, 2008), 99.

53. Gavin deBecker, *The Gift of Fear* (Boston, 1997), 92–102.

54. The trope is popular in right-wing rhetoric. An apparently straight-faced op-ed essay in the *Wall Street Journal* compares President George W. Bush to the superhero Batman, echoing Crusader religiosity in its demand that "Islamo-Fascists" must be "hounded to the gates of Hell." Andrew Klavan, "What Bush and Batman Have in Common," *Wall Street Journal,* July 25, 2008.

55. Jan Hoffman, "A Girl's Nude Photo, and Altered Lives," *New York Times,* March 26, 2011.

56. See Francis Parkman's account in *The Jesuits in North America in the Seventeenth Century* (1867; Lincoln, NE, 1997), 168–71.

57. Slotkin, *Regeneration through Violence,* 90. In Slotkin's reading Tompson's poems show the settlers caught up in the outrages, including cannibalism, that they attributed to the Indians.

58. See John Demos, *Entertaining Satan* (New York, 1983).

59. Jackson Lears explores the developments following the Civil War that led to the total war of 1914 in *Rebirth of a Nation: The Making of Modern America, 1877–1920* (New York, 2009).

60. Herman Melville, *Moby Dick,* ed. Elizabeth Renker (New York, 1998), 157.

61. "Tropical rainforests are disappearing at a rate of 2 percent per year. Populations of most large fish are down to only 10 percent of what they were in 1950. Many primates and all the great apes— our closest relatives—are nearly gone from the wild." See Jerry Coyne and Hopi E. Hoekstra, "The Greatest Dying," *The New Republic* online, September 24, 2007.

62. Barbara Tuchman, *The Proud Tower* (New York, 1966), 268.

63. See, e.g., *Nemesis: The Last Days of the American Republic* (New York, 2006).

64. Michael Klare, "A Planet on the Brink: Will Economic Brushfires Prove Too Virulent to Contain?" Posted at TomDispatch.com (February 24, 2009).

65. Jonathan L. Friedman, *Media Violence and Its Effect on Aggression: Assessing the Scientific Evidence* (Toronto, 2002).

66. Bill Moyers "NOW," PBS, September 12, 2008.

67. Moyers, September 12, 2008. The *New York Times* "reported that a mass email opposing the bill suggested that its supporters needed to be 'taken out by *any means*.' The bipartisan support collapsed, the bill died and right-wing talk-radio hosts took credit." A later chapter, "Rage for Order," examines aggressive immigration fantasies in the film *Men in Black*.

68. Robert C. Elliott, *The Power of Satire* (Princeton, 1960).

CHAPTER 2

1. Michael Barone, "Surge 101," *National Review Online*, December 29, 2007.

2. See Ernest Becker's account in *Escape from Evil* (New York, 1972), 103. The link between blood and soil was less sentimental in the Napoleonic era. In *War Is a Force That Gives Us Meaning*, Chris Hedges quotes *The London Observer* (November 18, 1822): "It is estimated that more than a million bushels of human and inhuman bones were imported last year from the continent of Europe into the port of Hull. The neighborhood of Leipzig, Austerlitz, Waterloo, and of all the places where, during the late bloody war, the principal battles were fought, have been swept alike of the bones of the hero and horse which he rode. . . . [They] have been . . . forwarded to the Yorkshire bone grinders [and] sold to the farmers to manure their lands."

3. The title Gordon M. Goldstein gives to a chapter of his collaboration with Bundy, *Lessons in Disaster: McGeorge Bundy and the Path to War in Vietnam* (New York, 2010).

4. Ken Jowitt, "Rage, Hubris, and Regime Change," *Hoover Institution Policy Review*, April and May 2003, http://www.hoover.org/publications/policyreview/3449481.html.

5. A senior Bush advisor thought to be Karl Rove famously told journalist Ron Suskind that he and others were "'in what we call the reality-based community,' which he defined as people who 'believe that solutions emerge from your judicious study of discernible reality.'" When Suskind mentioned empiricism, the advisor "cut me off. 'That's not the way the world really works anymore. We're an empire now, and when we act, we create our own reality.'" See "Faith, Certainty, and the Presidency of George W. Bush," *New York Times Magazine*, October 17, 2004.

6. As counterterrorism director Richard A. Clarke, for one, reported in *Against All Enemies* (New York, 2004).

7. An estimated 500 deaths a month, according to Steve Coll in "The General's Dilemma," *New Yorker*, September 8, 2008, 36. The invasion created as many as 2.5 million refugees.

8. Joseph Stiglitz and Linda Bilmes, "The Three Trillion Dollar War," *The Times*, February 23, 2008.

9. The editors were responding (July 16, 2009) to the Federal Report on the President's Surveillance Program (July 10, 2009).

10. Jowitt, "Rage, Hubris, and Regime Change."

11. Thom Shanker, "Despite Slump, U.S. Role as a Top Arms Supplier Grows," *New York Times,* September 6, 2009.

12. James Glanz and Andrew W. Lehren, "Use of Contractors Added to War's Chaos in Iraq," *New York Times,* September 6, 2009. They refer to the "Wild West chaos" of the war's early days.

13. Aaron Glantz, *Winter Soldier: Iraq and Afghanistan: Eyewitness Accounts of the Occupations* (Chicago, 2008).

14. Nick Turse, "A My Lai a Month," *The Nation,* November 13, 2008.

15. Richard A. Oppel Jr., "Iraqi Assails US for Strikes on Civilians," *New York Times,* June 2, 2006.

16. Consider an Iraqi mother John Lee Anderson describes in "Inside the Surge," New Yorker, November 19, 2007. Her son Amar went on a rampage to revenge his brother Jafaar, determined to kill ten Mahdi militiamen for every one of his brother's fingers. His mother, Um Jafaar, also fixated on this harvest of enemy life. She "took the body parts of Amar's victims, wrapped in cloth, to [Jafaar's] grave . . . and buried them there. 'I talk to my son, I tell him, "Here, this is from those who killed you, I take revenge. . . . I put them around the grave. So far, I have taken one hand, one eye, an Adam's apple, toes, fingers, ears, and noses. . . . But still my heart hurts. Even if we kill them all, I won't have comfort'" (66). Rage buffers her despair and sense of unbearable injustice. She is ritualistic in her magical thinking about the body parts, but also acts out creaturely motives. In effect, she feeds the butchered body parts to her dead son as if to replenish his spirit in a cannibal feast, not unlike the soldier described here who vowed to cut out enemy hearts for his dead friend.

17. See Deborah Nelson, *The War behind Me: Vietnam Veterans Confront the Truth* (New York, 2008).

18. Quoted in *The Fresno Bee,* October 10, 1965, when as governor of California, Reagan was working to suppress student unrest at Berkeley.

19. H. Bruce Franklin, *Vietnam and Other American Fantasies* (Amherst, MA, 2006), 73. The war in the Pacific was especially brutal on both sides, as Max Hastings recounts in *Retribution: The Battle for Japan, 1944–45* (New York, 2008). By the war's end, Allied bombs had killed no less than 1.8 million German civilians, whereas the official number of British civilian deaths is 100,297. For an account of the victors' rage, see Giles McDonogh, *After the Reich: The Brutal History of the Allied Occupation* (New York, 2007).

20. As Franklin notes, many regarded the campaign as a form of genocide. See *In the Name of America: A Study Commissioned and Published by Clergy and Laymen Concerned about Vietnam, January*

1968 (New York, 1968) and *Against the Crime of Silence*, ed. John Duffett (New York, 1968). For the role of racism in the war against Japan, see John Dower, *War without Mercy* (New York, 1993).

21. A trenchant analysis of the restructuring is Richard A. Gabriel and Paul L. Savage, *Crisis in Command: Mismanagement in the Army* (New York, 1978).

22. In Ricks, *Fiasco* (75–76).

23. See P. W. Singer's wide-ranging overview, *Wired for War* (New York, 2009).

24. David Barstow, "Behind TV Analysts, Pentagon's Hidden Hand," *New York Times*, April 20, 2008.

25. Jim Holt, "It's the Oil," *London Review of Books*, October 18, 2007. More up-to-date than Daniel Yergin's *The Prize* (New York, 1991) is Matthew Simmons, *Twilight in the Desert: The Coming Saudi Oil Shock and the World Economy* (New York, 2005). "Deputy Defense Secretary Paul D. Wolfowitz told Congress during the war that 'we are dealing with a country that can really finance its own reconstruction, and relatively soon.'" See Jeff Gerth, "Report Offered Bleak Outlook about Iraq Oil," *New York Times*, October 5, 2003.

26. Paul Blustein, "Wolfowitz Strives to Quell Criticism," *Washington Post*, March 21, 2005.

27. Frank Rich detailed the process in *The Greatest Story Ever Sold* (New York, 2007). See also Michael Isikoff and David Corn, *Hubris* (New York, 2006).

28. "Statement of Principles," June 3, 1997, newamericancentury.org.

29. See William Pfaff, *The Irony of Manifest Destiny: The Tragedy of America's Foreign Policy* (New York, 2010), and William Pfaff and Edmund Stillman, *The Politics of Hysteria* (New York, 1964). In *The Pursuit of the Millennium* (New York, 1961) Norman Cohn traces millenarian themes in Nazism and Soviet Communism.

30. Tom Engelhardt, "Stuff Happens: The Pentagon's Argument of Last Resort on Iraq," *Mother Jones*, November 21, 2008.

31. Evan Wright, *Generation Kill: Devil Dogs, Iceman, Captain America, and the New Face of American War* (New York, 2007), in Michael Massing, "Iraq: The Hidden Human Costs," *New York Review of Books*, December 20, 2007.

32. Dropped from the *National Review Online*, Coulter was unrepentant in her book, *How to Talk to a Liberal If You Must: The World According to Ann Coulter* (New York, 2004), insisting she advocated the same position "Now more than ever." On her website (June 30, 2004), Coulter was heedlessly triumphal and malicious: "The Americanization of Iraq proceeds at an astonishing pace, the Iraqis are taking to freedom like fish to water, and the possibilities for this nation are endless."

33. See Jared Diamond's "Vengeance Is Ours," *New Yorker*, April 21, 2008, 74.

34. Anderson, "Inside the Surge," 66.

35. See "A Guide for the Perplexed: Intellectual Fallacies of the War on Terror," Chalmers Johnson's perceptive review of Stephen Holmes's invaluable study *The Matador's Cape, America's Reckless Response to Terror*, TomDispatch.com (October 22, 2007).

36. In *The Shock Doctrine: The Rise of Disaster Capitalism* (New York, 2007), Naomi Klein traces the shock doctrine to Washington's Cold War fascination with the possibility of "wiping clean" an adversary's personality, as in brainwashing, to induce total compliance.

37. Chalmers Johnson, *Blowback: the Costs and Consequences of American Empire* (New York, 2004).

38. Maj. Gen. John Batiste "Root Causes of Haditha," *The Salt Lake Tribune*, June 9, 2006. Though his title focused on Haditha, the general never mentioned that the scandal involved rampage killing. His heartfelt criticism understood the personal dimension lacking in the neocons' fantasies of leverage, including references to the Abu Ghraib and Haditha scandals.

39. Klein, *Shock Doctrine*, 323–40.

40. Thomas B. Edsall and Juliet Eilperin, "Lobbyists Set Sights on Money-Making Opportunities in Iraq," *Washington Post*, October 2, 2003.

41. In "Billions over Baghdad," *Vanity Fair* (October 2007), Donald Barlett and James Steele, report bundled millions being carted at one point in a wheelbarrow, so shoveling is not merely a figure of speech here.

42. For background, see Pratap Chetterjee, *Halliburton's Army: How a Well-Connected Texas Oil Company Revolutionized the Way America Makes War* (New York, 2009).

43. Jane Corbin, "BBC Uncovers Lost Iraq Billions," June 10, 2008.

44. "U. S. Army: 'We will respond to contractor killings," CNN.com, April 1, 2004, quoting Brig. Gen. Mark Kimmitt.

45. Marjorie Cohn, "The Haditha Massacre," *Truthout | Perspective* (May 30, 2006), http://www.truthout.org/article/the-haditha-massacre.

46. Used against civilians it is an illegal chemical weapon, though Washington has not signed the International treaty restricting phosphorus munitions. BBC news (November 16, 2005) quoted an arms expert who said: "'It is not counted under the chemical weapons convention in its normal use but, although it is a matter of legal niceties, it probably does fall into the category of chemical weapons if it is used for this kind of purpose directly against people.'"

47. Dahr Jamail, "What I Saw in Fallujah," *New Statesman*, November 1, 2007.

48. Bill Van Auken, "Pentagon Plans Death Squad Terror in Iraq," *Newsweek*, January 13, 2005.

49. "Court Sentences 'Kill Team Soldier to 24 Years in Prison," *Spiegel Online*, March 24, 2011. Lt. Col. David Grossman's *On Killing* (New York, 1996) estimates that about 3 percent of soldiers can kill without inhibition.

50. Zogby poll, February 28, 2006.
51. In "The Wounded Platoon," PBS *Frontine*, May 17, 2010.
52. Dave Philipps, "Casualties of War, Part I: The Hell of War Comes Home," *Colorado Springs Gazette* (gazette.com), July 25, 2009.
53. Cohn, "The Haditha Massacre."
54. BBC, May 25, 2006, "Marines' Iraq Conduct Scrutinized."
55. Russell Carollo, "Suspect Soldiers: Did Crimes in US Foretell Violence in Iraq?" *Sacramento Bee*, July 11, 2008.
56. Josh White, "No Murder Charges Filed in Haditha Case," *Washington Post*, January 4, 2008.
57. The account of Needham's PTSD is based on Philipps, "Casualties of War," July 28, 2009.
58. Chris Hedges, "Body Bagger in Iraq," March 21, 2011, reporting on a memoir by Jess Goodell, Shade It Black: Death and After in Iraq: http://www.truth-out.org/body-bagger-iraq68624.
59. Philipps, "Casualties of War."
60. Paul von Zielbauer, "Testimony in Court-Martial Describes a Sniper Squad Pressed to Raise Body Count," *New York Times*, September 28, 2007.
61. Michael Belfiore, The Department of Mad Scientists, *How DARPA Is Remaking Our World, from the Internet to Artificial Limbs* (New York, 2010).
62. "Invisible Wounds of War: Psychological and Cognitive Injuries, Their Consequences, and Services to Assist Recovery," ed. Terri Tanelian and Lisa H. Jaycox, Rand Corp. Monographs, April 18, 2008.
63. Harvard University psychiatrist Roger Pitman "sees post-traumatic stress disorder as a perfectly natural process gone amok," since ordinarily strong memories of a dangerous situation can make for precautions and future survival. See William J. Cromie, "Pill to Calm Traumatic Memories," *Harvard University Gazette*, March 18, 2004.
64. Oliver Poole, "'Marines Are Good at Killing. Nothing Else. They Like It,'" *Daily Telegraph*, UK, January 6, 2006. URL: http://www.telegraph.co.uk/news/main.jhtml?xml=/news/2006/06/01/wbush101.xml.
65. Nick Turse, "(Un)fair Game: Targeting Iraqis as 'Big Game,'" Tomdispatch.com, October 25, 2007.
66. Turse, "(Un)Fair Game." Fantasies of the hunt drove the massacre that closed the first Gulf War, when US troops annihilated Iraqi convoys fleeing from Kuwait. "The slaughter continued after the cease fire. For example, on March 2, 1991, US 24th Division Forces engaged in a four-hour assault against Iraqis just west of Basra. More than 750 vehicles were destroyed, thousands were killed without any US casualties. A US commander said, 'We really waxed them.' It was called a 'Turkey Shoot.'" *International War Crimes Tribunal* (10), http://deoxy.org/wc/warcrim2.htm.

67. Raffi Khatchadourian profiled the force behind Wikileaks, the Australian Julian Assange in the *New Yorker,* June 7, 2010.

68. http://combatarms.mu.nu/.

69. A detailed account, emphasizing traumatic stress, is Jim Frederick, *Black Hearts: One Platoon's Descent into Madness in Iraq's Triangle of Death* (New York, 2010).

70. FBI affidavit in support of an arrest warrant for Steven D. Green, June 30, 2006.

71. "Josh White, Ex-Soldier Charged in Killing of Iraqi Family," *The Washington Post,* July 4, 2006. Green was convicted (May 8, 2009).

72. Brian Nicol, *Stalking* (London, 2006), 19.

73. In *Redacted* (2007), Brian DePalma loosely dramatized the murder of Abeer Qasim Hamza and her family. He tries to emphasize the repugnant criminality of the behavior, but he also reflexively criticizes berserk style-in-action by inventing within the film a soldier's homemade video diary and a terrorist website, both of which bring out the problems of complicity latent in style. The film has been attacked and not allowed into full distribution.

74. Robert C. Elliot, *The Power of Satire* (Princeton, 1960).

75. Human Rights First has reported on the US government's handling of the nearly 100 cases of detainees who have died in US custody since 2002, http://www.humanrightsfirst.org/us_law/etn/dic/index.asp.

76. "A major focus of the Committee's investigation was the influence of Survival Evasion Resistance and Escape (SERE) training techniques on the interrogation of detainees in U.S. custody. SERE training is designed to teach our soldiers how to resist interrogation by enemies that refuse to follow the Geneva Conventions and international law. During SERE training, US troops—in a controlled environment with great protections and caution—are exposed to harsh techniques such as stress positions, forced nudity, use of fear, sleep deprivation, and until recently, the waterboard. The SERE techniques were never intended to be used against detainees in U.S. custody. The Committee's investigation found, however, that senior officials in the U.S. government decided to use some of these harsh techniques against detainees based on deeply flawed interpretations of U.S. and international law." This was "a direct cause of detainee abuse and conveyed the message that it was okay to mistreat and degrade detainees in U.S. custody."

77. Seymour Hersh, "The General's Report," *New Yorker,* June 25, 2007.

78. Seymour Hersh, "The Gray Zone," *New Yorker,* May 24, 2005.

79. Joan Walsh, "The Abu Ghraib Files: Introduction," *Salon,* http://www.salon.com/news/abu_ghraib/2006/03/14/introduction/.

80. Kate Zernike, "Detainees Depict Abuses by Guard in Prison in Iraq," *New York Times,* January 12, 2005.

81. Lynddie England and others describe some of this background in Errol Morris's documentary "Standard Operating Procedure" (2008).

82. Seymour Hersh, "The General's Report."
83. "Other Government Agencies," in "The Abu Ghraib Files," *Salon* (Chapter 5, November 4–5, 2003): http://www.salon.com/news/abu_ghraib/2006/03/14/chapter_5/index.html.
84. See Andrew Sullivan, "Bush's Torturers Follow Where the Nazis Led," *Sunday Times*, October 7, 2007. Early in the war, Sec. Rumsfeld pressed for the adoption in Iraq of interrogation practices used in the prison at Guanatamo in Cuba and not sanctioned by the Geneva Conventions; and in a September 14, 2003, memo Gen. Sanchez complied.
85. Janis Karpinski, *One Woman's Army: The Commanding General of Abu Ghraib Tells Her Story* (New York, 2005).
86. Philippe Sands, *The Torture Team* (New York, 2008).
87. Jane Mayer, "Whatever It Takes," *New Yorker,* February 19, 2007.
88. Thomas E. Ricks, "The Descent into Abuse," *Fiasco,* 271–97.
89. David Bromwich, "Euphemism and American Violence," *New York Review of Books* (April 3, 2008), 30.
90. Under a 2004 law promulgated by the Coalition Provisional Authority.
91. Interview with John Cusack, http://www.huffingtonpost.com/john-cusack/the-real-blackwater-scand_b_67741.html.
92. By 2008 Hollywood had turned public unease over CIA kidnapping and torture into Gavin Hood's film *Rendition.*
93. Amy Joyce, "Planned Closings Stun GM Employees," *Washington Post,* November 22, 2005.
94. Chalmers Johnson, "Baseless Expenditures," tomgram.com, July 2, 2009. There are at least one thousand US bases in as many as 175 of the 192 countries in the United Nations.
95. Bryan Bender, "Pentagon Board Says Cuts Essential," *Boston Globe,* November 10, 2008.

CHAPTER 3

1. In a speech at a conference on banking regulation in Brussels, October 12, 2009.
2. Leo Cullum, *New Yorker,* December 15, 2008.
3. Matt Taibbi, "The Great American Bubble Machine," *Rolling Stone,* July 9–23, 2009.
4. George A. Akerlof and Robert J. Schiller develop and critique Keynes in *Animal Spirits: How Human Psychology Drives the Economy and Why It Matters for Global Capitalism* (Princeton, 2008).
5. Richard Parker, "Government beyond Obama," *New York Review of Books,* Vol. 56, No. 4, March 12, 2009. He adds, "even after productivity growth returned in the mid-1990s, average wages—which had stagnated for twenty years—continued to stagnate. In fact, between 2001 and 2007, wages grew not at all, something unprecedented in any previous recorded business recovery."

6. As Stephen D. King details in *Losing Control: The Emerging Threats to Western Prosperity* (New Haven, CT, 2010).

7. Bureau of Labor Statistics, Current Employment Statistics, Average Hourly Earnings in 1982 Dollars. Converted to 2008 dollars with CPI-U.

8. David Cay Johnston for Tax Analysts, "Scary New Wage Data," October 25, 2010, at http://www.tax.com.

9. In *The End of Easy Money and the Renewal of the American Economy* (New York, 2009), Peter S. Goodman sees the dominant motive as escapist magical thinking, underestimating the role of aggression and anxiety. The trope of binge gambling became a commonplace in the period. Vicky Ward incorporated the rampage killing trope of betrayal in *The Devil's Casino: Friendship, Betrayal, and the High Stake Game Played Inside Lehman Brothers* (New York, 2010).

10. Brady Willett, "Rubin's Cube," *FallStreet*, November 5, 2007, http://www.fallstreet.com/nov507.php.

11. The argument of Simon Johnson, former chief economist of the International Monetary Fund, in "The Quiet Coup," *The Atlantic*, May 2009.

12. Stephen Foley, "Paulson Reveals US Concerns of Breakdown in Law and Order," *Independent* (UK), July 17, 2009. Paulson gave a berserk-style title to his memoir of the meltdown *On the Brink: Inside the Race to Stop the Collapse of the Global Finance System* (New York, 2010).

13. John Kenneth Galbraith, *The Culture of Contentment* (New York, 1992).

14. In Garry Marshall's *Pretty Woman* (1990), love for a hooker with a heart of gold (Julia Roberts) tames one such buccaneer. See my *Post-Traumatic Culture*, 267–74.

15. For an incisive overview with data, see Donald R. Barlett and James B. Steele, *America: What Went Wrong?* (Kansas City, 1992).

16. Glenn Yago, "Junk Bonds," in *The Concise Encyclopedia of Economics*, http://www.econlib.org/LIBRARY/Enc/JunkBonds.html.

17. Dan Glaister, "Gekko Is Coming Back . . . but Will Greed Still Be Good?" *Guardian*, October 15, 2008.

18. Critical analyses of Greenspan's policies were as common as they were futile. See, e.g., William D. Rutherford, *Who Shot Goldilocks: How Alan Greenspan Did in Our Jobs, Savings, and Retirement Plans* (New York, 2008), and William Fleckenstein, *Greenspan's Bubbles: The Age of Ignorance at the Federal Reserve* (New York, 2008).

19. Savings were 8.9 percent of personal income in 1979, and reduced to 0.6 percent in 2007.

20. Nick Paumgarten, "The Death of Kings," *New Yorker*, May 18, 2009, 48.

21. A Ponzi scheme is a type of fraud based on fantasies of endless growth. The scheme pays off earlier investors with money raised from later victims until it runs out of new money and collapses.

22. Floyd Norris, "Since Alan Failed, the Job Must Be Impossible," *New York Times*, March 30, 2011.
23. Kevin Phillips, "Numbers Racket: Why the Economy Is Worse Than We Know," *Harper's Magazine*, May 2008.
24. Hanna Rosin, "Did Christianity Cause the Crash: How Preachers Are Spreading a Gospel of Debt," *Atlantic*, December 2009, 42.
25. Edward Wong, "Booming, China Faults U.S. Policy on the Economy," *New York Times*, June 17, 2008.
26. Russ Winter, "Berserker Funds in Commodities," *The Wall Street Examiner*, May 21, 2008, http://wallstreetexaminer.com/blogs/winter/?p=1664.
27. William Greider, "Goldman Sachs Socialism," *The Nation*, October 6, 2008.
28. CNBC News, October 6, 2008.
29. Nouriel Roubini, "The World is at Severe Risk of a Global Systemic Financial Meltdown and a Severe Global Depression," *Nouriel Roubini's Global EconoMonitor*, October 9, 2008. http://www.rgemonitor.com/index.php.
30. Jeremy Warner, "Mind-Boggling Growth in Derivatives," *The Independent*, November 18, 2006. "The volume of over-the-counter derivatives traded rose by a quarter in the first half of this year to $370 trillion, driven primarily by rapid growth in credit default swaps and interest rate derivatives."
31. "In 1985, there were only $1.6 trillion in home mortgages. And only $500 billion worth of them were in pools used to back securities. Twenty years later, total mortgage debt approached $10 trillion, with $7.5 trillion of it securitized." Bill Bonner, "The Bottom Has Fallen Out," *Daily Reckoning*, June 23, 2008.
32. Kenneth J. Gerbino, "Genève and Zurich Speech Notes," Keynote Address, Academe Finance Conference, June 4–6, 2008, Posted June 19, 2008, http://www.gold-eagle.com/editorials_08/gerbino061808.html.
33. Anthony Faiola et al., "What Went Wrong?" *Washington Post*, October 15, 2008.
34. Greenspan, "The Markets, Excerpts from Greenspan Speech on Global Turmoil," *The New York Times*, November 6, 1998.
35. Department of Defense news briefing, February 12, 2002.
36. Jim Puzzanghera, "Economic Rescue Could Cost $8.5 Trillion," *Los Angeles Times*, November 30, 2008.
37. A lucid overview is Steve Fraser, *Wall Street: America's Dream Palace* (New Haven, CT, 2008).
38. Bill Bonner, "Inevitable and Disgraceful, but Still Unpredictable," *Daily Reckoning*, November 28, 2008. Bonner was already sounding an alarm when he published *Financial Reckoning Day* (Hoboken, NJ, 2003).

39. Thomas Geoghagen, "Infinite Debt," *Harper's Magazine,* April 2009, 35.
40. By Scott Thill, *AlterNet.* Posted November 9, 2009.
41. Louis Uchitelle and N. R. Kleinfield, "On the Battlefields of Business, Millions of Casualties," *New York Times,* March 3, 1996, sec. A.
42. Steven Greenhouse, *The Big Squeeze: Tough Times for the American Worker* (New York, 2008).
43. *First Blood,* Dir. Ted Kotcheff (1982).
44. Postal employees are actually less likely to run amok than other workers. An independent commission in 1998 found 0.26 workplace homicides per 100,000 postal workers from 1992 to 1998. By comparison the rate was 2.10 per 100,000 for retail workers. The first post office rampage occurred on August 20, 1986, in Edmond, Oklahoma, when an ominously withdrawn and about to be fired letter carrier systematically shot to death 14 fellow employees.
45. Ford Fessenden, "They Threaten, Seethe and Unhinge, Then Kill in Quantity: Rampage Killers / A Statistical Report," *New York Times,* April 8, 2000.
46. In *Vietnam and Other American Fantasies,* H. Bruce Franklin has debunked the POW myth and the urban legend that returning Vietnam vets were mistreated.
47. Almost "every unit and officer that took part (and even many who did not) was able to enhance his career by being awarded a medal. It took the U.S. seven full battalions plus elements of two others to defeat fewer than 679 Cubans, no more than 50 of whom were trained combat soldiers." See Richard Gabriel, "Scenes from an Invasion—How the U. S. Military Stumbled to Victory in Grenada," *Washington Monthly,* February 1986.
48. The Romans' specialized slave workshops were the first factories.
49. Bernard D. Meltzer and Cass R. Sunstein, "Public Employee Strikes, Executive Discretion, and the Air Traffic Controllers," *The University of Chicago Law Review,* Vol. 50, No. 2 (Spring, 1983), 731–99.
50. Stephen Greenhouse, "Analysis: Victory for Labor, but How Far Will It Go?" *New York Times* (August 20, 1997). In *The Big Squeeze,* Greenhouse estimates that the number of professional "union avoidance" consultants in the country has risen from about a hundred in the 1960s to over two thousand today.
51. Thomas H. Davenport and Laurence Prusak, "Re-Engineering Revisited: What Went Wrong with the Business-Process Reengineering Fad, and Will It Come Back?" *Computerworld,* June 23, 2003.
52. Peter Gosselin, *High Wire: The Precarious Financial Lives of American Families* (New York, 2008).
53. Joseph Stiglitz, "Bleakonomics," *New York Times,* September 30, 2007. One sign of the reevaluation of free market theory is Lawrence D. Brown and Lawrence R. Jacobs, *The Private Abuse of the Public Interest* (Chicago, 2008).

54. Klein, *Shock Doctrine*, 6–7.

55. In his "Address to the Nation on the Situation in Southeast Asia," April 30, 1970, President Nixon used the term to justify his decision to widen the Vietnam War into Cambodia—which ultimately led to the Pol Pot regime's genocidal rampage.

56. "At each stage of the unfolding discovery of his world and the problems that it poses," says Becker in *The Denial of Death*, "the child is intent on shaping that world to his own aggrandizement. He has to keep the feeling that he has absolute power and control, and in order to do that, he has to cultivate independence of some kind, the conviction that he is shaping his own life," 37.

57. See Anne C. Heller's account in *Ayn Rand and the World She Made* (New York, 2009).

58. Andrew Clark, "Hedge Fund Hotel Yields Up Secrets," *Guardian*, March 7, 2009.

59. David Corn, "Alan Shrugged," *Mother Jones*, October 24, 2008.

60. James K. Galbraith, "Causes of the Crisis," *The Texas Observer*, May 1, 2009.

61. Paul Craig Roberts, "American Economy, R.I.P.," *Online Journal*, September 11, 2007. Roberts was assistant secretary of the Treasury in the Reagan Administration. In the 1960s CEOs took home about 30 times the pay of an average worker and the ratio had been around 30 to 1. In the new century the ratio has reached 200–300 to 1.

62. Holman W. Jenkins Jr., "The New Economy's Sore Losers," *Hoover Institution Policy Review*, April and May 2003.

63. Peter C. Whybrow, *American Mania: When More Is Not Enough* (New York, 2005).

64. "The automobile industry has been one of the losers in the new American economy. US consumers spent less on new automobiles in 2007 than they spent on 'brokerage charges and investment counselling'; in 1979, they had spent ten times as much." Emma Rothschild, "Can We Transform the Auto-Industrial Society?" *New York Review of Books*, January 29, 2009, 8.

65. *Consumer Reports* Vol. 2, No. 6 (1937), 32.

66. At his retirement in 1990, GM's Roger Smith had his benefits gratuitously doubled. "The vote on what was once an obscure compensation issue has become something of an embarrassment for G. M.'s board. . . . The board adopted the change last fall, although some directors have indicated privately that they were unaware that it would almost double Mr. Smith's pension, from $700,000 to about $1.25 million a year, an official close to the board said yesterday." Anise C. Wallace, "G. M. Holders Likely to Back Rise in Executive Pensions," *New York Times*, May 24, 1990.

67. "The Bright Side of the G. M. Disaster, Jim Kingsdale's Energy Investment Strategies," posted by Kingsdale on December 15, 2008

in *Energy Policy, The Economy,* http://www.energyinvestmentstrategies. com.

68. William Greider, "Political and Financial Bedlam," Dollars & Sense Blog, September 30, 2008. Section 8 in the Treasury's three-page summary of Paulson's plan mandated that his supremacy was to be guaranteed: "Decisions by the Secretary pursuant to the authority of this Act are non-reviewable and committed to agency discretion, and may not be reviewed by any court of law or any administrative agency," http://dollarsandsense.org/blog/2008/09/political-and-financial-bedlam-william-greider.html.

69. Anatole Kaletsky, *Times online,* October 6, 2008.

70. Nassim Taleb and Pablo Trian, "Bystanders to This Financial Crime Were Many," *Financial Times,* December 7, 2008. They add, "Listening to us, risk management practitioners would often agree on every point. But they elected to take part in the system and to play bystanders. They tried to explain away their decision to partake in the vast diffusion of responsibility. . . . Most poignantly, the police itself may have participated in the murder. The regulators were using the same arguments. They, too, were responsible."

CHAPTER 4

1. Gregor Peter Schmitz and Gabor Steingart, "Crisis Plunges US Middle Class into Poverty," *Spiegel Online,* April 23, 2009.

2. Andrew Clark, "Big Increase in US Suicides at Work," *Guardian,* August 21, 2009. "The number of people who killed themselves at work in the US rose 28% to an all-time high last year, in a grisly statistic that sparked speculation it was due to stress linked to the economic recession."

3. William K. Black, "How the Servant Became a Predator: Finance's Five Fatal Flaws," new deal 2.0, http://www.newdeal20.org/?p=5330. See also his *The Best Way to Rob a Bank Is to Own One* (Austin, 2008). Black was an investigator of the 1980s Savings-and-Loan scandal.

4. Joe Conason, "Bring Wall Street Crooks to Justice," *New York Observer,* September 24, 2008.

5. George Packer, "The Ponzi State," *New Yorker* (February 9 and 16, 2009), 85.

6. Sprott Asset Management, "Welcome to the 2008 Meltdown," *Markets at a Glance,* January 2008, 1. See also Bonner and Wiggin, *Financial Reckoning Day.*

7. Dan Mitchell, "Walker, Fiscal Ranger," *New York Times,* March 10, 2007.

8. Bill Bonner, "The Dead Cat Bounce," *Daily Reckoning,* July 28, 2008.

9. Matt Taibi, "Wall Street's Bailout Hustle," *Rolling Stone,* February 17, 2010.

10. The title of George A. Akerlof and Paul M. Romer, *Looting: The Economic Underworld of Bankruptcy for Profit* (Toronto, 1993) draws on the trope of mafia and (institutional) killing for profit.

11. Eliot Spitzer, "Predatory Lenders' Partner in Crime: How the Bush Administration Stopped the States from Stepping In to Help Consumers," *Washington Post*, February 14, 2008.

12. Eliot Spitzer, "What Clayton Knew," *Slate*, October 19, 2010, http://www.slate.com/id/2271647/.

13. "Cleveland Mayor Frank G. Jackson Says Subprime Lending Practices No Different Than 'Organized Crime,'" *UPI*, January 11, 2008.

14. Michael Shank, "Chomsky on Iran, Iraq, and the Rest of the World," *Foreign Policy in Focus*, February 16, 2007, http://www.fpif.org/fpiftxt/3999.

15. "Chavez Threatens US Oil Cutoff," Associated Press, February 10, 2008.

16. Zygmunt Bauman, *Wasted Lives: Modernity and Its Outcasts* (Cambridge, UK, 2004), 63. Bauman quotes from Francois de Bernard, *La Pauvrete durable* (Felin, 2002), 37–39. See also Richard Rubenstein, *The Age of Triage*.

17. Richard Rorty, "Globalization, the Politics of Identity and Social Hope," *Philosophy and Social Hope* (New York, 1999), 229–39.

18. Ed Vulliamy, "How a Big US Bank Laundered Billions from Mexico's Murderous Drug Gangs," *The Observer* (UK), April 3, 2011.

19. Jerome C. Glenn and Theodore J. Gordon, *2007 State of the Future*. The Millennium Project, 2007. See also Misha Glenny, *McMafia: A Journey through the Global Criminal Underworld* (New York, 2008).

20. Julian Borger, "Organised Crime: The $2 Trillion Threat," *Guardian*, September 12, 2007.

21. On the right, Austrian School economist Murray Rothbard, who regarded government as "a gang of thieves," held in his *World Market Perspective* (1984) that banks have been primary drivers of American policy.

22. In his 1987 PBS program "The Secret Government: The Constitution in Crisis," Moyers defines "[t]he Secret Government [as] an interlocking network of official functionaries, spies, mercenaries, ex-generals, profiteers and superpatriots, who for a variety of motives, operate outside the legitimate institutions of government." See, e.g., John Perkins, *The Secret History of the American Empire: Economic Hit Men, Jackals, and the Truth about Global Corruption* (New York, 2007).

23. Arian Campo-Flores and Monica Campbell, "Bloodshed on the Border," *Newsweek*, December 8, 2008.

24. Allen Rucker and David Chase, *The Sopranos, A Family History* (New York, 2003).

25. Steve Eder, "Insider Trading Case As Much Sopranos as Wall Street," *Reuters*, October 5, 2009.

26. Bosses of the Camorra, the Neapolitan mafia, watch their murders reported on TV news, and call killing "doing a piece," as in doing piecework or contract labor, and as if mob murder is a kind of manufacturing. See Roberto Saviano, *Gomorrah* (New York, 2007). Camorristi have gone global, selling toxic waste, money laundering, drug smuggling, etc. According to Saviano, the Camorra has no code or ideology beyond "the most aggressive neoliberalism."

27. F. William Engdahl, "The Financial Tsunami Part IV: Asset Securitization," Financial Sense Editorial Archives (February 8, 2008), http:// www.financialsensearchive.com/editorials/engdahl/2008/0208.html.

28. See Robert Darnton, "Peasants Tell Tales," in *The Great Cat Massacre* (New York, 1984).

29. Price Pritchett, *New Work Habits for a Radically Changing World*, 51.

30. Klein, *Shock Doctrine*, 424–25.

31. Klein, *Shock Doctrine*, 425.

32. Glen O. Gabbard, *The Psychology of the Sopranos: Love, Death, and Betrayal in America's Favorite Gangster Movie* (New York, 2002), xii.

33. Peter C. Whybrow, *American Mania: When More Is Not Enough* (New York, 2005).

34. After describing CEO John Thain's extravagances Maureen Dowd concluded, "How are these ruthless, careless ghouls who murdered the economy still walking around (not to mention that sociopathic sadist Bernie Madoff?)—and not as perps?" in "Wall Street's Socialist Jet-Setters," *New York Times*, January 27, 2009.

35. Carrie Johnson, "Enron's Fastow Gets 6 Years," *Washington Post*, September 27, 2006.

36. In Nicholaus Mills, *Culture in an Age of Money: The Legacy of the 1980s in America* (Chicago, 1990).

37. Eric J. Fry, "Pinstriped Psychopaths," in "The Rude Awakening" blog, July 8, 2005. In their book *Snakes in Suits* (New York, 2006), Paul Babiak and Robert D. Hare argue that a surprising number of workplaces employ psychopaths. While psychopaths make up 1 percent of the general population, Babiak and Hare found that 3.5 percent of the executives they worked with "fit the profile of the psychopath." Psychopathic employees are pathological liars who get away with doing little or no work. See also Robert Monk's bracing *A Traitor to His Class* (New York, 1999).

CHAPTER 5

1. Ernest Becker, *Escape from Evil* (New York, 1975), 4.

2. See, e.g., T. F. Denson et al., "The Angry Brain: Neural Correlates of Anger, Angry Rumination, and Aggressive Personality," *Journal of Cognitive Neuroscience* 21: 734–44.

3. Scott Tobias, Review of "Death Sentence," The A. V. Club, August 30, 2007.

4. Jonathan Simon, "Governing Through Crime: How the War on Crime Transformed American Democracy and Created a Culture of Fear" (New York, Oxford University Press, 2007), 59. In *Huffington Post,* January 14, 2010, Anis Shivani analyzed Bush's messianic authoritarianism in a review of his memoir *Decision Points* (2010).

5. Steven V. Roberts, "Ronald Reagan Is Giving 'Em Heck," *New York Times,* October 25, 1970.

6. Anne-Marie Cusac, *Cruel and Unusual: The Culture of Punishment in America* (New Haven, CT, 2009), 132.

7. David Cole, "Can Our Shameful Prisons Be Reformed?" *New York Review of Books,* November 19, 2009, 41.

8. *Time Magazine,* "The Youth Crime Plague," July 11, 1977.

9. Tom Hayden, "The Myth of the Super-Predator," *Los Angeles Times,* December 14, 2005.

10. See Lawrence D. Spiegel, "The Phenomenon of Child Abuse Hysteria as a Social Syndrome: The Case for a New Kind of Expert Testimony," *IPT Journal,* Vol. 2, No. 1 (1989), and Susan Kiss Sarnoff, "Assessing the Costs of False Allegations of Child Abuse: A Prescriptive, *IPT Journal* 9 (1997).

11. See Richard Of she and Ethan Watters, *Making Monsters: False Memories, Psychotherapy, and Sexual Hysteria* (New York, 1994). For an analysis of a popular children's book that exploits this hysteria, see "Vampire Abuse" in my *Post-Traumatic Culture* (Baltimore, 1998), 199–211.

12. Susan P. Robbins, "The Social and Cultural Context of Satanic Abuse Allegations," *IPT Journal* 10 (1998).

13. "Kids Recant Abuse Claim after Dad Jailed 20 Years," AP, July 11, 2009.

14. *The Courage to Heal: A Guide for Women Survivors of Child Sexual Abuse,* ed. Ellen Bass and Louise Thornton (New York, 1988), 128. Frederick C. Crews offers a bracing overview of the MPD craze and responses in "The Revenge of the Repressed," Parts I and II, in *New York Review of Books,* November 17 and December 1, 1994.

15. Susan A. Clancy, *The Trauma Myth: The Truth about the Sexual Abuse of Children and Its Aftermath* (New York, 2009). See also Paul R. McHugh, *Try to Remember: Psychiatry's Clash over Meaning, Memory, and Mind* (New York, 2008).

16. Dahlia Lithwick, "Cruel but Not Unusual," *Slate,* April 1, 2011.

17. Antonin Scalia, "God's Justice and Ours," www.prodeathpenalty. com/scalia.htm.

18. David Grann, "Trial by Fire: Did Texas Execute an Innocent Man?" *New Yorker,* September 7, 2009, 51. The first condemned man freed by DNA evidence was Kirk Bloodsworth, in 1993. For good reason the Federal government helps fund DNA testing provided for in the Innocent Protection Act, though the protection cannot be comprehensive.

19. John Paul Stevens, "On the Death Sentence," *New York Review of Books,* December 23, 2010.

20. Patrik Johnsson, "Armed America: Behind a Broadening Run on Guns," *Christian Science Monitor,* April 13, 2009.

21. "The number of people under supervision in the nation's criminal justice system rose to 7.2 million in 2006, the highest ever, costing states tens of billions of dollars. . . . The cost to taxpayers, about $45 billion, is causing states such as California to reconsider harsh criminal penalties." See Darryl Fears, "New Criminal Record: 7.2 Million: Nation's Justice System Strains to Keep Pace with Convictions," *Washington Post,* June 12, 2008. See also Anne-Marie Cusac, *Cruel and Unusual: The Culture of Punishment in America* (New Haven, CT, 2009) and *The Real War on Crime: The Report of the National Criminal Justice Commission,* ed. Steven Donziger (New York, 1996).

22. Adam Liptak, "US Prison Population Dwarfs That of Other Nations," *International Herald Tribune,* April 23, 2008. For an analysis of prison demography, see Glenn C. Loury et al., *Race, Incarceration, and American Values* (Cambridge, MA, 2009).

23. Daniel MacCallair and Mike A. Males, *Striking Out: The Failure of California's "Three-Strikes and You're Out" Law.* (San Francisco, CA, 1999). Full version published by the *Stanford Law and Policy Review* (Fall 1999).

24. Proposal: Under the terms of Proposition 184, if a criminal has had one previous serious or violent felony conviction, the mandatory sentence for a second such conviction is doubled. After two violent or serious felony convictions, any further felony, nonviolent or not, will trigger a third strike; the mandatory sentence will then be the greater of: (1) three times the term ordinarily required, (2) 25 years, or (3) a term determined by the court. Crimes committed by a minor of at least 16 years of age count as strikes. The amount of credit that a second or third strike felon can apply toward eventual release is reduced from one half to one-fifth, and probation is not an alternative.

25. Systematic critiques of the law are Jerome H. Skolnick, "Wild Pitch: 'Three-Strikes, You're Out' and Other Bad Calls on Crime," *The American Prospect,* No. 17 (spring 1994).

26. John Nichols, "Bill O'Reilly's San Fran Rant," CBS News, http://www.cbsnews.com/stories/2005/11/15/opinion/main1044750.shtml. Talk show celebrity Glenn Beck has openly toyed with murder on the air: "I'm thinking about killing Michael Moore and I'm wondering if I could kill him myself, or if I would need to hire somebody to do it. No, I think I could. I think he could be looking me in the eye, you know, and I could just be choking the life out of him. Is this wrong?"

27. Elaine Rapping, "Aliens, Nomads, Mad Dogs," *Mythologies of Violence in Postmodern Media,* ed. Christopher Sharrett (Detroit, 1999), 263.

28. N. C. Aizenman, "New High in US Prison Numbers," *The Washington Post,* February 29, 2008.

29. Laura Sullivan, "Folsom Embodies California's Prison Blues," on "All Things Considered," NPR, August 13, 2009.

30. Solomon Moore, "California Prisons Must Cut Inmate Population," *New York Times,* August 4, 2009.

31. Robert S. Boyd, "Will Robot Killers Be Allowed to Fire on Their Own?" McClatchy Newspapers, March 25, 2009.

32. See *Georges Bataille,* ed. Stuart Kendall (Chicago, 2007).

33. See Marina Warner, *No Go the Bogeyman* (1998), republished as *Monsters of Our Own Making* (Louisville, KY, 2007), 132–33.

34. Dave Cullen, "The Depressive and the Psychopath," *Slate,* April 20, 2004.

35. Quoted in Joel Achenbach and Dale Russakoff, "Teen Shooter's Life Paints Antisocial Portrait," *Washington Post* (April 29, 1999).

36. Bnet (Business Network), March 1, 1999.

37. Achenbach and Russakoff.

38. Fessenden, *New York Times,* 2000.

39. Mike Davis, *Ecology of Fear* (New York, 1998), 339–40.

40. For an expanded version of this argument, see "Aliens Amok" in *Popping Culture,* ed. Murray Pomerance and John Sakeris (Boston, 2007), 147–58.

41. Jennifer Bennett, *Slate,* May 30, 2008.

42. Gail Bederman, *Manliness and Civilization: a Cultural History of Gender and Race in the United States* (Chicago, 1995), 200. For Roosevelt's attitude toward race suicide, see 199–206.

43. "Ancient civilizations were usually the victims of their own success, as the Hebrew prophets saw. Their prosperity became their pride, and toppled them: in a typical pattern, their wealth attracted large hordes of foreign invaders, who for a time might furnish labor, mercenary armies, and even new energy . . . but imperial success attracted either more vicious invaders or rival empires, who eventually brought down these great nations in their pride." See Herbert N. Schneidau, *Sacred Discontent* (Berkeley, 1976), 107–08.

44. See "The Politics of Monstrosity" in Chris Baldick's *In Frankenstein's Shadow* (Oxford, 1987), esp. 14–21.

45. See *The Movies Begin,* Vol. 5 (VCR cassette), from Film Preservation Associates, 1994.

46. The film's markers for Jewishness are the entertainment world's usual mix of profound historical symbols and shtick. Like the neighborhood delicatessen he patronizes, Rosenberg's old-fashioned jewelry shop denies the ruthlessness of the Arquillians' threat to annihilate humankind. Stalked by a monster, a subliminal neo-Nazi, Rosenberg evokes the Holocaust survivors who took shelter in New York. His assassin tellingly sneers that humans are themselves pests to be exterminated. The galaxy Rosenberg has secreted in a jewel is reminiscent of the jewels that Jews hid during their expulsion from their homes in Spielberg's *Schindler's List* (1993). Like a Diaspora Jew, the Arquillian Rosenberg carries a homeland with him in an aesthetic, quasi-abstract "jewel" or form. The Arquillians' demand for the contested galaxy

echoes the situation of nuclear-armed Israel and its clashes with Palestinians over the "lost" lands of Eretz Israel. In *The Age of Triage* (Boston, 1983), Richard L. Rubenstein calls his chapter on the Holocaust "The Unmastered Trauma" and demonstrates that competition between Jews and others was central to the tragedy and is often overlooked today (128–64). Although Jews had lived in Europe for centuries, insofar as they remained unassimilated, they were tacitly immigrants.

47. Rubenstein, *Age of Triage*, 1.

CHAPTER 6

1. "As he announces his plans for the ethnic cleansing of Canaan," says Jack Miles, "the Lord does not, to repeat, seem angry with the Canaanites, but the effect is genocidal all the same, and there is no escaping it." See Jack Miles, *God: A Biography* (New York, 1995, rpt. 1996), 117.

2. Reza Aslan surveys groups around the world that view their earthly struggles in cosmic terms. See *How to Win a Cosmic War* (New York, 2008). Like Samuel Huntington's *The Clash of Civilizations and the Remaking of World Order*, Aslan's book emphasizes the power of ideas to drive behavior.

3. Ruth Stein, "Evil as Love and Liberation," in *Terror and Apocalypse,* ed. Jerry S. Piven et al., (Writer's Showcase Press, 2002), 107. See also her *For Love of the Father: A Psychoanalytic Study of Religious Terrorism* (Stanford, CA, 2010).

4. Quoted in Joel Achenbach and Dale Russakoff, "Teen Shooter's Life Paints Antisocial Portrait," *Washington Post* (April 29, 1999).

5. Mervyn Bendle, "The Apocalyptic Imagination and Popular Culture," *Journal of Religion and Popular Culture*, XI (Fall 2005).

6. "Gunman Wrote of Revenge," Springfield, MA, *Union-News*, July 31, 1999.

7. *People*, August 16,1999, 121.

8. *Jonestown: The Life and Death of Peoples Temple*. American Experience, PBS.org.

9. Jeanne Mills, *Six Years with God* (New York, 1979).

10. Mary McCormick Maaga includes a transcript of the Jonestown tape in *Hearing the Voices of Jonestown* (Syracuse, NY, 1998).

11. "The suicides were so well organized that the potion for the children was prepared in a different container (at a lesser strength, I assume) than the potion for the adults" (Maaga's note).

12. Richard N. Ostling, "Of God and Greed," *Time*, June 24, 2001.

13. Bruce Wilson, "Palin-Attended Church Event Featured Samurai Sword Ceremony," *Huffington Post*, July 17, 2009.

14. Frank Schaeffer, "How I (and other Pro-Life Leaders) Contributed to Dr. Tiller's Death," *Huffington Post*, June 1, 2009.

15. Gabriel Winant, "O'Reilly's Campaign against Murdered Doctor," *Salon,* May 31, 2009. Kathleen Parker, "Carnival of the Fire-Breathers," *Washington Post,* June 3, 2009.

16. Jeff Sharlet, "Jesus Killed Mohammed: The Crusade for a Christian Military," *Harper's,* May 2009, 34.

17. Bruce Wilson, "John Ensign Linked to 'Do-it-Yourself' Exorcism Movement," *Huffington Post,* July 14, 2009.

18. Bruce Wilson, "Fighting Demons, Raising the Dead, Taking over the World," *Religion Dispatches,* April 1, 2009, http://www.religiondispatches.org/archive/politics/1273/fighting_demons,_raising_the_dead,_taking_over_the_world.

19. The research debunking recovered memory and multiple personality is extensive. An incisive account of the craze is Joan Acocella, "The Politics of Hysteria," *New Yorker,* April 6, 1998. More comprehensive is Ian Hacking, *Rewriting the Soul* (Princeton, 1995). For MPD as a cultural fantasy, see my *Post-Traumatic Culture,* Ch. 7.

20. For details, see Ch. 7 of my *Post-Traumatic Culture,* esp. 194–211.

21. George Frederick Drinka, MD sketches this process in *The Birth of Neurosis: Myth, Malady and the Victorians* (New York, 1984).

22. See D. Frankfurter, *Evil Incarnate: Rumors of Demonic Conspiracy and Ritual Abuse in History* (Princeton, 2006). In *Demon Lovers* (Chicago, 2002), Walter Stephens demonstrates that witchcraft fantasies can be understood as attempts to believe in supernatural religion. Fundamentalist Christians' professed horror at demonic influence in Halloween, Harry Potter, and Satanic ritual child abuse, says Stephens, is a case of "forlorn hope masquerading as morbid fear" (367).

23. Hitler's secretary Traudl Junge describes the trancelike atmosphere that engulfed her in *Until the Final Hour: Hitler's Last Secretary* (New York, 2004).

24. In "The Politics of Hysteria," Acocella reports that Dr. Braun came to believe that even florists were part of the satanic cult, sending color-coded flowers to his hospitalized patients (76).

25. David Grann, "Trial by Fire: Did Texas Execute an Innocent Man?" *New Yorker,* September 7, 2009, 62.

26. For an overview of this development, see Kevin Phillips, *American Theocracy: The Peril and Politics of Radical Religion, Oil and Borrowed Money in the 21st Century* (New York, 2006).

27. Jon Basil Utley, "America's Amageddonites," Foreign Policy in Focus (October 10, 2007), www.fpif.org. See also Chris Hedges, *American Fascists: The Christian Right and the War on America* (Free Press, 2006).

28. George Monbiot, "US Policy Towards the Middle East Is Driven by a Rarefied Form of Madness. It's Time We Took It Seriously," *The Guardian,* April 20, 2004.

29. Utley, "America's Armageddonites."

30. Mike Davis, *Ecology of Fear* (New York, 1998). In "The Irresistible Urge to Destroy New York on Screen," *New York Times*, December 26, 2007. Sewell Chan toted up 18 films.
31. Jared Orsi, in *Humanities and Social Science Net Online*, September, 1998, http://www.h-net.msu.edu/reviews/showrev. cgi?path=11745907095636.
32. See, e.g., Ronald H. Fritze, *Invented Knowledge: False History, Fake Science and Pseudo-Religions* (London and Chicago, 2009), 168.
33. Robert Jay Lifton, "American Apocalypse," *The Nation*, December 22, 2003.

Conclusion

1. James Truslow Adams made the phrase popular with *The Epic of America* (New York, 1931).

INDEX

1984 (Orwell), 162
24 (television drama), 86–88, 90

Abu Ghraib prison, 65, 82–86, 89,
  118
Acocella, Joan, 238nn19, 24
Adams, Henry, 47
Adams, James Truslow, *The Epic of
  America,* 239n1
Adkisson, Jim, 52
Agnew, Vice President Spiro, 148
Ahmadinejad, Mahmoud, 90
Aizenman, N. C., 235n28
Akerlof, George A., and Paul M.
  Romer, *The Economic Underworld
  of Bankruptcy for Profit,* 232n10
Akerlof, George A., and Robert
  J. Schiller, *Animal Spirits How
  Human Psychology Drives the
  Economy,* 226n4
Albucher, Ronald C., and Israel
  Liberson, 218n423
Aldridge, David, 216n14
Alexander the Great, 38
Allin, GG, 19, 20
Al-Janabi, Abeer, Qassim Hamza, 79
Al Maliki, Prime Minister Nouri, 60
Al Qaeda, 57, 71, 78, 87
Al-Zarqawi, Abu Musab, 69
Anastasia, Albert, 155
Anderson, John Lee, 221n16, 222n34
Anderson, Rev. Steven, 219n50
Anderson, Wes, *The Fantastic
  Mr. Fox* (film), 133
Andreasen, Nancy C., 215n11

Antichrist, 52
Apocalypse Now (film), 192
Applewhite, Marshall, 209
Archer, Christian J., *World History
  of Warfare,* 216n9
Ardagh, Sir John, 48
Arkin, Ronald, 162
Armageddon (film), 207, 208
Armour, Stephanie, 218nn35, 37
Aschembach, Joel, and Dale
  Russakoff, 236nn35, 37, 237n4
Aslan, Reza, *How to Win a Cosmic
  War,* 237n2
Assange, Julian, 225n67
Atta, Mohammed, 182–86,195
Attila (the Hun), 168
Avildsen, John G., *Joe* (film), 149

Babiak, Paul, and Robert D. Hare,
  Snakes in Suits, 233n37
Bacevich, Col. Andrew, 65
Bakker, Rev. Jim, 196
Baldick, Chris, *In Frankenstein's
  Shadow,* 236n44
Ball, Alan, *True Blood,* 20
Barlett, Donald R., and James B.
  Steele, 223n41; *America: What
  Went Wrong?,* 227n15
Barnum, P. T., 46
Barone, Michael, 55, 220n1
Barstow, David, 222n24
Barton, Mark O., 184–86, 191
Bass, Ellen, and Louise Thornton,
  The Courage to Heal, 234n14
Bataille, Georges, 164

Batiste, Maj. Gen. John, 69, 223n38
Bauman, Zygmundt, 129, 130, 132, 232n16
Beady, Willett, 227n11
Beauty and the Beast (film), 147
Becker, Ernest, 23, 24, 26, 28; *Denial of Death,* 216n11, 218n34, n46, 230n56; *Escape from Evil,* 29, 32, 35, 39, 115, 137, 145, 216n12, 220n2, 233n1
Bederman, Gail, *Manliness and Civilization,* 236n42
Beethoven, Ludwig, 40
Belfiore, Michael, 76, 224n61
Belile, Cpl. Joshua, 80–82
Bender, Brian, 226n95
Bendle, Mervyn, 237n5; *The Matrix,* 184
Bennett, Jennifer, 236n41
Bennett, William, 150
Bennis, Warren, 117, 118, 122
Bernall, Cassie, 168, 169
Berry, Wendell, 28, 217n27
Bigelow, Katherine, *Strange Days,* 204
Bikel, Ofra, and Rachel Dretzin, 201
Bin Laden, Osama, 39, 43, 67, 74, 163, 184
Binson, Diane, and William Woods, *Gay Bathhouses and Public Health Policy,* 216n7
Bishop, Amy, 30
Blache, Alice Guy, *The Making of an American Citizen,* 176
Blacker, Kay H., and Joe P. Tupin, 216n4
Black Panthers, 187, 190
Black, William, 127, 231n3
Blackwater, 70, 90, 91, 135
Blade Runner, (film), 162
Blahyi, Milton, 2
Bloodsworth, Kirk, 234n18
Bluestein, Paul, 222n26
Blunt, Rep. Roy, 208
Bolt, Robert, 153
Boesky, Ivan, 97

Bonner, William (Bill), 106, 228n31, 231n8; *Financial Reckoning Day,* 228n38, 231n6
Borger, Julian, 232n20
Bowen, Stuart W., Jr., 91
Bowlby, John, 109
Boyd, Robert S., 236n3
BP, Deepwater Horizon, 95
Braun, Dr. Bennett, 201–04, 238n24
"Breaking Bad" (television drama), 131
Bremer, L. Paul, 68
Briones, Cpl. Roel, 71, 73
Britton, Rhonda, 122
Bromwich, David, 89, 226n829
Brown, D., and Lawrence R. Jacobs, *The Private Abuse of the Public Interest,* 229n53.
Bryant, Anita, 121
Buddha, 188
Buffalo Bill, 46
Buffet, Warren, 8, 90, 102, 105
Bundy, McGeorge, 56, 220n3
Burgus, Patty, 201, 203
Bush, Pres. George W., 57, 58, 67, 78, 83, 89, 90, 116, 132, 148, 206, 215 n. 8, 219n54, 220n5
Butterfield, Fox, 216n13

Calley, Lt. William, 61, 75
Cameron, James, 76
Campos-Flores, Arian, and Monica Campbell, 232n23
Canetti, Elias, *Crowds and Power,* 217n23
Carmen (opera), 20
Carollo, Russell, 224n55
Center for Defense Information ("Strauss Military Reform Project"), 92
Chaplin, Charlie, 10; *Modern Times,* 110, 111, 119–22
Charcot, Jean-Martin, 201
Chase, David, "Sopranos," 131, 133
Chatterjee, Pratap, *Halliburton's Army,* 223n42

Chavez, Pres. Hugo, 129
Cheney, Vice Pres. Dick, 58, 215n8; and Halliburton, 69, 83, 90, 129
Chirac, Pres. Jacques, 206
Chomsky, Noam, 129
Clancy, Susan A., 152; *The Trauma Myth*, 234n15
Clark, Andrew, 230n58, 231n2
Clarke, Richard A., *Against All Enemies*, 220n6
Cohn, Marjorie, 73, 223n45, 224n53
Cohn, Norman, 205, 217n15, 222n29
Cole, David, 234n7
Coll, Steve, 220 n. 7
Columbine High School, 1–3, 10, 20, 165–69; Dylan Klebold, 20, 165, 166, 183; Eric Harris, 41, 165–69, 181–83
Conason, Joe, 231n4
Conrad, Joseph, *Heart of Darkness*, 191
Coppola, Francs Ford, 191
Corbin, Jane, 223n43
Corn, David, 230n59
Cosmatos, George, 109
Coyne, Jerry, and Hope E. Hoekstra, 219n61
Coulter, Ann, 6, 163, 222n32
Courage to Heal, 151, 234n14
Crews, Frederick, 234n14
Crimson Tide (film), 171
Cromie, William J., 224n63
Cullen, Dave, 236n34
Cullum, Leo, 226n2
Cusack, Anne-Marie, *Cruel and Unusual: The Culture of Punishment in America*, 234n6
Cusack, John, 226n91
Custer, Gen. George Armstrong, 105

Dahmer, Jeffrey, 82, 164, 186
Daily Show, The, 43
D'Amato, Gus, 7
Dante, 21
Darby, John Nelson, 207

Darnton, Robert, *The Great Cat Massacre*, 233n28
Darwinism, 46
Davenport, Thomas H., and Lawrence Prusak, 229n51
Davis, James, 32–37
Davis, Lennard, *Obsession*, 219n51
Davis, Mike, 170; *Ecology of Fear*, 208, 236n39, 239n30
Davis, Richard Allen, 157
Day after Tomorrow, The (Film), 208
Deadwood (drama), 46
Death Sentence (film), 148
Death Wish (film), 148, 159
DeBecker, Gavin, 219n53; *The Gift of Fear*, 42, 43
Deep Impact (film), 209
Defense Business Board, 92
Delaney, Sam, 216n8
DeLay, Rep. Tom, 208
Demos, John, 219n58
Denson, T. F., 233n2
DePalma, Brian, *Redacted* (film), 225n73
Dewan, Shaila, 217n28
Dexter (television drama), 131, 163–67
Diamond, Jared, 222n33
Director, Roger, 87
Dowd, Maureen, 233n34
Dreier, Marc S., 124
"Dr. Green," 203
Drinka, Dr. Frederick, *The Birth of Neurosis*, 238n21
Dr. Strangelove (film), 187
Du Bernard, Francois, 232n16
Duffett, John, ed., *Against the Crime of Silence*, 222n20
Dunlap, "Chainsaw Al," 111
Durkheim, Emil, 30
Dutton, Donald, 35, 217n19, n26

Eastridge, Pvt. Kenneth, 71, 74–76
Ebbers, Bernard, 115, 144

Eder, Steve, 232n25
Edsall, Thomas B., and Juliet
    Eilperin, 223n40
Elliott, Robert C., *The Power of
    Satire*, 220n68, 225n74
Emmerich, Roland, 17, 208
Engdahl, F. William, 233n27
Engelhardt, Tom, 222n30
England, Lynddie, 225n81
Ensign, Sen. John, 199
Escobar, Pepe, 77

Fabing, Howard, 1, 215n1
Faiola, Anthony, 228n33
Fallujah (Iraq), 57, 59, 68, 70
Falwell, Rev. Jerry, 172, 196
Fastow, Andy, 133, 144
Ferguson, Colin, 32
Fessenden, Ford, 215n4, 229n44,
    236n38
Figgis, Mike, *Leaving Las Vegas*, 19,
    143
First Blood (film), 229n43
Fitzgerald, F. Scott, 40; *The Great
    Gatsby*, 117, 133, 136, 211–13
Fleckenstein, William, *Greenspan's
    Bubbles*, 227n18
Flemke, Elizabeth, and Katherine R.
    Allen, 216n1
Foley, Stephen, 227n12
Ford, Dennis, *The Search for
    Meaning*, 217n29
Ford, Henry, 119, 120
Frankenheimer, John, *The
    Manchurian Candidate*, 201
Frankenstein (Mary Shelley), 31,
    164, 176
Frankfurter, D., *Evil Incarnate:
    Rumors of Demonic Conspiracy
    and Ritual Abuse in History*,
    238n22
Franklin, H. Bruce, *Vietnam
    and Other American Fantasies*,
    221n19, n20, 229n46
Fraser, Steve, *Wall Street: America's
    Dream Palace*, 228n37

Frederick, Jim, *Black Hearts: One
    Platoon's Descent into Madness*,
    225n69
Freud, Sigmund, 53, 201
Friedman, Jonathan, 51, 219n65
Friedman, Milton, 112–15
Friedman, Thomas, 125
Fritze, Ronald H., *Invented
    Knowledge: False History, Fake
    Science, and Pseudo-Religion*,
    239n32
Fromm, Erich, 26, 83, 217n16
Fry, Eric J., 233n37
Fuld, Richard, 101
Fumento, Michael, 17
Furrow, Buford O'Neill, 176
Fuselier, FBI Agent, 168

Gabbard, Glenn, *The Psychology of
    the Sopranos*, 233n32
Gabriel, Richard, 229n47
Gabriel, Richard A., and Paul I.
    Savage, *Crisis in Command:
    Mismanagement in the Army*,
    222n2, n21
Galbraith, James K., 230n60
Galbraith, John Kenneth, 109;
    The Culture of Contentment,
    227n14
Garland, David, *Peculiar Institution:
    America's Death Penalty in an
    Age of Abolition*, 154
Geoghagen, Thomas, 229n39
Gerbino, Kenneth J., 228n32
Gerbner, George, 42, 219n52
Gerth, Jeff, 222n25
Gibney, Alex, 83, *The Smartest Guys
    in the Room*, 143
Giddens, Anthony, *Modernity and
    Self-Identity*, 181
Gilgamesh, 27
Gladwell, Malcolm, 216n5
Glaister, Dan, 227n17
Glantz, Aaron, 221n13
Glanz, James, and Andrew W.
    Lehren, 221n12

Glenn, Jerome C., and Theodore Gordon, *State of the Future*, 232n19

Glenny, Misha, McMafia: *A Journey through the Global Criminal Underworld*, 232n19

Goebbels, Joseph, 29, 65

Goffer, Zvi, 131, 132

Goldstein, Gordon M., 220n4

Goldstein, Laurie, and William Glaberson, 217n31, 218n36, n38

Goldwater, Barry, 44

Goleman, Daniel, 14, 216n2

Goodell, Jess, 224n58

Goodman, Peter S., *The End of Easy Money and the Renewal of the American Economy*, 227n9

Gordon, Howard, 87

Gosselin, Peter, *High Wire: The Precarious Financial Lives of American Families*, 229n52

Graner, Cpl. Charles A., Jr., 85

Grann, David, 234n18, 238n25

Great Gatsby, The, 40, 211–13

Greaves, Anne, 185

Green, Pfc. Steven D., 80, 225nn.70, 71

Greenberg, Michael, 36, 218n43

Greenhouse, Steven, 107, 229n50; *The Big Squeeze: Tough Times for America's Workers*, 229nn42, 50

Greenspan, Alan, 94, 96, 98, 100, 104, 105, 112, 116, 128, 227n18, 228n34

Greenwald, Michael, "*Iraq for Sale*" (film), 85

Greider, William, 123, 228n27, 231n68

Gross, Michael Joseph, 218n48

Grossman, Lt. Col. David, *On Killing*, 223–33, 34n49

Hacking, Ian, *Rewriting the Soul*, 238n19

Haditha (Iraq), 59, 71–73, 77

"Hadji Girl" (song), 80–81

Hagee, Gen. Michael, 71, 72

Hague Peace Conference, 48, 49

Hammond, D. C. "Corey," 203

Hammond, Peter, 7

Hare, Robert, 145

Harry Potter, 6

Hastings, Max, *Retribution: The Battle for Japan*, 221n19

Hayden, Tom, 150, 234n9

Heaven's Gate (cult), 209

Hedges, Chris, 224n58; *American Fascists*, 238n27; *War Is a Force That Gives Us Meaning*, 220n3

Heins, Rebecca, 167, 168

Heller, Anne C., *Ayn Rand and the World She Made*, 230n57

Hersh, Seymour, 84, 85, 225nn77, 78, 226n82

Hitler, Adolf, 25, 31, 38, 40, 51, 67, 120, 148, 172, 198, 238n23

Hoffmann, E. T. A., 40

Hoffman, Jan, 219n55

Hogarth, William, *The Reward of Cruelty*, 164

Holmes, Sherlock, 163

Holmes, Stephen, *The Matador's Cape: America's Reckless Response to Terror*, 223n35

Holt, Jim, 222n25

Holyfield, Evander, 8

Homer, *The Iliad*, 1, 2, 22

Hood, Gavin, *Rendition* (film), 226n92

Hooper, Tobe, *Texas Chainsaw Massacre*, 116, 158

Horney, Karen, 24, 38; *Neurosis and Human Growth*, 218n45

Hubbert, M. King, 65

Huffington, Michael, 157

Hunt for Red October, The (film), 171

Huntington, Samuel, *The Clash of Civilizations*, 237n2

Huron and Iroquois ritual, 45

Hussein, Bilal, 70

Hussein, Saddam, 57, 66, 67, 71, 74

Incredible Hulk (film), 7, 8, 14
Independence Day (film), 17, 209
Ingraham, Laura, 87–89
Innocent Blood (film), 164
Irving, Edward, 207

Jack the Ripper, 164
Jackson, Mayor Frank G., 232n13
Jalava, Jarkko, 218n40
Jamail, Dahr, 223n47
Jean, Grace, 27
Jenkins, Holman W. Jr., 116, 117,
    230n62
Jesus, 188, 199
Joe (film), 149
John Birch Society, The, 190
Johnson, Carrie, 233n35
Johnson, Chalmers, 50, 91,
    223n35, 226n94; *Blowback:*
    The Costs and Consequences of
    America's Empire, 223n37
Johnson, Pres. Lyndon, 44, 62, 78,
    187, 190
Johnson, Simon, 227n11
Johnsson, Patrik, 235n20
Johnston, David Cay, 227n8
Jones, Bill, 157, 161
Jones, Rev. Jim (Peoples Temple),
    32, 186–96, 209
Jones, Pastor Terry, 41
Jonestown: *The Life and*
    Death of the People's Temple (film),
    237n8
Jowitt, Ken, 58, 220nn2, 4, 221n10
Joyce, Amy, 226n93
Junge, Traudl, 238n23

Kaczynski, Ted (Unabomber), 163
Kaletsky, Anatole, 124, 231n69
Kaplan, H. I., and B. J. Sadock,
    The Comprehensive Textbook of
    Psychiatry, 215n11
Karpinski, Col. Janis, 86; *One*
    Woman's Army, 226n85
Katz, Jack, 216n6
Keaton, Buster, 10

Kendal, Stuart, ed., *Georges Battaile,*
    236n32
Kennedy, Bobby (assassination), 186,
    189
Kennedy, Pres. John F.
    (assassination), 44, 189
Kerry, Sen. John, 30
Keynes, John Maynard, 94;
    Keynesianism, 109
Keystone cops, 10
Khatchadourian, Raffi, 225n67
Kill Bill (film), 39
Kimmett, Maj. Gen. Mark, 223n44
King, Martin Luther, 194;
    (assassination), 186, 189
King Philip's War, 45
King, Stephen D., *Losing Control:*
    The Emerging Threats to Western
    Prosperity, 227n6
Kingsdale, Jim, 123, 230n67
Kinsolving, Lester, 191
Kipling, Rudyard, 1
Kirkland, Lane, 111
Klaas, Marc, 158
Klaas, Polly, 157, 200
Klare, Michael, 50, 219n64
Klavan, Andrew, 219n54
Klein, Naomi, 69, 90, 113, 114, 201;
    The Shock Doctrine, 223nn36,
    39, 330n54, 233nn30, 31
Koch, Fred, 32
Kopel, David, 155
Koresh, David (Branch Davidians),
    163, 196
Kotcheff, Ted, *First Blood,* 22, 108,
    229n43
Kreutzer, William (Fort Bragg
    shooting), 169
Kubrick, Stanley, *Dr. Strangelove,*
    29, 49, 187
Kunstler, James, 50
Kunze, Michael, 217n24

LaHaye, Tim, 206; *Armageddon,* 207
Landis, John, *Innocent Blood* (film),
    164

Lansky, Meyer, 143
Larsson, Steig, 39
Lay, Ken, 115, 143
Leadership Secrets of Attila the Hun, The, 109, 144
Lears, Jackson, 219n59
Led Zeppelin, 298
Lee, Ang, 7
Lee, Tom (Virginia Citizens' Militia), 155
Leed, E. J., 30, 217n30
Left Behind (series), 206
Legacy, The (film), 156–60
LeMay, Gen. Curtis, 44, 63
Lenin, Vladimir, 188
Lethin, Col. Clarke, 77, 78
Levin, Jack, 126
Lifton, Robert J., 78, 209, 239n33
Lincoln, Pres. Abraham, 56, 57
Liptak, Adam, 235n22
Lithwick, Dahlia, 234n16
Lombroso, Cesare, 34
Longo, Robert, *Johnny Mnemonic* (film), 120
Loughner, Jared, 33, 34
Loury, Glenn C., *Race, Incarceration, and American Values,* 235n22

Maaga, Mary McCormack, *Hearing the Voices of Jonestown,* 237nn10, 11
MacAndrew, Craig, and Robert Edgerton, *Drunken Comportment: A Social Explanation,* 15, 216n3
MacCallair, Daniel, and Mike A. Males, *Striking Out: The Failure of California's Three Strikes . . . Law,* 235n23
Machiavelli, Nicolo, 113
MacKay, Charles, *Extraordinary Delusions and the Madness of Crowds,* 94
Madoff, Bernard, 107, 124, 211
mafia, 41, 91, 128–44, 155, 156, 164, 165, 188, 190, 196

Maguigad, E. L., 215n5
Mahan, Capt. (Admiral) Alfred Thayer, 48, 49
Making of an American Citizen, The (film), 176
Manchurian Candidate (film), 33
Manson family, 38, 190
Marine Rifle Creed, The, 55
"Marines' Iraq Conduct Scrutinized" (BBC), 224n54
Marshall, Gary, *Pretty Woman* (film), 227n14
Marx, Karl, 94; *Kapital,* 136
Massing, Michael, 222n31
Matrix, The (film), 120, 162, 184
Mauer, Marc, and Ryan S. King, 149
Mayer, Jane, 86–88, 218n33, 226n87
McCain, Sen. John, 39
McDonough, Giles, *After the Reich: The Brutal History of the Allied Occupation,* 221n19
McFadden, Robert D., 218n32
McHugh, Paul R., *Try to Remember: Psychiatry's Clash over Meaning, Memory, and Mind,* 234n15
McKee, Geoffrey B., *Why Mothers Kill: A Forensic Casebook,* 215n7
McNamara, Robert, 63, 121
McVeigh, Timothy, 22, 163, 196
Meehan, Capt. Shannon R., 55
Meltzer, Bernard D., and Cass R. Sunstein, 229n49
Melville, Herman, *Moby Dick,* 46, 47, 50, 111, 219n60
Men in Black (film), 170–79, 220n67
Meyers, Stephanie, *Twilight,* 20
Mifflin, Marcus, 71
Miles, Jack, *God: A Biography,* 237n1
Miller, Christine, 192
Miller, Maj. Gen. Geoffrey, 84
Millon, T., and R. D. Davis, 216n10
Mills, Jeanne, 186, 187, 189–91, 193; *Six Years with God,* 237n9
Mills, Nicholas, *Culture in an Age of Money,* 233n36

Minh, Ho Chi, 148
Mitchell, Dan, 231n7
Modell, John, and Timothy
  Haggerty, 217n30
Monahan, John, 218n39
Monbiot, George, 207, 238n28
Monk, Robert, *A Traitor to His
  Class*, 233n37
Moore, Michael, *Roger and Me*,
  121–23, 133, 179
Moore, Michael J., *The Legacy*
  (film), 156, 159, 235n26
Moore, Solomon, 236n30
More, Thomas, 153
Movies Begin, The (film), 236n45
Moyers, Bill, 131, 219n66, 220n67,
  232n22
Murdoch, Rupert, 158
Murphy, H. B. M., 216n4
My Lai (Vietnam), 60, 61, 71, 75, 149

Napoleon Bonaparte, 38
Needham, John, 73, 74, 224n57
Nelson, Deborah, *The War Behind
  Me: Vietnam Veterans Confront
  the Truth*, 221n17
*Nemesis: The Last Days of the
  American Republic*, 219n63
New Jerusalem, 46
New Yorker (cartoons), 41, 94, 111, 145
Nichols, John, 235n26
Nicol, Brian, 80, 225n72
Nixon, Pres. Richard M., 90, 128.
  148, 149, 230n55
Nizza, Mike, 218n44
Noland, Doug, 93
Noonan, Peggy, 39
Norris, Floyd, 100, 228n22
"Nurse Jackie" (television drama), 131

Obama, Pres. Barack, 39, 41, 52
O'Brien, Tim, *Going after Cacciato*, 64
Ofshe, Richard, and Ethan Watters,
  *Making Monsters: False Memories,
  Psychotherapy, and Sexual
  Hysteria*, 234n11

Operation Speedy Express
  (Vietnam), 60
Oppel, Richard A. Jr., 221n15
O'Reilly, Bill, 158, 198
Orsi, Jared, 239n31
Orwell, George, 162
Ostling, Richard, N., 237n12
Ousama-bin-Munquidh, 20

Packer, George, 231n5
Pagano, Rev. Ken, 155
Palin, Sarah, 39, 198
Parker, Kathleen, 198, 238n15
Parker, Richard, 226n5
Parkman, Francis (Jesuit), 45, 219n56
Patterson, Orlando, *Slavery and
  Social Death*, 217n17
Paulson, Hank, 97, 123, 124, 130,
  227n13
Paumgarten, Nick, 99, 100, 227n20
Paycheck, Johnny, 42
Paye-Layleh, Jonathan, 215n3
Pazder, Dr. Lawrence,
  and Michelle Smith, *Michelle
  Remembers*, 201
Perkins, John, *The Secret History of
  the American Empire*, 232n22
Pfaff, William, *The Irony of Manifest
  Destiny: The Tragedy of America's
  Foreign Policy; The Politics of
  Hysteria*, 222n29
Philipps, Dave, 224nn52, 57, 59
Philips, Todd, *Hated*, 19
Phillips. Kevin, 228n23; *American
  Theocracy*, 238n26
Phuc, Kim, 44
Pinochet, Gen. Augusto, 83, 113, 114
Pitman, Roger, 224n663
Piven, Jerry, ed., *Terror and
  Apocalypse*, 237n3
Plato, 6
Podvoll, Edward, *The Seduction of
  Madness*, 36
Poe, Edgar Allen, 210
Pollack, Andrew, 215n8
Pollack, William, 215n13

Pomeranz, Murray, ed., *Popping Culture*, 219n52, 236n40
Ponzi (Ponzi scheme), 100, 103, 107, 124, 227n21
Poole, Oliver, 77, 224n64
Post-Traumatic Culture, 7, 216n4, 218n32, 227n14, 238n20
Pritchett, Price, *New Work Habits for a Radically Changing World*, 110, 233n29
"Project for a New American Century" (PNAC), 66
Puzo, Mario, *The Godfather*, 14
Puzzanghera, Jim, 228n36
Pyszczynski, Tom, *In the Wake of 911*, 217n14

Ralegh, Sir Walter, 45
Ramadi (Iraq), 71, 74
Rambo, 9, 22, 107–9, 116, 119, 121
Rand, Ayn, *The Fountainhead*, 115, 116
Rank, Otto, 28, 29, 205, 217n25
Ranucci, Sigfrido, "Fallujah: The Hidden Massacre," 70
Raping, Elaine, 235n27
Ratner, Michael, 135
Reagan, Michael, 51
Reagan, Pres. Ronald, 50, 51, 62, 63, 97, 98, 108, 109, 111, 112, 121, 149, 196, 205, 221n18
Reich, Robert, 144
Reifenstahl, Leni, *Triumph of the Will* (film), 120
Reynolds, Kimberly, 156
Reynolds, Mike, 156–60
Rich, Frank, *The Greatest Story Ever Sold*, 222n27
Ricks, Thomas, *Fiasco*, 88, 222n22, 226n88
Ringer, Robert, *Winning through Intimidation*, 109
Robbins, Susan P., 234n12
Roberts, Paul Craig, 116, 230n61
Roberts, Steven V., 234n5
Robocop (film), 162
Rodriguez, Jazon, 26

Roeder, Scott, *A Time for Anger*, 198
Roger and Me (film), 121–23, 133, 179
Rolling Stones, 19
Roosevelt, Pres. Theodore, 46, 172
Roper, Lyndal, 217n24
Rorty, Richard, 130, 232n17
Rosen, Gary, 215n8
Rosin, Hannah, 228n24
Ross, Alex, 219n49
Ross, Deputy Sheriff Fred, 122
Ross, Edward A. ("race suicide"), 172
Rossing, Barbara R., 207
Roth, Henry, 177
Rothbard, Murray, *World Market Perspective*, 232n21
Rothschild, Emma, 230n64
Roubini, Nouriel, 102, 228n29
Rovem Karl, 220n5
Rubenstein, Richard, I., *The Age of Triage*, 237–38nn46, 47
Rubenstein, Richard L., 178, 179
Rubin, Robert, 96, 130
Rucker, Allen, and David Chase, *The Sopranos* (film), 232n24
Rucker, Philip, 92
Rumsfeld, Sec. Donald, 68, 69, 85, 90, 104, 226n84
Rutherford, William D., *Who Shot Goldilocks*, 227n18
Ryan, Gov. George, 152
Ryan, Rep. Leo, 191, 192, 195

Sachs, Roberta, 201
Sacks, Oliver, 36, 218n43
Salander, Lisbeth, 39
Salt (film), 39
San Marco, Jennifer, 3
Sanchez, Gen. Richardo, 226n84
Sands, Philippe, *The Torture Team*, 226n86
Santa Claus, 122, 123
Sarnoff, Susan Kiss, 234n10
Savage, Michael, 72; *Liberalism Is a Mental Disorder*, 51
Saviano, Robert, 233n26

Scalia, Antonin, 147, 152–54, 234n17
Schaeffer, Rev. Frank, *A Christian Manifesto*, 198, 237n14
Schneidau, Herbert, *Sacred Discontent*, 236n43
Schreiber, Flora Rheta, *Sybil*, 201
Schwarzenegger, Arnold, 38, 61, 162
Scorcese, Martin, *Casino* (film), 143
Scott, Ridley, *Blade Runner*, 162
Scurlock, James, *Maxed Out* (film), 106, 128
Seabrook, John, 215n9
Shakespeare, William; Coriolanus, 22; Macbeth, 22; *Merchant of Venice*, 101; *1 Henry IV*, 102; Romeo and Juliet, 19
Shank, Michael, 232n14
Shanker, Thom, 221n11
Shanley, Mary, 201, 202
Sharlet, Jeff, 238n16
Sharrett, Christopher, ed., *Mythologies of Violence in Postmodern Media*, 235n27
Shay, Jonathan, 1, 9, 21, 60, 62, 79; *Achilles in Vietnam*, 215n2, n12
Shelley, Mary, 164, 176
Sherman, Rep. Brad, 101
Sherry, Michael S., 63
Shipman, Tim, 218n47
Shivani, Anis, 234n4
Siegel, Bugsy, 143
Silberman, Charles, 3, 215n6
Simmons, Matthew, *Twilight in the Desert*, 222n25
Simon, Jonathan, 234n4
Simpsons, The (film), 148
Singer, P. W., *Wired for War*, 222n23
Skolnick, Jerome H., 235n25
"Slaglerock Slaughterhouse" (blog), 78, 79
Slotkin, Richard, 217 n. 20; *Regeneration through Violence*, 219n57
Smalls, Biggie (Christopher Wallace), 150
Smith, Adam, 112

Smith, Roger, 122, 230n66
Smitz, Gregor Peter, and Gabor Steingart, 231n1
Sonnenfeld, Barry, *Men in Black*, 170–79
Soros, George, *The New Paradigm for Financial Markets*, 102
Soencer, Clyde Ray, 151
Spiegel, Lawrence D., 234n10
Spielberg, Steven, 208, 236n46
Spitzer, Eliot, 128, 232nn11, 12
Stalin, Josef, 188
Star Wars (film), 191, 203
Stein, Ben, 116
Stein, Ruth, 183, 186, 237n3
Steinem, Gloria, 205
Steinhauer, Jennifer, 217n18
Stephens, Walter, *Demon Lovers*, 238n22
Stevens, John Paul, 154, 155, 225n19
Stevenson, Robert L.; *Dr. Jekyll and Mr. Hyde*, 7, 129, 143
St. George, 39
Stiglitz, Joseph, E., 93, 101, 220n8, 229n53
Stoen, Tim, 193
Stoker, Bram, *Dracula*, 126, 142
Stone, Oliver, *Wall Street* (film), 97, 145
Sullivan, Andrew, 226n84
Sullivan, Laurs, 235n29
Superman, 6, 121
Surnow, Joel, 86–90
Surowiecki, James, 9, 215n10
Suskind, Ron, 220n5

Taguba, Gen. Antonio, 85
Taibbi, Matt, 94, 125, 226n3, 231n9
Taleb, Nassim, and Pablo Trian, 230n70
Tanelian, Terri, and Lisa H. Jaycos, 224n62
Tarentino, Quentin, 17
Tasso, Torquato, 134
Taxi to the Dark Side (film), 83

Tchaikovsky, Peter Ilyich, *Pathetique* Symphony, 120
Temoshok, Lydia, and Clifford Attkisson, 216n4
Teran, Susan, 169
Terminator, The (film), 39, 61, 76, 77, 120, 162–64, 204
Terry, Randall, 198
Texas Chainsaw Massacre (film), 116, 158
Thain, John, 233n34
The Who, 19
Thelma and Louise (film), 6
Thill, Scott, 229n40
Tiller, Dr. George, 198
Toback, James, 7
Tobias, Scott, 233n3
Tompson, Benjamin, *New Englands Crisis*, 45; *New Englands Tears*, 46
Trajan's column, 56
Tristan and Iseult, 6
Trump, Donald, 99
Tuchman, Barbara, 48, 219n62
Tufts, Col. Henry, 62
Turner Diaries, The, 196
Turner, Patrick (Crash Café), 167
Turse, Nick, 78, 217n21, 221n14, 224n65, n66
Tyson (film), 7, 8
Tyson, Mike, 7, 8, 10

Uchiltelle, Louis, and N. R. Kleinfield, 229n41
Ullman, Harland, and James, B. Wade, 76
Umberger, Mary, 107
Unruh, Howard B., 2
Ut, Nick, 44
Utley, John Basil, 208, 238n27, 238n29

Vallely, Paul E., 65
Van Auken, Bill, 223n48
Vela, Sgt. Evan, 75
Verhoeven, Paul, 162; *Total Recall* (film), 204

Virginia Tech, 1, 3
Vito, Gennaro, ed. *Criminology, Theory, Research, and Policy*, 218n4
Volcker, Paul, 106
Vulliamy, Ed, 232n18

Wagner, C. Peter, 199
Walker, David, 127
Wall Street (film), 145
Wallace, Anise C., 230n66
Walsh, Joan, 225n79
Walton, Jonathan, 101
Wan, James, 148
Warchowski, Andy, 162
Ward, Vicki, *The Devil's Casino*, 227n9
Warner, Jeremy, 228n30
Warner, Marina, *No Go the Bogeyman*, 236n33
War of the Worlds, 172
Warren, Elizabeth, 106
Waxman, Rep. Henry, 69, 135
Weather Underground, 148
"Weeds" (television drama), 131
Weiser, Stanley, 97
Welch, Jack, 116
Wells, H. G., *War of the Worlds*, 172
Whalen, Christopher, 115
Wheeler, Winslow, 92
White, Josh, 224n56, 225n71
Whybrow, Peter C., *American Mania: When More Is Not Enough*, 117, 140, 230n64, 233n33
Wilde, Oscar, 13
Winant, Gabriel, 238n15
Wilson, Bruce, 237n13, 238nn17, 18
Wilson, James Q., 149
Wilson, Gov. Pete, 157, 158
Wikileaks, 59, 78
Willingham, Cameron Todd, 154, 204, 205
Winner, Michael, 159
Winter, Russ, 228n26
"Wire, The" (television drama), 132

Wodjakowski, Maj. Gen. Walter, 86
Wolfowitz, Paul, 66, 222n25
Wong, Edward, 228n25
Woodford, Jeanne, 161
World Trade Center, 41
"Wounded Platoon, The," 224n51
Wright, Evan, 67, 217n22;
    Generation Kill, 222n31
Wuterich, Staff Sgt. Frank D., 72

Yago, Glenn, 227n16
Yates, Andrea, 3
Yergin, Daniel, The Prize (film), 222n25

Zernike, Kate, 225n80
Zibardo, Philip G., 154
Zielbauer, Paul von, 224n60
Zillman, Dolf, 14, 216n2
Zogby (poll), 224n50